S0-BYA-857

PRIVATE LIFE UNDER SOCIALISM

The author and Mr. Hu Yanjun (in long coat) standing in front of Mr. Hu's house in 1991. Note the decorative wall inscribed with the poem that Mr. Hu wrote to express the new family ideal. See the Introduction for details.

YUNXIANG YAN

Private Life under Socialism

Love, Intimacy, and Family Change in a Chinese Village
1949–1999

STANFORD UNIVERSITY PRESS

STANFORD, CALIFORNIA

Stanford University Press
Stanford, California

© 2003 by the Board of Trustees of the
Leland Stanford Junior University.
All rights reserved.

Printed in the United States of America
on acid-free, archival-quality paper.

Library of Congress Cataloging-in-Publication Data
Yan, Yunxiang, 1954–
    Private life under socialism : love, intimacy, and family change in a
Chinese village, 1949–1999 / Yunxiang Yan.
        p. cm.
Includes bibliographical references and index.
    ISBN 0-8047-3309-0 (cloth : alk. paper) — ISBN 0-8047-4456-4 (pbk. :
alk. paper)
    1. Family—China—Xiajia (Heilongjiang Sheng) 2.
Marriage—China—Xiajia (Heilongjiang Sheng) 3. Intergenerational
relations—China—Xiajia (Heilongjiang Sheng) 4.
Courtship—China—Xiajia (Heilongjiang Sheng) 5. Communism and
family—China—Xiajia (Heilongjiang Sheng) 6. Xiajia (Heilongjiang
Sheng, China)—Social conditions—20th century. 7. Xiajia (Heilongjiang
Sheng, China)—Social life and customs—20th century. I. Title.
HQ684.Z9.X539 2003
306.8'0951'84—dc21

                                                2002013327

Original Printing 2003

Last figure below indicates year of this printing:
12   11   10   09   08

Typeset by Classic Typography in 10/14 Janson

To James L. Watson, guru and friend

Contents

Figures

Tables

Preface

It has been nearly fifteen years since this book was first conceived in the form of a research proposal. In the academic year 1987–88, I diligently pored through the existing studies of the Chinese family and kinship, a sub-field that I had chosen as part of my Ph.D. training in anthropology at Harvard University. I was instantly attracted to the interesting and complex issues I read about, yet at the same time I was puzzled by the absence of a discussion of individual agency: most scholarly accounts focused on the structural principles and collective behavior of the domestic group. That was at odds with my understanding of family life in the People's Republic of China, where the family institution has undergone radical and rapid changes since 1949. After I began to teach, my students expressed the same feeling that something was missing from the readings I assigned to them. The questions they asked most frequently were: "Why is the Chinese family so economic, and are people always so rational?"

There are two possible answers to this puzzle. One answer is that the Chinese family was indeed an economic organization, with little room for other aspects of private life such as intimacy, emotionality, and individual freedom. The other answer is that, in order to emphasize the unique features of the Chinese family and compare it with the American/Western family, many studies omitted elements of everyday life that were deemed insignificant or too familiar to readers in the West. As my own research on the subject developed and progressed, I became convinced that the latter explanation is more likely correct.

Generally speaking, academic studies have presented three models of the Chinese family. The first is the economic family, proposed mainly by Western

social scientists, who regard the domestic group primarily as a corporate organization characterized by a common budget, shared property, and a household economy with a strict pooling of income. The second may be called the
political family, shown primarily by feminist scholars to have deeply rooted
inequalities and power dynamics; their studies explore the resulting political
dimension of the Chinese family. Studies of the relationship between the
family and the state may also be included in this type. The third is the cultural family; as portrayed mainly by Chinese scholars and cultural elite, these
studies emphasize the overarching and enduring influence of traditional values, particularly Confucian ethics, on family behavior. The individual remains at the margins in all three models, and the emotional world of flesh-
and-bone people has usually been overlooked.

Yet without individuals and their lived experiences the family would have
not existed and family life would have not been possible. My research shows
that the contemporary Chinese family, while certainly economic, political,
and cultural, is also personal and emotional. Like its counterpart in American
society, Chinese family life is characterized by the moral experiences of individuals, whose concerns about privacy, intimacy, emotionality, and individual
rights are as important as economic gains. By focusing on the personal and
emotional, I hope this book may provide a new way of understanding private
life in China and balance the previous emphasis on the structure and collectivity of the Chinese family.

In retrospect, I realize how much my longitudinal fieldwork in Xiajia village
benefited from my having spent my youth there in the 1970s. As my fieldwork
evolved, I often found myself a stranger in the community where I grew up
because the social landscape, the people, and my relationship with the villagers had changed so dramatically. Thus I had to relearn what I thought I
already knew. As times changed, so did the mentality of the villagers, many
of whom viewed the same social phenomenon differently or even provided
different narratives of the same event at different times. To capture the dy-
namism in people's behavior and mentality, particularly that of village youth
who are most sensitive to social changes in larger settings, I simply followed
and documented the life course of more than two dozen individuals, a process
that would have been impossible had I not shared my own life experiences
with them in the 1970s.

I do not intend to portray this rural community as representative of Chinese society as a whole. On the contrary, in this case study I am primarily concerned with how the villagers lived their private lives under socialism and how their local history was shaped by social conditions. I also want to note that the trends of change described in this book, including the privatization of the family, the increasing importance of intimacy and emotionality in family life, the rise of individuality, and the growing crisis of civility, have long occurred in cities and many parts of rural China, as shown by several large-scale national surveys of family change and numerous empirical studies. This is because all Chinese people have lived with the same socialist state since 1949, a state that played a decisive role in transforming Chinese private life. Consequently, the social issues and moral dilemmas that people in Xiajia village have to deal with are largely the same as those dealt with by people nationwide. These same issues and dilemmas also exist in most of the world's societies and thus are relevant to people around the globe. Nevertheless, because people always respond to changes and challenges from the outside world in accordance with local conditions and by exercising their own agency, the specific form and content of their responses vary greatly. Therefore, it is only through local particularities and historical specificities that we may deepen our understanding of the general trends of social change and of the moral experiences of the people. In this sense, I am confident that the implications of this case study have relevance far beyond the boundaries of the village.

During my long intellectual journey since 1987 I have accumulated vast debts to many friends and colleagues and received financial support from a number of institutions, without whose help it would have been impossible to complete this book.

The first person I want to thank is James L. (Woody) Watson, my guru and friend. Woody was the most enthusiastic supporter of the research project from its inception and was untiring in offering advice and critically reading several drafts of the manuscript. As an inspiring and encouraging mentor, Woody has played a decisive role in my intellectual development; as a good friend, he has been extremely warm, caring, and always available. To Woody I owe a debt of such great dimensions that a simple acknowledgment is insufficient; hence the dedication of this book to him.

Similarly, words are inadequate to express my gratitude to Arthur Kleinman and Joan Kleinman, who have far exceeded their obligations in offering support and help ever since I became Arthur's student in 1986. They read several drafts of the manuscript that became this book and offered so many valuable comments that I lost count. I am above all indebted to Arthur for his theoretical inspiration. This book represents my own attempt to write an individual-centered ethnography of moral experience—the kind of anthropological enterprise that Arthur and Joan have long advocated.

I am deeply grateful to the residents of Xiajia village, Heilongjiang province, in northeastern China, for receiving me on two occasions. In 1971, at the age of seventeen, I traveled hundreds of miles from a village in Shandong province to Heilongjiang as a destitute migrant searching for a new home with enough food. During my wanderings from one place to another while performing various temporary jobs, the villagers of Xiajia generously took me in. I thereafter lived in Xiajia as an ordinary farmer until I entered Peking University for my undergraduate education in 1978. In the spring of 1989 I returned to the village as a Ph.D. student from Harvard University to carry out my first anthropological fieldwork; that visit was followed by a series of field research trips in 1991, 1993, 1994, 1997, 1998, and 1999. Each trip began with one or two reunion parties and ended with a long and warm farewell; in between there were equally memorable times as the villagers tried their best to fulfill my seemingly endless curiosity about their work, life, family, and community. Among the villagers, I am especially grateful to Mr. Hu Yanjun, a friend for more than thirty years, whose knowledge, humor, and intellect were instrumental in helping me with the specifics of my fieldwork and who played an important role in my research design. I frequently solicited his opinion on how to deepen and widen my investigations. I cannot imagine how difficult, if possible at all, my eleven years of longitudinal fieldwork would have been without the help and support of the villagers and several friends in the local government.

Many friends and colleagues read parts of or the entire manuscript and generously offered insightful comments. They are my heroes, and I am almost certain the following is an incomplete list: Cameron Campbell, Myron Cohen, Deborah Davis, Stephan Feuchtwang, Maris Gillette, Marjorie Goodwin, Susan Greenhalgh, Stevan Harrell, Douglas Hollan, William Jankowiak, Jun Jing, William Lavely, James Lee, Bonnie McDougall, Jonathan Parry, Isabelle

Thireau, Jonathan Unger, Wang Feng, Rubie Watson, and Martin Whyte. I am also grateful to Joseph Bosco, Karen Brodkin, Choi Chi-cheng, Lothar von Falkenhausen, Linda Garro, Guo Yuhua, Xiaoxia Gong, Philip Huang, Jean Hung, Nancy Levine, Liu Dik-Sung, Paula Paderni, Shen Yuan, Sun Liping, and Yang Nianqun for their insights, which were equally important in formulating and clarifying many of my arguments. I owe special thanks to Liang Xiaoyan for sharing with me her acute observations of social change in China and for her critiques of several important points that appear in the concluding chapter.

I was also lucky to find a transcontinental community for invaluable discussions while writing. Françoise Sabban generously invited me to be a visiting associate professor at the Centre d'Etudes sur la Chine Moderne et Contemporaine, Ecole des Hautes Etudes en Sciences Sociales (EHESS) in May 2000. This wonderful opportunity enabled me to write Chapter 8 in a small yet charming apartment in northern Paris, while presenting other draft chapters in three lectures at EHESS. During the following month, thanks to Charles Stafford's kind hospitality, I visited the Anthropology Department at the London School of Economics and presented my research results on two occasions. During my stay in Europe I also delivered materials from this book at the Institute of Sinology at Leiden University, the Center for Asian and South Asian Studies at the University of Amsterdam, and the Institute of Anthropology at Oxford University. In 2001, I gave public lectures at the Institute of Sociology and Anthropology of Peking University and at the Institute of Sociology of the Chinese Academy of Social Sciences. I would like to thank Leo Douw, Stefan Landsberger, Luo Hongguang, Ma Rong, and Frank Pieke for their hospitality and the participants in these seminars for questions, comments, and critiques. Their input greatly strengthened the book; all the remaining weaknesses and errors in the study, needless to say, are entirely my own responsibility.

Two respected scholars carefully reviewed the manuscript for Stanford University Press, providing me with long lists of penetrating questions and helpful advice. I cannot thank them in person because they remain anonymous, but I want them to know how much I appreciate their contributions. As early as 1997, Muriel Bell of the Stanford University Press was one of the most enthusiastic supporters of this project, and her subsequent encouragement, attention, and editorial expertise carried me through the entire course of writing. As always, I am grateful to Nancy Hearst, whose moral support and skillful editorial assistance made the writing much more pleasant. I also want to thank Jonathan Jackson for compiling the index.

Part of Chapter 3 is based on materials from my article "Courtship, Love, and Premarital Sex in a North China Village," published in *The China Journal*, no. 48 (2002). Part of Chapter 4 was previously published under the title "The Triumph of Conjugality: Structural Transformation of Family Relations in a Chinese Village," in *Ethnology* 36, no. 3 (1997). Chapter 8 is based on an article that appears in the French journal *Etudes Rurales* (nos. 161–62, July 2002), which is entitled "Planning Birth: Changes in Fertility Culture in a Chinese Village." I thank these journals for their permission to include the materials here.

Thanks are due to the following institutions for financial support: the National Science Foundation, the Wenner-Gren Foundation, the Chiang Ching-kuo Foundation for International Scholarly Exchange (USA), the University of California President's Office (for its Research Fellowship in Humanities), the International and Overseas Studies Program at UCLA, and the Academic Senate of UCLA. I also owe thanks to my colleagues in the Anthropology Department at UCLA for providing a collegial and stimulating intellectual environment. I am grateful to Department Chair Joan Silk and Dean Scott Waugh in the Division of Social Sciences for permitting me to take a year-long leave in 2000 to concentrate on writing.

Finally, my deepest appreciation goes to Betty Leung, my fiancée. When Betty and I met in 1999, I had just started to draft the first chapter, and now, while completing this preface, I am looking forward to our wedding in August. Over the past three years Betty has transformed my life with laughter and love. It is thus needless to say anything more about her contribution to this book.

YUNXIANG YAN

LOS ANGELES, FEBRUARY 2002

PRIVATE LIFE UNDER SOCIALISM

Introduction

The Chinese Family and the Study of Private Life

On a summer day in 1990, Mr. Hu Yanjun, a 46-year-old man in Xiajia village, wrote the following eulogy to the ideal family:

> The family is a harmonious whole
> that is created by the universe;
> containing the personal happiness of family life,
> it is the origin of well-being
> and the symbol of warmth.[1]

Later that year Mr. Hu renovated his house and landscaped the courtyard, constructing a billboard-like decorative wall (about two by two-and-a-half meters) on the right side of a formal entrance arch, facing the street. He then had a local artist inscribe his family eulogy onto the wall. Underneath the huge Chinese character *jia* (family) that occupied half of the wall, the main text was inscribed in a classical style of calligraphy in red against a yellow background with sky-blue and white borders. Mr. Hu's original purpose was to use his family ideal to educate his children and grandchildren about the beauty and significance of the family in one's life, something he had been trying to do for years. Once the project was completed, the inscription on the wall and his new courtyard became a landmark in Xiajia and the neighboring villages.

Having worked as a main cadre in Xiajia for many years before his retirement in 1988, Mr. Hu is a very capable man and probably the most powerful father in the village, living in a rich and close-knit extended family of ten people in three generations, including two daughters-in-law and three grandchildren.[2] Although he did not even completed his secondary school education because of family difficulties in the early 1960s, Hu likes to read and write. He has written several dozen poems and short essays expressing his feelings and his understanding of life, people, and the world, which he shares with his children and other relatives. Mr. Hu has always been concerned with the emotional and spiritual quality of family life. He told me that, in addition to frequent family meetings on important issues, he spent his leisure time with his two married sons, watching TV, listening to popular music, or playing mahjong. He considers his best and most successful effort to be a special family party for family members and relatives visiting from other villages and cities during the 1991 Chinese Spring Festival.

With more than forty people in attendance, the family party began at 7:30 P.M. and ended at 2:00 A.M the next day. It was full of fun, laughter, and emotional communication. Most of the younger guests—Mr. Hu's children, nephews, and nieces—contributed entertainment, including speeches, songs, and jokes, which they worked on for weeks before the party. Mr. Hu had assigned a special task to his only daughter (who then at the age of 19 was studying at an occupational school): to comment on the strengths and weaknesses of each family member. To everyone's surprise, when commenting on her father, she criticized him for not treating her mother well. She said, as quoted by Mr. Hu: "In my memory you rarely talked with my mother unless you had to; you always went out after dinner, spending time with your colleagues instead of with my mother. Now you have retired from the office and have begun to spend more time with us, but you still do not spend much time with my mother." The daughter's open criticism, as Hu recalled, shocked him and moved his wife to tears. For a while, everyone at the party was speechless. After that encounter Mr. Hu indeed tried to improve his own conjugal relationship, something he had neglected for many years. His efforts were admired by his fellow villagers, who agreed that people should do more to improve family harmony and build a happier family life.

Here, the intriguing point is that Mr. Hu and his fellow villagers regarded the family as a warm place for personal happiness where emotionality and affectionate ties hold a central place. Moreover, they also believed that the ideal of family happiness could be achieved through efforts to increase understanding and affection among family members. In other words, the family became, in both the villagers' life aspirations and lived experiences, a new haven for individuals that was actualized in a somewhat dramatized form during the Spring Festival party at Mr. Hu's house. The importance of personal happiness in family life and the centrality of the individual—the two most important implications of Mr. Hu's story—however, are rarely studied in existing scholarly accounts of the Chinese family.

The Corporate Family and the Missing Individual

Because my goal in this book is to study how individual villagers in one community live their private lives, I do not attempt to provide a comprehensive review of the literature of the Chinese family, which is too rich to be covered in only a few pages. Suffice it to say that, given the primacy of the family in Chinese society, family change has long been a central concern among China scholars. In addition to early and general surveys of the Chinese family (see, e.g., Lang 1946; Levy 1949), we find an abundance of ethnographic accounts of the family institution and family life, many of which, however, are embedded in accounts of the Chinese kinship system.[3]

The dominant approach in the study of the Chinese family is the "corporate model," which sees the family primarily as an economic entity composed of rational, self-interested members. According to this approach, the Chinese family is an organization characterized by a common budget, shared property, and a household economy that relies on a strict pooling of income. Family-owned property serves as the most important mechanism to shape the actions of maximizing persons. A key feature of the Chinese family is its flexibility and entrepreneurial ability to make the best of both family resources (capital and labor) and outside opportunities in larger social settings. Variations in family structure, and by implication, family change, therefore, are ultimately determined by the economic self-interest of the domestic group as a corporate enterprise (see, e.g., Baker 1979; Cohen 1970, 1976; Fei [1947] 1992; Freedman [1961] 1979; Gallin and Gallin 1982; Harrell 1982; A. Wolf 1985).

To date, Myron Cohen's 1976 book remains the most comprehensive and influential work on the subject, in which he proposes a powerful analytic framework of the Chinese family, showing the countless variations in corporateness over the family cycle. According to Cohen (1976), the Chinese family consists of three organizational elements: the estate, the economy, and the group. Responding to different social conditions, the actual structural composition of these three elements may vary greatly, and the key element that determines whether married brothers stay together or live separately is the individual act of self-management. This is an important contribution that simultaneously deconstructs and perfects the corporate family model. Emphasizing the rationality and management skills of the villagers, Cohen also critiques the "dumb Chinese peasant" rhetoric common both to the Chinese elite and to some Western scholars at that time, a theme that he elaborates in detail later (see Cohen 1993).

Equally important is Margery Wolf's (1972) groundbreaking ethnography on women in rural Taiwan families, which alters earlier conceptions of the Chinese family as a harmonious group. Wolf reveals the complex nature of the domestic sphere in which women actively mobilize resources and attempt to advance their own interests and construct another family of their own—the "uterine family." Defined as a women's unit built on sentiments and personal loyalties that die with its members, the concept of the uterine family constitutes the first attempt to challenge and deconstruct the corporate model of the Chinese family.

Since the 1980s, feminist scholars have unpacked the family from a gender perspective and shed new light on family change and women's liberation in China. They argue that although the socialist revolution made some changes in marriage customs and intergenerational relations, it failed to realize the party-state's promise of gender equality and family reforms because of the deep-rooted ideology and structure of the patriarchal family (K. A. Johnson 1983; Stacey 1983; and M. Wolf 1985). Ellen Judd reexamines the issue of the state and family change in the contemporary context of rural reforms, focusing on the interplay between power and gender (Judd 1994). Although the feminist studies focus on the life experiences of women, none of them questions the corporate nature of the Chinese family, which most scholars accept as a given.

Many studies of family change in the postcollective era emphasize the increasingly important role that family labor has played in the rural economy. These studies reveal complicated patterns of family behavior that reflect distinctive regional economies, ethnic cultures, overseas connections, and local histories, as well as the influence of state policies (see esp. Croll 1987; G. Johnson 1993; Harrell 1993; S. Huang 1992; Lavely and Ren 1992; and Selden 1993). Nevertheless, influenced by the corporate model, most analyses continue to focus on changes in family size and household composition. Although the younger generation's demands for conjugal independence have been recognized in some of these studies (see, e.g., Cohen 1992, 1999; Selden 1993), the nuclearization of the family, together with a few important customs such as marriage patterns, postmarital residence, and family division, remains the ultimate standard by which family change is measured in rural China (see essays in Davis and Harrell 1993; a notable exception is Whyte 1995).

On another front of scholarly inquiry, the corporate model has been employed to explain the record-breaking economic performance of Chinese populations (which began in Taiwan, Hong Kong, and Singapore and has continued more recently in mainland China). Some scholars challenged the dominant view that the Chinese family is an obstacle to economic development by pointing out the corporate features of the Chinese family (see Berger and Hsiao 1988). The predatory and irrational policies of former Chinese governments are now regarded as the primary reasons that China did not develop more rapidly earlier. Once these governments got "out of the way," the positive contributions of the Chinese family to development became apparent (Harrell 1985; Wong 1985).[4] A more balanced view holds that the Chinese family contains a mixture of tendencies, some favorable and others unfavorable to development. It is the outside forces and institutions that determine whether positive or negative tendencies predominate in household farming and family business (Whyte 1996).[5]

In this connection, Susan Greenhalgh's work on the family firm is particularly noteworthy; she begins to take the corporate model apart by revealing the neglected political dimension of the Chinese family. She points out that the corporatism of the contemporary family is actually the reinvention of a tradition found in a particular national and global political economy that gave aspiring entrepreneurs few choices but to build their firms with their families. The notion of the unified, cohesive, mutually supportive family, far from being a reality, is a political construction that conceals broad inequalities between genders and generations (Greenhalgh 1994b).

In short, despite a few attempts to modify or challenge the corporate model, most existing studies place a heavy emphasis on the corporate nature of the Chinese family, particularly its "collective action" in responding to social change in larger settings. Accordingly, it is the public domain—economic, political, and jural—of domestic life that attracts the most scholarly attention, while the private and personal domain is by and large overlooked. None of the above-mentioned critiques of the corporate model has gone far enough to bring out the individual experiences in family life. When commenting on Judith Stacey's 1983 book, Rubie Watson correctly points out: "For a book about the family, there is not much here about the internal dynamics of domestic life" (1985b: 62). This comment can be applied to many other works that either explicitly or implicitly employ the corporate model, in which the structural principles, behavioral norms, and state policies weigh much more than individual agency and interpersonal dynamics. As a result, the individual has long been missing from scholarly discourse on rural family life in China. Thus far, we know more about the family as an institution than about the individuals who live within the institution, more about changes in family structure than we know about changes in actual family life, and more about family life in cities than that in the countryside.[6]

Here I must note that the corporate model is indeed a powerful framework for characterizing the traditional family in China, that many of its generalizations may remain valid for current family life, and that my own research was inspired and initially guided by the same theoretical framework. It was only during my fieldwork for this book over the eleven years from 1989 to 2000 that I gradually realized that the corporate model, while shedding light on many issues, cannot explain some other equally important areas of family life. As far as contemporary family life is concerned, it is at least inaccurate to assume that individuals always put family interest above personal interest. Emotionality, desires, and personal freedom have become so important in everyday negotiation and contestation among family members that an individual would be unlikely to sacrifice his or her interests simply for the sake of reproducing the family.

Moreover, the family is also a cultural construct, "a 'socially necessary illusion' about why the social division of obligations and rights is natural or just" (Coontz 1988: 14). A new perception about what a family ought to be may shape individual behavior within the family and transform the family institution. Thus the pursuit of family economic interests is insufficient to explain all the changes in family life, such as individual demands for intimacy and privacy. This is particularly true in contemporary China, where the standard of living has significantly improved since the 1980s and people can make choices in accordance with necessity and with personal life aspirations. For instance, the emotional family that Hu Yanjun of Xiajia village wrote about and tried to realize is fundamentally different from the Chinese family in our received wisdom, which is highly disciplined, hierarchical, and corporate in nature. Therefore, major revisions of the corporate model and a search for a new approach to studying the private lives of individuals are now in order.

Toward a Private Life Approach

While Mr. Hu and other villagers in Xiajia taught me the limitations of the corporate model through their positioned views and lived experiences, I was also inspired by Philippe Ariès and Georges Duby's *A History of Private Life* to search for a new approach to studying the Chinese family. Calling the history of private life untouched ground, Duby states: "We started from the obvious fact that at all times and in all places a clear, commonsensical distinction has been made between the public—that which is open to the community and subject to the authority of its magistrates—and the private" (Ariès and Duby 1987: viii). However, this five-volume work is all about Western Europe, mostly French society. As the editors and authors comb through historical records, it becomes clear that the family in Western Europe, which was previously subsumed by communal forms of sociability, emerged as the focus of private life by the eighteenth century and separated itself more sharply from the public in the nineteenth century: "It became something it has never been: a refuge, to which people fled in order to escape the scrutiny of the outsiders; an emotional center; and a place where, for better or for worse, children were the focus of attention" (Ariès 1989: 8).[7]

The greatest benefit to me from reading the book was acquiring a basic understanding of the dual transformation of private life. First, the family, which in many societies previously served only as a social institution of production and reproduction, gradually evolved to be a center of private life and a refuge for individuals. Second, as the family became a private haven, individual family members began to have personal lives within the domestic sphere, hence the double meaning of private life—that of the family and that of the individual. This proposition is elaborated elegantly by Antoine Prost in his analysis of the spread of the notion of privacy from the upper class to all walks of social life in France. Writing on the changing nature of the modern family, Prost maintains:

> In fact, the family has ceased to be a powerful institution; its privatization has amounted to a deinstitutionalization. Society is moving in the direction of what might be called 'informal families.' At the same time, however, it is within the family that individuals have won the right to an autonomous private life. Private life has assumed two interconnected forms: within the private life of the family the private life of the individual unfolds. (Prost 1991: 51)

Now a question arises: is the family also a private haven in contemporary rural China? Alternatively, do Chinese villagers also have individual personal lives within the family? It may be true that the family in rural China before the 1949 revolution was primarily a social institution and that villagers had little private life within the family (this remains questionable, however). But when talking about contemporary rural families, my answer to this question is strongly affirmative. The family eulogy by Mr. Hu and his New Year party provide clear proof.

After years of fieldwork on family change in Xiajia village, I was convinced that although the practice of radical socialism in rural China did not, as leaders of the Chinese Communist Party (CCP) intended it to, construct a new type of socialist family, it indeed produced significant changes in family relations and family ideology, such as an increase in youth autonomy, a decline of parental power, and a rise of young women as active agents in family politics.

Moreover, notions of romantic love, free choice in spouse selection, conjugal independence, and individual property that emerged during the collective era (1956–80) have become increasingly important in the domestic sphere since the 1980s. Rural collectivization and other socialist practices during the first three decades of the People's Republic of China brought an end to many of the public functions previously performed by the family; the family was privatized and ceased to be the overarching mode of social activities in rural China. This trend has continued in the postcollective era (1980 to the present) because decollectivization restored only family farming, not the entire familial mode of social organization. As a result, a similar dual transformation of private life has occurred: the family has become a private haven where the private lives of individuals thrive, and individual identity and subjectivity have emerged as well.[8]

Here, following the French historians, the private is defined broadly as a zone of immunity for individuals, a realm that is, ideally, not open to the scrutiny of the community and not subject to the intrusion of public authority. The core of this private realm is the family, the sphere of domesticity, secrecy, and privacy in the sense of rights protecting the individual against public authority (see also Moore 1984). One of the central questions in this book is whether, when collectivization broke up the previous system of social hierarchy based on kinship, it also created the antithesis of collectivity—namely, individuality. Similarly, when the state reconstructed the public in rural communities, how were the boundaries of the private also redefined?

To document and examine these changes, a new private life approach needs to be developed. Unlike the corporate model, the new approach will enable the researcher to examine family change from the perspective of individual agents and to explore areas that have been overlooked, such as emotionality, desire, intimacy, privacy, conjugality, individuality, and new forms of sociality. The first step toward such a private life approach, therefore, is to have an individual perspective that prioritizes the moral experience of individuals in a local world (to follow Arthur Kleinman's theory), rather than a perspective that prioritizes ethical discourse.

According to Kleinman, "Moral experience is always about practical engagements in a particular local world, a social space that carries cultural, political, and economic specificity" (1999: 365). In contrast, ethical discourses are principle-based abstract articulation and debate over codified values, and they aim to be normative (1999: 363–64).[9] While acknowledging the importance of both, Arthur and Joan Kleinman have been advocating a new ethnography of moral experience since the early 1990s. Experience is defined as the felt flow of interpersonal communication, negotiation, contestation, and other sorts of engagements; it is "the intersubjective medium of social transactions in local moral worlds" (Kleinman and Kleinman 1991: 277; see also Kleinman 1999: 358–59).

In light of this theory of moral experience, it becomes clear to me that private life, viewed as a moral process, exists in the felt flow of interpersonal, intersubjective engagements and transactions in a local moral world. The family cannot always take precedence over its individual members, and a new focus in studying family life should be the lived experience of individuals. This is precisely what the corporate model of the Chinese family has missed, and it should be the departure point of the private life approach.

Methodologically, one of the best ways of studying the private lives of individual villagers is to do a fine-grained participatory ethnography, because it is "an engagement with others that brings the ethnographer into the ordinary, everyday space of moral processes in a local world" (Kleinman 1999: 413). The renewed interest in experience-near, individual-centered ethnography in medical-psychological anthropology has begun to influence biomedicine, cultural studies, and related fields (Hollan 1997; Hollan 2001; Kleinman 1999). According to Douglas Hollan, a strong advocate of individual (person)-centered ethnography, Robert LeVine first used the term *person-centered ethnography* in 1982 to refer to the experience-near ways of describing and analyzing human behavior, subjective experience, and psychological processes. The core of this research method or approach is an emphasis on the individual: "A primary focus of person-centered ethnography is on the individual and on how the individual's psychological and subjective experience both shape, and are shaped by, social and cultural processes" (Hollan 1997: 219). It is therefore better termed an *individual-centered ethnography*.

In a sense, the call for experience-near, individual-centered ethnography is a return to tradition—the tradition of a detailed narrative of everyday life based on long-term and thorough fieldwork in a local community. But its new focus is on individual experience and agency rather than social structure or cultural norms. This is what I try to accomplish in this book, a major lesson of which is that individual-centered ethnography relies heavily on repeated fieldwork in one field site and longitudinal studies of the same local world. This is the method I used to gather the material for this book.

As indicated in the Preface, I lived in Xiajia village, Heilongjiang province, for seven years during the 1970s and conducted fieldwork there seven times between 1989 and 1999. Except for the first two trips, during which I focused on gift exchange and social networks, individual experiences in the private sphere were the focus of my research agenda from 1993 to 1999. More often than not, however, I ended up talking with villagers about anything but their private lives per se. For a variety of reasons, such as concerns with social face (*mianzi*), shame, and modesty, Xiajia villagers, like people elsewhere, were reluctant to reveal information about their intimate engagements with loved ones, their positive and negative feelings toward family members and other people, secrets regarding their achievements or failures in life, and so on.[10] It took tremendous time and effort on the part of both the villagers and the ethnographer to establish a solid ground of mutual trust and understanding. Only thereafter was I able to observe real life dramas and to collect accounts of moral experiences from my informants. It is well known that sometimes informants provide false information purposely,[11] and this is particularly true when they are asked to talk about their private lives simply because they have something more directly at stake in the private sphere. In this respect, repeated fieldwork can come to the rescue: the same informant who lies in the first interview may reveal his or her actual experience in the third or the seventh interview.

In 1991, for example, a woman who fell in love with and eventually married a man against strong parental objections in the early 1970s denied all the local stories about her romance. She even invented a narrative in which her parents played a leading role to arrange the happy union. She firmly told me that she never had any special feelings toward her husband before their wedding, despite the fact that he and I had worked together in the same collective during the 1970s and I was thus a "witness" to their romance. It was not until 1998 that she admitted her active role in their courtship and emotionally recalled some of the details of their love affair. This occurred during my fifth long chat with her and after many short conversations between 1991 and 1998. The trigger for her openness was what she considered the outrageously improper behavior of the younger generation in courtship, including her daughter's involvement in premarital sex, which I learned about through another channel—the family of the girl's boyfriend. And it seemed rather accidental on that particular day for us to talk about the sex-related behavior of the young generation, because I had gone to her home to look at her newly remodeled house, which included newly separate bedrooms and a bathroom, and we had intended to discus interior decoration.

Admittedly, had the woman told me the story of her romance in 1991 instead of 1998, the recollection would have been slightly or significantly different (but she would not have told me of it in 1991, for the reasons mentioned above). Interestingly, her account was still different in several important details from the story that I had heard from other sources at different times (including the 1970s). Yet, we cannot fully understand this woman's moral experience without also knowing most (though not all) of the positioned views—hers and others'—regarding it. For this reason alone, the advantages of repeated fieldwork in the same site are obvious.

Moreover, fieldwork is also a process of moral engagement for the ethnographer (see Kleinman 1999). Ethnographers participate, from time to time, in the lives of the people they study and put their own decency and morality on the line. The more frequently an ethnographer visits the same field site and the longer her or his relationship with the informants lasts, the more responsibility he or she feels to accurately represent the moral experiences of the informants, which in turn leads to more fieldwork and self-discipline on the part of the ethnographer. This is because moral experience can only be understood through moral experience, just as a true gift can only be reciprocated with another gift.

Hollan identifies three approaches in doing individual-centered ethnography, which, respectively, emphasize personal accounts of subjective experience, participant observation of behavior and of what is at stake for informants, and embodiment of subjectivity on the tacit, visceral, unspeakable aspects of life experience (Hollan 1997; Hollan 2001). Each has its own limits, because life as lived is not life as experienced: "No matter how much we know about the concrete details of a person's life, we can never really know how this person experiences a particular event without asking him or her about it" (Hollan 1997: 227). An ideal way of studying the felt flow of individual experiences, in my opinion, is to combine all three approaches in a longitudinal study of a local world. I believe that, had I not asked about the enclosure of a separate bedroom in the woman's new house, we would not have talked about her daughter's sexual behavior, and she definitely would not have opened herself to recall her love affair of more than twenty years earlier. And the whole episode would not have been possible had I not chatted with her so many times since my first fieldwork in 1989.

With the individual perspective and the method of person-centered ethnography, this study represents my first attempt to apply a private life approach to studying the family and private life. Strictly speaking, this is only a partial attempt. As stated at the outset, I examine the rural family both as a social institution and as a private haven, which means that I draw upon the corporate model of the Chinese family as much as I critique it. One of the themes that I address throughout this book is the shifting role of the family from a social institution to a private haven for individuals—in other words, the rise of the private family. However, while the importance of the corporate family has declined, the private family is still in the process of developing. The weight of the private family in one's personal life also varies greatly across the boundaries of age, generation, gender, and personality, a factor that limits the depth of my inquiry. As James Watson notes: "In fieldwork you live where people live, you do what people do, and you go where people go" (1997: viii). In both real and symbolic terms, I can only go as far as my informants have been; hence the vacillation of my ethnographic descriptions between the corporate and private family in the following chapters.[12]

The Organization of the Book

Chapter 1 provides an overview of the changing local moral world in Xiajia village in northeastern China. I first examine the political economy in the community, with a focus on village leadership and the reach of the socialist state into local society. Then I take a closer look at the major aspects of public life, such as sociability, morality, political participation, and the provision of public goods, and review the local kinship organization and social networks. Social changes in these three dimensions over the past five decades have contributed in major ways to the dual transformation of private life in this rural community.

In Chapter 2, I start the narrative of the rise of the private family with its emotional pretext—romantic love and spouse selection. Through a careful examination of nearly 500 marriages, I document the development of romantic love in courtship between 1949 and 1999. By the end of the 1990s, the focus of change in spouse selection had shifted from the rise of youth autonomy against parental control over their marriage to the saliency of the individual experience of romance and intimacy, a significant change that is explored in detail in Chapter 3. By tracing the origin of a local custom in the 1970s that allowed an engaged couple to spend time alone in an institutionalized time and space, I examine the emerging popularity of premarital sex and argue that sexual intimacy contributes to the development of affectionate love. A close look at the local forms of love expression and the changing discourse about the ideal spouse shows that a romantic revolution in spouse selection has occurred in both practice and ideology. Together these two chapters dispel the prevailing myth that Chinese villagers are not interested in or capable of romantic love. I call for more scholarly attention to the emotional world in rural society.

Chapter 4 is concerned with the structural change of family relations—the newly emerged centrality of the husband-wife relationship in the domestic sphere or, as I call it, the triumph of conjugality. Three important aspects of conjugality are examined: intimacy and conjugal love, division of labor and decision-making, and the redefinition of the gender role in the spousal relationship. While the horizontal conjugal tie replaced the vertical parent-son relationship as the central axis of family relations in both nuclear and stem households, parental authority and power further declined and the previously unprivileged members of the family—women and youth—began to acquire their own space and independence. The triumph of conjugality over patriarchy signals a turning point in the evolutionary history of the Chinese family.

In Chapter 5, I turn to the spatial transformation of private life as reflected in a wave of house remodeling in Xiajia village, focusing on how villagers defined, and were defined by, spatial relations in their house plans. Two kinds of privacy emerged: the privacy of the family and the privacy of individuals within the family. These in turn altered the previous pattern of intrafamilial relations. It becomes clear at the end of my inquiry that the villagers' pursuit of family privacy and personal space represents a logical development of love, intimacy, and conjugality.

Property rights are discussed in the context of family division and marriage transactions in Chapter 6. By examining three interrelated changes in the custom of family division and one radical development in the practice of bridewealth, I demonstrate the increasing importance of individual property rights in the politics of family property, tracing its origins to the collective period. Changes in this aspect of family life also reveal the disarray of the corporate structure of rural family organization.

The transformation of private life has not always been easy; it is a process full of confusion, anger, despair, and suffering in both emotional and material terms. Generally speaking, several generations of parents have gradually lost their power, privilege, prestige, and secure position at home. In Chapter 7, I examine the living conditions of elders and the sense of crisis regarding old-age security among aging parents 45 and older. Taking into account the views of both the senior and junior generations, I argue that the traditional mechanism of intergenerational reciprocity has broken down and that it has been replaced with a new logic of balanced exchange. To cope with the change, parents employ a variety of strategies to invest in old-age security, thus redefining the notion of filial piety.

The crisis of filial piety is one of the causes that led to the making of a new fertility culture, an important change that is discussed in Chapter 8. Birth control is an area where the Chinese state has significantly reshaped the family and family life in urban and rural areas alike. Ethnographic evidence shows, however, that villagers are not merely victims of the state policies of strict population control; instead, from the inception of the birth control regulations, different individuals have adopted different strategies, ranging from confrontation, passive resistance, and cooperation to adaptation to the new fertility values. By analyzing individual responses to the state-sponsored program, particularly those of young parents who chose to have only one child—an only daughter in some cases—I analyze the sociocultural reasons for the emergence of a new fertility culture.

In the concluding chapter I argue that what has occurred over the past five decades represents the transformation of private life in a dual sense: the rise of the private family and of the private lives of the individuals within the family. The essence of this transformation lies in the development of individuality, rather than in household size or family structure, though the latter have changed significantly as well.

Then I address the rise of the individual and the role of the socialist state in transforming family life. Rural youth, particularly young women, have played a major role in transforming the family institution through their expression of the three major components of their subjective world: autonomy, emotionality, and desires. The development of individual identity and subjectivity, however, is unbalanced and incomplete because the newly emerged individualism tends to emphasize individual rights and personal interests while downplaying a person's obligations to the community and other individuals. In other words, many individuals have lost a basic sense of civility and have thus become uncivil.

The socialist state has played a key role in the transformation of private life and in the formation of the uncivil individual. The state was a major force in initiating or causing profound changes in both the family and the local moral world between 1949 and 1999. From the 1950s to the 1970s, several generations of youths were sometimes encouraged and sometimes led by the state to challenge patriarchal and communal power; they gradually gained more autonomy and independence in their private lives yet became dependents of the collectives and the state in public life. While opening up new horizons for individual development in certain aspects, the retreat of the state that started in the early 1980s also created a social vacuum of moral values and behavioral norms that was soon to be filled by sweeping consumerism and other values of utilitarian individualism of late capitalist society. Contextualizing the changes in the private sphere in the larger social setting shows that the decline of public life, the near-absence of community power, the increasingly predatory local government, and the accelerating pressure of competition in a market-oriented economy all contributed to the rapid spread of egotism and the rise of the uncivil individual.

The transformation of the private sphere, after all, is inevitably linked to, and often a response to, the larger transformations in the public sphere and society as a whole. Thus this study begins with a careful survey of the changing local moral world in which villagers live their public and their private lives.

CHAPTER ONE

The Changing Local World

Political Economy, Public Life, and Social Networks

Xiajia village is located at the southern edge of Heilongjiang province in northeastern China. Approximately fifty kilometers south of the provincial capital and twenty-four kilometers southeast of the county seat of Shuangcheng, Xiajia is a farming community whose primary crop is maize. Until the 1960s, the village was encircled by farmland on the north and east and by grassy marshlands on the south and west; the majority of the marshland was transformed into irrigated rice paddies in the late 1970s. Neighboring villages are one to three kilometers away. Five kilometers south of Xiajia, the Lalin River separates Heilongjiang from Jilin province. Throughout its history summer floods threatened the village's lower farmland until a network of canals was constructed in the 1970s. During dry years, however, the village enjoys fertile, black soil.

In comparison with other villages in many parts of China south of the Great Wall, Xiajia is a young community, with a history of little more than a hundred years. This is common for villages in Shuangcheng County, because the region was opened for settlement only in the early nineteenth century by the Qing government. In the late nineteenth century the first settlers built small shanties on farmland that is now the center of Xiajia, and the community was officially recognized as an administrative village in the late 1930s. The village continued to grow thereafter, as a production brigade consisting of four production teams during the collective period and again as an administrative village during the postcollective era. By the summer of 1998, Xiajia had a population of 1,492 in 381 households.[1]

For the men and women in Xiajia, however, the village is much more than an administrative unit—it is the local moral world where they live and die and where "certain things really matter: power, position, prestige, material resources, ethnic identity, social order, ultimately survival. Because vital interests and values are at stake, everyday social activities are *moral*" (Kleinman and Kleinman 1997: 102, emphasis in original). Rather than drawing a general picture of the local moral world, I will concentrate on the three dimensions that are most relevant to the private lives of Xiajia residents (for additional details about the village, see Yan 1996: 24–38). I first examine the political economy in Xiajia, focusing on village leadership and the reach of the socialist state into the local moral world. Next I describe public life and offer a brief review of changes in sociability, public morality, political participation, and the provision of public goods since the Communist revolution in 1949. In the third section I take a closer look at local kinship organization and social networks, which constitute perhaps the only nongovernmental dimension of the local world after the 1949 revolution.

Village Cadres and the Changing Face of the State

Before the Communist revolution, land ownership in Xiajia village was concentrated in the hands of a few Manchu landlords and some rich Han farmers; less than 25 percent of the land was cultivated by independent small farmers. Most villagers worked as long-term tenants or short-term contract laborers for the big landowners.[2] The Communists took over the southern region of Heilongjiang province in 1946–47; as a result Xiajia villagers witnessed the accompanying dramatic social changes three years before the founding of the People's Republic.

In Xiajia and the surrounding area, land reform was launched in late 1946. The prior social hierarchy was completely altered during this radical attempt at social transformation. Landlords were denounced and humiliated in mass rallies, and most of their property was confiscated and redistributed among the poor. More important, everyone was assigned a class label in accordance with their economic status and occupation at the time of land reform. Class labels included "poor peasant," "middle peasant," "rich peasant," and "landlord." The latter two labels, plus "counterrevolutionary" and "rotten element" (reserved for those who challenged the Communist regime or committed crimes), were assigned to class enemies, also known as the "four bad elements." To a great extent these class labels determined people's life chances throughout the 1960s and 1970s, when the focus of national politics was on "class struggle."[3]

Another legacy of the land reform campaign was the displacement of wealth as the basis of power and privilege in the local world; in its stead, impoverishment became the symbolic capital in the new society. It has been said that during one struggle session a shepherd who had become the village head stated, in all seriousness: "Thanks to the party, it is now those of us who lay green shit who have the final say" (a reference to the fact that before the revolution people were so poor that their major source of food was wild herbs).

As in other parts of rural China, poor, uprooted young men became the new leaders during land reform (see Friedman, Pickowicz, and Selden 1991: 95; Ruf 1998: 72–74). Owing to their previously marginal status in local society, they were extremely loyal to their party superiors. During the subsequent collectivization campaign from 1953 to 1957, Xiajia was subject to most of the irrational social experiments sponsored by the state because the leaders were determined to make Xiajia a model community of socialist transformation. Consequently, Xiajia villagers suffered more than those in neighboring villages during the height of the Great Leap Forward (1958) and the 1959–61 famine. Fortunately, the next generation of leaders refocused their efforts during the 1960s and 1970s, concentrating on agricultural production instead of political campaigns. Average payment for a day's work in Xiajia collectives was between 1.10 and 1.30 yuan from the late 1960s through the 1970s; this increased to as much as 2.50 yuan per day in a production team on the eve of decollectivization in 1983. Xiajia was thus among the richer villages in northern China, where the average daily wage in most villages was only about 0.50 yuan.

It is not surprising that when the rural reforms reached the stage of decollectivization both the cadres and many villagers in Xiajia had difficulty accepting the fact that the collectives were to be dismantled. Much like the political campaign for collectivization during the 1950s, decollectivization was carried out with compelling force from above, regardless of local responses and reservations. At the end of 1983, Xiajia collectives were dismantled overnight and most of the collective property was privatized, including the tractors and other heavy agricultural machines. Farmland, the fundamental means of production, was divided into two categories: subsistence-grain land (*kouliang tian*) and contract land (*chengbao tian*). Everyone in the village was entitled to two *mu* of rationed land (about one-third of an acre), and every adult male laborer received ten mu of contract land. The villagers' obligations to provide the state with cheap requisitioned grain applied only to the contract land. Decollectivization in 1983 once again altered the order of social life to a great extent, separating the postcollective or reform era from the collective period (1953–83) (see Yan 1992).

Partially because of poor transportation facilities (only an unpaved road linked the village to the major road to the county seat), there was no rural industry in Xiajia village during the collective period. Several grain-processing factories and husbandry farms were established in the 1990s, all of which were small family businesses. By the end of the 1990s, the majority of villagers still relied on farming to meet their basic needs and to pay state taxes and various local levies. Family sideline occupations provided some desperately needed cash income. By the summer of 1999, more than 30 percent of Xiajia families were raising dairy cows in order to sell milk to a joint venture Nestle factory in the county seat, and several dozen families ran chicken or pig farms. But almost all these operations were small sidelines rather than formal businesses. Dairy cows could generate considerable cash income; yet, because capital was limited and raising cows expensive, most families could only afford to raise one or two. Only three households considered raising chickens to be a serious business, but their maximum capacity was no more than 500 hens.

After the late 1980s, temporary jobs in the cities became another important source of cash income and, for those villagers who were too young to receive contract land in 1983, such jobs were also a major means of survival. In 1991 there were 106 Xiajia laborers working regularly outside the village for longer than three months per year; this figure increased to 167 in 1994. The trend continued throughout the second half of the 1990s; an increasing number of unmarried young women also joined the force of temporary migrant laborers. But as urban unemployment rates increased and national economic growth slowed down in the 1990s, it became more and more difficult for villagers to find jobs in the cities, and the rewards declined as well.

Xiajia's heavy reliance on agriculture has been one of the major obstacles to economic development since decollectivization. As a result the village has gradually been transformed from a rich village into a marginally unsuccessful farming community. The average per capita income in Xiajia has remained slightly below the national average ever since the rural reform—it was 528 yuan in 1988 and 616 yuan in 1990, while the national average in these two years was 545 yuan and 623 yuan, respectively. The situation was exacerbated during the 1990s, and the living conditions of most villagers showed little sign of improvement since the 1980s. Official figures during the same period, however, were less reliable as the village economy stagnated and cadres were under pressure to inflate their achievements. For instance, the reported per capita income in 1997 was 2,700 yuan, a figure that even the village cadres openly admitted was false. Nevertheless, all villagers I interviewed agree that living conditions had improved since the collective period. Households that had been able to take advantage of the new opportunities of the reform era had become quite affluent in recent years, in sharp contrast with others that had been left behind (see Yan 1992).

Another major change in Xiajia's political economy was the rapid decline of village leadership, as reflected in the differences among four party secretaries who held power during important turning points in village politics and cadre behavior.

The party secretary from 1952 to 1960 was typical of the generation of land reform cadres. An illiterate and extremely poor farm laborer in the late 1940s, he became one of the first young militant activists during land reform and was promoted to the top leadership position in Xiajia mainly because of his loyalty to the party and his superiors. He attempted to implement all the irrational policies of the Great Leap Forward campaign, causing Xiajia residents to suffer much more than their neighbors. Relying on the full support of his superiors and the coercive force of the village militia, he controlled Xiajia tyrannically, earning the nickname "big wolf." A frequently cited example of his ruthlessness was that he ordered a villager—one of his senior kinsmen—to be tied up and beaten because the villager had complained about missing a meal in the public canteen. However, the party secretary lived in the same humble conditions as the village poor, and he was widely recognized as a clean cadre, free of economic corruption. He believed in the party dictates and worked wholeheartedly for the local government, efforts that in theory should also have served the interests of the Xiajia residents. For this reason, many villagers were ambivalent about him: on the one hand, they hated him for inflicting famine and poverty on the village; on the other hand they respected him for his commitment to public duty and his selfless character.

Although the subsequent three party secretaries from 1962 to 1987 shared similar pragmatic work styles and all made contributions to the stability and prosperity of the village, the man who held office from 1978 to 1987 was the most popular because the collective economy achieved great progress under his leadership. Like his predecessor, he used overt coercion to exercise his power and he controlled the social life of villagers tightly. He confessed to me that he could not even remember how many people he had beaten during his ten-year tenure as party secretary. Given the predominance of the patriarchal tradition among village cadres, it was natural that he and his colleagues first resisted decollectivization in the early 1980s and then encountered tremendous difficulties dealing with villagers who were no longer dependent on the cadre management of production. He told me that after decollectivization "doing thought work" was no longer effective and people no longer respected the authority of cadres.[4] Even worse, the party did not appreciate its own cadres' political achievements, and upper-level state officials withdrew their support of village cadres just when the latter needed it most. During a violent public conflict with a villager in 1987 the township government pretended to know nothing about it and did not support the party secretary. "It is meaningless to be a cadre now," he said in explaining why he resigned after that incident. Obviously, as a figure whose term of office spanned two periods, he found it difficult to adapt to the new type of power relationships after the reforms and thus had no choice but to quit.

The loss of meaning in being a "revolutionary cadre" did not affect the next party secretary, who held office from 1987 to 1993. This was because he simply did not care about political rewards and public interest. During an interview in 1989, he explained: "The society has changed now. Who cares about the party and the state? Even the top leaders in Beijing are only interested in getting rich. Why am I doing this job? Simple—for money. I was not interested in the title of party secretary, but I do like the salary of 3,000 yuan." Two years later I was told that this cadre had designed his strategy around the three "nos": saying nothing, doing nothing, and offending no one. When I checked this with him myself, he did not hesitate to admit it. As a result of his passive leadership, social order deteriorated and a small group of young thugs bullied villagers, even on several occasions beating up cadres (see Yan 1995). Taking advantage of this situation, many villagers refused to pay local taxes and levies. However, this man did have something to be proud of: his family was transformed from one of the poorest to one of the richest in the village, and the families of his two sons also moved to the top of the "rich list" by the early 1990s. He resigned from the top post in 1993 and moved into an apartment in the county seat for a comfortable retirement. Rumors have it that he had amassed more than 200,000 yuan for his family by the time he resigned, while the village owed a debt of 800,000 yuan to both state banks and private lenders. Judging from the fact that he purchased three apartment units (two for his two married sons) in the county seat at a price of more than 60,000 yuan each, it can be assumed that he indeed did reap a fortune during his tenure.

After a brief chaotic period of power struggles among more than a dozen political players in 1993–94, a man in his early thirties emerged as a new type of village leader. This man formerly had been a well-known troublemaker and had a record for minor criminal offenses, including battery, theft, and attempted robbery. Thanks to his criminal reputation, he was first appointed as a public security cadre and then promoted to village head by an incapable party secretary during this transitional period, in the hope that he could help keep the village thugs under control. Relying on a small gang of violent youth, this bully-turned-cadre was indeed able to collect the unpaid levies that villagers owed to the local government and to stop the widespread logging of public trees by others. As a long-term informant for the local police department, he led police raids on private homes at night and helped the authorities arrest the leading thug. These achievements made him an excellent village cadre in the eyes of the township government. In 1995 he was appointed party secretary in Xiajia, despite the fact that he was not even a party member at the time (the recruitment procedure was, of course, completed soon thereafter).

As party secretary he became even more corrupt and abusive, openly taking bribes, appropriating state loans to the village for his own private use, and pocketing public funds. He was involved in extramarital affairs with three women and reportedly used his political power to seduce or force several other women to engage in casual sex with him. He often beat up villagers who failed to pay their levies on time, and he asked local police to handcuff and detain those who dared to challenge his authority. He spent a large amount of public funds for gifts (often in the form of cash) to his superiors and the local police chief, securing firm support from the local government. He was thus promoted as a model village party secretary for three consecutive years and rewarded with a salary increase and bonuses each year. His abusive behavior caused much discontent and anger among the villagers, and in 1996 a group of villagers began to file complaints against him with the county government. He was finally removed from the post after a mass protest involving more than 300 villagers in 1998. But his removal led to another round of political chaos because several ambitious upstarts, including the fallen party secretary's younger brother, competed for the top position, a drama that was still unfolding when I completed my fieldwork in the summer of 1999.

The sketch of these four party secretaries can also be applied to the village leadership in general; most cadres during each historical period shared similar ideological motivations and sociopolitical standing, and more important, they shared a similar relationship with national political trends. Thus the fall of the first party secretary also ended the careers of the village head, the village militia head, and a deputy party secretary, all of whom were illiterate but devoted to the public good and to carrying out the dictates of the revolution. The second party secretary represented a new generation of political elites during the collective period: they exerted a rhetorical political power as well as an iron-fist work style (many village cadres had earlier served in the army). They won the support of the villagers mainly through their effective management of collective farming and public projects, such as canal construction and land reclamation. Except for the former brigade accountant, however, none of the major leaders during the collective period was able to remain in office after the late 1980s because village politics in the postcollective period had been radically transformed.

According to many villagers, cadres in the new era of market-oriented reforms shared the same urge to use their official position to enrich themselves, shamelessly becoming involved in economic corruption and caring little about the good of the community and the villagers. Because of the absence of rural industry in Xiajia and the surrounding area, political power remained the easiest and most lucrative way of getting ahead. Take cadre salaries as an example. While the village economy and household income stagnated during the 1990s, the salary of the party secretary increased from 3,000 yuan in 1991 to more than 9,000 yuan in 1998; other village cadres also received pay raises. Their salaries were actually extra income because they still had their full share of contract land, which is the major source of household income for ordinary villagers. In addition, cadres have more access to public funds and can offer their family members opportunities to earn quick cash from nonfarm work (see Yan 1992).But the most serious damage that the party secretary from 1987 to 1993 did to Xiajia, according to many villagers, was to allow the evil wind to prevail over good trends (*xiefeng ya dao zhengqi*), as illustrated by the rise of the fourth party secretary in the late 1990s.

The fourth party secretary, together with his small gang of violent and unruly youth, represents the emergence of local bullies as a legitimate political force. As noted above, he was promoted to party secretary before he was officially recruited into the party, which indicates both his lack of moral authority and the changing political trend at the grassroots level. To maintain his power to collect taxes and levies (the reason that he was promoted to this post in the first place), he formed alliances with other thugs in the village, appointing them village head, deputy party secretary, and officers or members of the village security team; hence the transformation of the entire village leadership. What disturbed Xiajia villagers most is that when some of these bully-turned-cadres broke the law they could seek protection from the local government. For instance, although the village head, who was the right-hand man of the party secretary, was caught sexually assaulting a woman in 1997, he received only an internal warning from the local government. He lost his job only after his transgression was exposed in the provincial newspaper by an angry villager's letter.

The local government protected unpopular and unethical village cadres for its own survival. In order to complete the tasks that previously were overseen by the collectives, the township government expanded from about twenty officials and staff in the early 1980s to more than sixty people in the late 1990s, despite the central government's efforts to reduce the size of the bureaucracy.

More than 50 percent of the new officials were hired with so-called extra-budgetary funds—that is, revenue generated by the local government. Because there were no successful collective enterprises in this town, the only way to support the ever-expanding local government was to increase the extractions from villagers. When the villagers resisted paying local taxes, fees, levies, and surcharges, the local government hired more policemen and other officials to enforce collection, thus requiring more funding. Hence a vicious circle. It was against this background that the bullies-turned-cadres in Xiajia provided the local government with a seemingly more efficient way to carry out unpopular tasks, because the village cadres were paid with public funds from the village, which, of course, also came from levies on the villagers.

The Xiajia case is neither unique nor the worst in rural China. The gradual evolution of village leadership from radical rebels to a technocratic elite during the collective period is one of the themes that Richard Madsen explores in his 1984 study.[5] Accounts of such changes can also be found in a number of case studies (see Chan, Madsen, and Unger 1992; Friedman, Pickowicz, and Selden 1991; Ruf 1998; and Siu 1989). It is also widely recognized that in underdeveloped, noncommercialized rural regions local governments tend to be predatory, using the state apparatus to extract and distribute unproductive rents, rather than entrepreneurial in developing the local economy (see Baum and Shevchenko 1999: 344–46).[6] Reports of local cadres imposing exorbitant levies and fines on overburdened villagers and using public funds to enrich themselves are widely published both in and outside of China (see Gao 1999; Kung 1994; Oi 1991). As Baum and Shevchenko note, "Some of the appropriation has been institutional in nature, involving excessive exactions by local officials on behalf of their cash-starved state agencies" (1999: 345). The institutional predation therefore legitimizes the individual predators.

One development that has not received much attention from Western scholars is the rise of local bullies as a legitimate political force in the countryside, particularly in the underdeveloped northern regions. In China the problem was first addressed by scholars and reform-oriented officials as the deterioration of the relationship between the cadres and the masses (see Anonymous 1997; and Li Jiangyuan 1998). In her 1998 book, He Qinglian describes how thugs and bullies dominated local towns and villages in the early 1990s. She uses the phrase *heibai heliu* (the merger of black and white) to describe the trend whereby local bullies seek alliances with local cadres or simply take over an office (see He 1998: 282–319). Examining the continuing trend of heibai heliu, Sun Yuandong asserts that it has become a widespread phenomenon in the rural north; in many places, he points out, local thugs and bullies not only control village offices but also have taken positions in state agencies and legal apparatuses (Sun 1999: 39). It should be noted that social historians have long noted the replacement of gentry-type local leaders by bullies and tyrants in the rural north during the Republican period, owing to increasing state penetration, the overextraction of taxies and levies, and the breakdown of cultural traditions (see Duara 1988; and P. Huang 1985). The revival of local bully power in the postcollective era deserves a full-scale study in its own right.

The changing village leadership serves as the best indicator of the changing relationship between the state and the villagers. In the eyes of the Xiajia villagers, the socialist state as embodied in the central government is located more than 1,000 kilometers away in Beijing, thus relating to their everyday life only in terms of abstract national policies. It is the local government represented by township officials and village cadres that implements national policies and sponsors political campaigns. For the villagers, state policies are important only when they are implemented locally, and the socialist state is powerful only in the ways that it affects their personal lives. For instance, discrimination against people of "bad" class origins was less severe in Xiajia than in a village in Shandong province where I spent five years in my youth, and it thus had less influence on marriage and the family among the "bad class" people even during the heyday of radical socialism (cf. Croll 1981). Yet the birth control program has been much more effective in Xiajia than in other villages. The difference is mainly due to how local cadres carry out state policies.

Elsewhere I note that policy implementation in Xiajia village has been transformed from an inflationary to a deflationary process. During the 1950s and 1960s village cadres tried to maximize state policies because of their ideological and political devotion to the revolutionary cause. The pragmatic leaders of the 1970s and the early 1980s managed to maintain a balance between meeting state demands and caring for local interests. In contrast, the minimalist cadres in the postcollective era made little effort to implement state policies, except for completing the "hard tasks," such as birth control and tax and levy collections (see Yan 1995: 228–30). This trend continued during the

1990s. By the end of the 1990s village cadres had become much more predatory in completing the hard tasks, while completely ignoring or resisting
other state policies, such as the regulations on reducing the peasant burden
or the directives for village democratic elections. This has led to the increase
of the state's extractive capacity in a more coercive and destructive form, although the new extractions from peasants do not necessarily go to the central state. But, the state's other capacities, such as its regulatory and normative capacities, have been seriously undermined by self-serving cadres at
both the township and village levels.[7] Local cadres seem to have become a
special interest group of "entrepreneurial brokers," to borrow a term from
Prasenjit Duara (1988: 42–57). Many local cadres actually act against the
long-term interest of the state, even though they may help the state to increase its extractive capacity in the short run.

   The reach of the state into local society, therefore, has been both strengthened and weakened in the postcollective era, but the changes have not occurred in the same areas. There is no doubt that the state has become much
less intrusive in the villagers' everyday lives—public and private—and the
state has also stopped dictating villagers' economic activities. However, a series of decentralization and fiscal reforms also have led to the withdrawal of
state-sponsored public projects and social and cultural programs at the local
level. The retreat of the state has translated into a decline in the provision of
public goods and the expansion of cash-starved local governments. A predatory local government has to rely on the state apparatus (such as policemen
and the courts) and tyrannical cadres (including local bullies) to extract taxes
and levies from villagers, a circumstance that leads to a rapid increase in state
penetration of local society.[8]

   For individual villagers, however, the most important issue is not how
deeply the state reaches into society, but what the state can do for them. An
intrusive state that provides more services to villagers may be regarded as
benevolent; conversely, an absentee state may be seen as irresponsible and
impotent. What occurred in the 1990s was the worst possible combination:
the burden of taxes and levies increased and the provision of public goods
was reduced. It is true that the restoration of household farming has enabled
villagers to avoid the extremely unfair expropriation of surplus agricultural
production by the state through the collective system, but the villagers now
pay more attention to what the state openly takes away from their harvests.

Many complain that the state has abandoned the peasants who, not long ago, were regarded as the privileged backbone of the revolution (see Unger 1984). The changing face of the state from intrusive yet paternalistic to distant and extractive has caused a great deal of confusion, disappointment, and alienation among Xiajia villagers, especially with regard to public life and community.

The Rise and Fall of Public Life

I first became interested in public life when I noted the inability of Xiajia residents to spend leisure time outside their private homes. One result of the 1983 decollectivization was to give the villagers unprecedented spare time: they needed to work for no more than two months per year, normally spending a week on spring planting, three or four weeks on summer hoeing, and another week on the harvest. The radical reduction in work time was due to greater efficiency under household farming and the wider use of agricultural machinery, chemical fertilizers, and pesticides. When herbicides were introduced in the region in the late 1990s, even the summer hoeing was hardly necessary, and villagers had even more spare time. It is true that the lack of work at home motivated many men and women, mostly youth, to seek temporary jobs in cities; but because of the economic changes at the national level finding a city job was not always easy. Temporary jobs in the cities usually lasted only three to six months during the warm seasons, and then the workers returned home to rejoin the army of idle villagers.

Noticeably, Xiajia residents spent their increasingly abundant spare time almost entirely in their homes, either in front of a television or at a mahjong table, because there was so little to do in the community. I was told repeatedly that there had not been a public event for years, and the village cadres made no effort to initiate public projects, cultural programs, or villagewide meetings. After the demolition of the collective headquarters, villagers did not even have a new place to gather and socialize informally. "There is no human spirit (*renqi*) on the streets. The village is dead," commented an amateur actor who had been part of the village performance troupe during the collective period. Indeed, Xiajia's public life in the postcollective era has declined rapidly in many respects: political participation, public goods provision, cultural activities, morality, and sociality in general have all suffered.

For those villagers who experienced collectivization, the change in political participation is all the more striking. For instance, ever since the land reform campaign, meetings and public rallies had become part of village life, whether the villagers liked them or not. In addition to political meetings related to seemingly endless national campaigns, there were also regular commune meetings (*sheyuan dahui*) to address production and distribution issues in the collectives. Many villagers also belonged to party-sponsored organizations, such as the Youth League, the Women's Association, the village militia, and the Association of Poor Peasants, which held their own meetings and activities. For party members, there were additional regular party meetings and study lessons (for a detailed study of village political life, see Chan, Madsen, and Unger 1992).

In most cases mass participation in village politics was initiated and directed by local cadres as the agents of the socialist state (except during political campaigns that aimed at local cadres, such as the Four Cleanups and the Cultural Revolution), and villagers' participation was not entirely voluntary. Many villagers recalled that they often felt bored and overburdened by these endless evening meetings because they were already busy with their daily work in the collectives, in their private plots, and at home. However, over the years, villagers became accustomed to participating in such activities, and occasionally meetings were exciting and meaningful when the villagers felt their participation made a difference. An elderly party member told me that the entire party branch had held four meetings to debate the recruitment of a young activist whose family class label was not "poor peasant." The young man later became the respected party secretary who held office from 1978 to 1987.

While living in Xiajia during the 1970s I also attended several important mass meetings that were meaningful to all the members of our production team. One such meeting in 1973 discussed the retention of the team head who wished to step down because of poor health and his anger over a small group of rebellious youth. The meeting lasted for more than five hours on a chilly autumn evening, as the participants discussed various strategies to keep the team head (who did not attend the meeting), openly criticized the young troublemakers, and also enthusiastically discussed ways to improve the production team. The event ended dramatically: three youths went to the team head's home to apologize and, when the latter still hesitated to attend the mass meeting, one of the youths picked him up and carried him on his back to face the masses. My own migration to this village in 1971 was also the subject of a tense discussion at a mass meeting of the production team. Later I learned that public opinion had been split because many felt it was unfair to force the production team to assume the burden of accepting me for the benefit of the entire brigade, which also included three other production teams.

The last memorable mass meeting was held in 1983, when the villagers received their shares of farmland and participated in a lottery to buy draft animals, agricultural machines, and production tools from the dismantled collectives. The well-built collective headquarters, consisting of more than twenty rooms and a huge courtyard, was subsequently demolished, as was the village auditorium that could seat more than four hundred people. Mass participation in village politics and community affairs dropped sharply thereafter, owing partly to household farming and partly to the changes in the village leadership. Many Xiajia residents noted that there had not been a single mass meeting in the village since 1987 when the minimalist party secretary took power. The village party branch (*dangzhibu*) virtually stopped functioning because party members never met after the early 1990s, and not a single individual was recruited into the party during the entire decade (except for the bully–turned–party secretary). The other organizations (such as the Youth League and the village militia) have completely disappeared, leaving a purely nominal structure in the annual reports submitted to the county government each year. Whenever a directive or a new policy was sent down from the upper levels, the village cadres simply passed it on to villagers through the broadcast system, along with the fine that would be levied should villagers fail to comply. The public accounts remained confidential, and ordinary villagers had no idea that the village was in debt on the order of 800,000 yuan by the late 1990s, despite the fact that they had been forced to pay more levies and fees each year. The villagers told me that the cadres did not want to hold mass meetings because they could not account for the missing public funds and the other problems caused by their irresponsible leadership.

When asked about the village elections promoted by the central government in the 1990s, Xiajia residents did not appear to take them seriously. By 1999 there had been three elections in the village. In each the party secretary sent his most-trusted emissary (either his brother or his mistress) to visit the villagers' homes to ensure that they voted for the "right" candidates, by physically handing them the "correct" ballot to be deposited in the box. Once, when a villager's wife would not listen to the advice of the party secretary's mistress because she despised her, the village office cut off her family's electricity the next day. This was a fatal blow to the family's food processing business, so the woman's husband had to offer gifts to both the party secretary and his mistress, begging for forgiveness.

The only visible signs of mass political participation in the late 1990s were the efforts by some villagers to lodge formal complaints against the party secretary. In addition to sending letters to the relevant government agencies at the county level and above, villagers twice launched an organized appeal and protest in front of the county government office building and planned to do the same in front of the Party Discipline Committee at the provincial level. At the climax of this political event, more than three hundred signatures were collected to lodge a formal complaint against the party secretary, and in 1998 there was a villagewide refusal to pay an unreasonable levy. However, these activities were initiated by a group of villagers who had been either formal cadres or activists during the collective period, and the dispute thus evolved into a prolonged power struggle between the current and the past party secretaries (see Yan 2001). The masses were interested only when they were promised some immediate gains, such as the elimination of a 300 yuan per household levy during the 1998 protest. On most occasions, the majority of villagers remained on the sidelines watching the two camps fight it out.

Parallel to the decline of mass political participation, there has been a reduction in the provision of public goods since the early 1980s. During the collective period, commune members received all their subsistence supplies from the collectives, from grain to cooking fuel. The collectives also provided financial aid for family emergencies, free schooling for children, old-age support for childless elderly, and, during the 1970s, basic medical care. More important, the collectives also provided the capital and organizational power to complete a series of infrastructure construction projects, such as an antiflood canal in the early 1960s, land reclamation and the installation of electricity in the 1970s, and road construction and afforestation during the 1970s and the early 1980s. The village school was expanded twice during the collective period, and an elaborate village auditorium was built along with the huge headquarters buildings for the four production teams. Working for these projects, which villagers still benefit from today, was also an important mode of public participation.

In contrast, the provision of public goods has been a serious problem in the postcollective era. Owing to the shortage of both public funding and strong leadership, there has been no major infrastructure construction since the mid-1980s, and all the previously collectively funded social programs, such as medical care and free schooling, have been canceled. When small-scale projects need to be completed, cadres contract them out as commercial projects to their relatives and collect extra levies from the villagers. For example, in 1997 the party secretary contracted a project to replace the electricity poles to a private construction team headed by his close relative, and the final cost was three times what had been planned. Rumor had it that both the party secretary and his relative appropriated a large proportion of the collected funds for this project. The resentment of villagers eventually grew into the mass protest noted above. Low-interest loans from the state-owned Agricultural Bank and other agencies had been an important source of funding for poor families during the collective period. But now cadres simply withhold most of the loans and use the money to pay the huge debts of the village office, or to relend at high interest rates.

The worst change, according to many villagers, is the deterioration of public order. Xiajia had been a safe and peaceful community during the collective period, and there was no need to lock one's house from the inside during the night (admittedly, villagers owned few valuables at that time). The situation changed after the late 1980s when a group of unruly youth began to steal private property at night and roam the streets during the day. The then party secretary did nothing to improve public security (continuing to adhere to his minimalist strategy of three "nos"), and the village was quickly taken over by violent youth and thugs. Theft of private and public property increased yearly, forcing Xiajia residents to lock their houses and build walled courtyards. For two years there was even no phone service in the village office because the iron wires used as telephone lines were always stolen.

Another serious problem is arson in the villagers' corn-stem stacks. Villagers use corn stems as cooking fuel and pile them up in huge stacks in the fields, taking only a small portion home when needed. The fires in the stacks do not threaten houses or property in the village, but they can cost the victims a year's worth of cooking fuel and have become a common strategy of attack or revenge. When the political struggle between the current and past party secretaries intensified in the winter of 1998, such arson occurred almost weekly. Strangely, not a single arsonist was apprehended because the local police department made little effort to investigate such relatively minor crimes. One police officer told me that the budget allowed the police to concentrate on only the major cases. But, villagers complained that the police, like the local government, cared little about the safety and property of the ordinary people; all they really cared about was helping village cadres to collect taxes, levies, and fees. Whatever the reason, the passivity of the local police has also contributed to the deterioration of public security.

Community-based social and cultural activities constitute the third area of public life that has declined since the late 1980s. Again, the decline began with the end of the collective period when the villagers, especially the village youth, were mobilized to participate in public activities sponsored by the collectives. The village performance troupe, movies, sports activities, and organized volunteer work were most frequently mentioned as examples during my interviews with villagers.

From the late 1950s to the early 1980s, Xiajia village had a well-organized performance troupe to entertain villagers during slack seasons; it also served as a propaganda team during the political campaigns. The troupe belonged to the village community (Xiajia Brigade) and its members were paid by the collectives in work points. The male members were permanent, but the female members changed every few years because women normally stopped performing after marriage. During the Chinese Spring Festival the troupe also played a leading role in organizing the annual *yangge* parade, a popular folk dance performed collectively on the streets. Over a period of twenty-plus years, the troupe provided free entertainment, served as a center of popular culture, and also created a social space for talented youth, some of whom became teachers and cadres; others left the village for higher education.

The production brigade also showed movies and organized sports activities during the slack seasons. A film projection team was invited from the county cultural bureau; a portable generator was used to operate the film projector, and movies were shown outside on a huge screen hanging from two poles. There were regular sports activities as well as an annual basketball tournament that began among the production teams and village units such as the local school and the tractor station. Some especially good players formed a village team to participate in a tournament at the commune level. Villagers looked forward to these annual public events as the highlight of their social lives.

The Youth League, village militia, and Women's Association also did volunteer work during the 1960s and 1970s, such as helping childless elderly people with household chores, cleaning up the streets, or simply doing extra farm work without pay. Study groups were also an important part of public life, especially during periods of strong ideological influence, such as during the "Study Mao's Work" campaign in the early 1960s and the "Criticize Lin Biao and Confucius" campaign in the early 1970s.

Despite the heavy influence of political campaigns and Communist ideology during this period, villagers were still able to enjoy much of the new public life created by the collectives on behalf of the state. A new public morality was on the rise, albeit one that was heavily politicized. During my interviews throughout the 1990s, older villagers fondly and nostalgically recalled the experiences of their youth and contrasted them with their critical views of contemporary youth. As one informant explained: "In the 1960s we young people all had endless energy and good thoughts. We wanted to do good things for the collectives and for everyone in the society." He then told me about an occasion in 1963 when a middle-aged woman who was seriously ill needed a blood transfusion. When the village party branch and Youth League issued a joint call for blood donors, sixteen young men and women lined up in front of the village office. My informant was one of two chosen to donate blood, and he told me that he felt extremely honored. During our 1994 interview, he said: "Unfortunately, the class label of the woman's family was middle-peasant. Had she been a poor peasant, I am sure there would have been many more people willing to donate blood." Given the traditional fear of losing blood shared by most Chinese, especially peasants, it is clear that the new public morality motivated the youth at that time.

All of these public activities were sponsored and organized by the collectives, and the kind of sociality generated in this social space inevitably bore the imprint of the official ideology of the party-state, emphasizing the submission of individuals to an officially endorsed collectivity. Perhaps the best example of such an "organized sociality" is the broadcasting system. In the early 1970s, the production brigade installed a loudspeaker in every house, normally right above the bed in the main room. Individual villagers could not control either the content or the time of the broadcasts—they were all controlled at the local broadcasting station at the commune level, of which the brigade was an extended branch. Villagers could not even choose not to listen because the loudspeakers did not have on/off switches, so they were showered daily with official news, political scripts, cadre speeches, and various entertainment programs, regardless of their individual wishes.

After decollectivization in 1983, these sociocultural activities came to an end because they all relied on both the organizational and the financial resources of the collectives. Several individuals turned the performance troupe into a private business, but it failed to profit and lasted only two years. This was also the fate of the annual yangge dance parade. The basketball court became an abandoned lot filled with weeds because there was no one to keep it up. Since the Youth League and other organizations stopped functioning, there have been no organized activities of any sort, not to mention volunteer work. When the entertainment function of radio broadcasting was replaced with television and cassette players, the speakers inside villagers' houses quickly disappeared in the postcollective era.

With the rapid decline of public life, leisure activities shifted to private homes. The media influx of information and images from the cities and foreign countries has replaced the former organized sociality with a powerful but mostly imaginary space whereby villagers develop and pursue new life aspirations. The rise of a TV culture since the 1980s is particularly noteworthy. One evening in 1978 I joined several young Xiajia villagers on a five-mile walk to another village to watch television on the first set in the local area. By 1991 there were 135 TV sets in Xiajia alone, including eight color TVs; by the end of the 1990s, virtually every household owned at least one, and some had two. While still under state control, Chinese television has also changed profoundly to adapt to market competition. In addition to the conventional propaganda, many programs introduce new values and ideas (see Lull 1991; and Zha 1995). As early as 1991 I found myself watching "Hunter"—the American TV police series—in Xiajia village; the same show had played on channel 25 in Boston several months earlier. In the summer of 1997, I joined a small group of villagers watching a typical Taiwanese soap opera about love, marriage, and money for several weeks. The young villagers, particularly the young women, were attracted to the comfortable middle-class lifestyle as well as to the modern values of family life depicted in the TV series. When older villagers had difficulty following the plot, the young audience explained the story to them, while at the same time lecturing them about modern family life. In 1998, I saw two large pictures of pop stars (a Hong Kong man and a Japanese woman) hanging in the bedroom of a 19-year-old, the second son of an old friend. The father told me that his son was a fan of several pop stars and that his dream was to become a professional singer.

These anecdotes illustrate that, in an increasingly integrated world created by the global flow of information and images, the imaginary social space that villagers can appropriate has expanded far beyond the physical and social boundaries of Xiajia. However, unlike in the cities or in developed rural regions where commercialized arenas, such as dancing halls, bowling alleys, restaurants, and coffee shops, have replaced state-controlled public space (see, e.g., the essays in Davis 2000), a newer kind of public space had yet to emerge in Xiajia village. Instead, the continuing decline of public life in the community had caused villagers to retreat into their private homes to spend their leisure time with family members, relatives, and close friends; hence the growing importance of the family, kinship, and social networks.

Kinship Organization and Social Networks

As a result of immigration throughout its history, Xiajia village currently consists of more than thirty agnatic groups. The largest one is the Xia, with 104 households, a fact reflected in the name of the village, which translates literally as "Xia's home." Besides the Xia, there are seven sizable agnatic groups, such as the Xu and the Wang, each with more than fifteen households. Moreover, village endogamy has been practiced for several generations in Xiajia, so many villagers are bound by affinal ties rather than agnatic relations.[9] Its origins can be traced back to the early settlement period, but it became even more popular during the collective period, resulting from a new type of courtship and marriage, one characterized by romantic love and conjugal affection (discussed in Chapters 2 and 3).[10]

Before the 1949 Communist revolution, the significance of patriliny and agnatic solidarity was ritually demonstrated and reinforced during the annual Qingming (grave-sweeping) Festival. The Xia lineage collectively owned land and trees near the ancestral tombs. During the Qingming Festival, Xia males gathered to visit their ancestors' tombs, located six kilometers away from the village. After the visit a banquet was provided at the home of the lineage head. Similar gatherings were held on the eve of the Chinese New Year when the year-end ritual of ancestor worship was performed in the homes of the senior males of each sublineage. Other major agnatic groups in Xiajia village had similar practices, but they were smaller than that of the Xia. These agnatic groups also constituted the major organized form of social and economic activity for most ordinary villagers. The overall power of lineage organization in Xiajia village, however, was never as strong as that along the southeast coast (see Baker 1968; Freedman 1966; Potter 1970; J. Watson 1975; R. Watson 1985a). Thus for Xiajia villagers, the family was all they could depend on in their struggle of survival in the frontier environment (for similar situations in Taiwan, see Gallin 1966; and Harrell 1982).

During the post-1949 period, especially after the high tide of radical collectivization that was aimed at destroying traditional patterns of social organization, the power of the patrilineage in Xiajia diminished considerably. The ancestral land and trees were redistributed among villagers during land reform and a public cemetery was established outside the southeastern gate of the village. The Xia, and other groups whose ancestral tombs were far away from Xiajia, began to bury their dead in the public graveyard. The lineage-wide Qingming visit to the ancestral tombs and the associated banquet no longer took place. What remained were only unorganized, family tomb visits during the fifth days of the first and seventh months of the lunar calendar and during the Qingming Festival, but these visits were more sentimental (or memorial) than religious. Domestic ancestor worship during the Spring Festival continued until the Cultural Revolution (1966); it was only partially resumed in some families during the early 1980s and gradually died out by the end of the 1990s. Some core notions of lineage ideology, such as filial piety, male preference, and generational superiority, were also attacked during the repeated political campaigns. Despite such efforts and the state's hostility toward large kinship organizations, however, the importance of kinship per se has not declined. Instead, kinship ties have been absorbed into the more general and open-ended structure of *guanxi* networks.[11]

The Chinese notion of *guanxi*, which may be translated roughly as "social networks," is multilayered and has been a central concern among China scholars in recent decades. Scholarly accounts tend to regard guanxi as one element of a uniquely Chinese normative social order (see, e.g., King 1991; Kipnis 1997; Hwang 1987) or to treat guanxi as a practical means for advancing specific personal interests (Walder 1986; Yang Ping 1994). My study in Xiajia, however, shows that villagers perceive their guanxi networks as the very foundation of society—the local moral world in which they live their lives and the flow of interpersonal experience occurs (Yan 1996). Guanxi in such a local moral world constitutes a total social phenomenon in the Maussian sense, because it provides one with a social space that at once incorporates economic, political, social, and recreational activities.[12]

A careful analysis of patterns of gift exchange, the most important means for building up and maintaining guanxi in everyday life, shows an important change over the past several decades.[13] By the 1990s, the overall structure of guanxi networks in Xiajia was characterized by a heavy reliance on friendship ties, as opposed to (official) kinship relations, the involvement of a large number of fellow villagers, and an active role of affines.[14] More important, Xiajia villagers have gone beyond the boundaries of the kinship system to build networks through all kinds of personal relations based on friendship: friends, colleagues, and fellow villagers (locally called *tunqin*, which literally means "relatives by coresidence"). It is this stress on extended relatedness, as opposed to inherited or blood-based relatedness, that attracted my attention after my first fieldwork in 1989 because such relatedness has to be made and maintained and therefore depends heavily on individual choice and agency (see Yan 1996: 105–21).

Equally important, the local world is also moral and emotional, which is reflected in *renqing* ethics. The local term *renqing* can be roughly translated as "human feelings," but in practice it has multiple meanings. The fundamental principle of interaction and communication at the individual level is encapsulated in renqing ethics, which should be understood primarily as a set of moral norms that guide and regulate one's behavior. Renqing is also the socially accepted pattern of emotional responses in the sense that one takes others' emotional responses into consideration. One's failure to fulfill the obligation of reciprocity, or to show no consideration for others' feelings and emotional responses, is regarded as an immoral act and thus a violation of renqing ethics. Furthermore, renqing serves as an important standard by which villagers judge whether one is a proper social person. In other words, it is renqing that gives meaning to everyday engagements, interactions, and transactions among villagers. Without renqing, life is less meaningful and people are dehumanized (see Yan 1996: 122–46).

Nevertheless, this local moral world is by no means the only arena within which villagers play their social roles. As a result of economic reforms and decollectivization, villagers find themselves more and more often dealing with people from the outside world. When villagers encounter outsiders, they tend to resort to what they know best—that is, renqing ethics and guanxi networks. This leads not only to the expansion of old guanxi networks but also to the cultivation of new short-term and instrumental personal connections. More important, when many instrumental connections are recruited into guanxi networks, and when people have to utilize the gift as a means to get things done, guanxi and renqing are transformed into what I call their extended forms. In its new extended form guanxi becomes a means of entering "back doors," and renqing is regarded mainly as an exchangeable resource, something that is primarily instrumental and less emotional or moral. By the end of the 1990s, the extended forms of guanxi and renqing had gradually assumed an important role in social exchange within the community. Some villagers hosted family ceremonies only for the purpose of collecting monetary gifts, some tried to avoid the obligation of proper reciprocity, and others even took advantage of renqing-based trust to cheat friends and neighbors in business transactions.

The decline of public life and the instrumentalization of guanxi and renqing have led some villagers to search for alternatives. In 1997, I unexpectedly discovered two religious groups in the village, one Protestant and the other Catholic; and a third group that was also Protestant emerged two years later. The Catholic group had about twenty members who gathered twice a week at the house of the group leader, a 28-year-old woman with a middle school education. When I visited her home again in 1998, she and her husband had converted half of their home into a church, with the holy cross and candles on a center altar and homemade benches in rows in the two-room family church. It was called *qidaodian*, meaning "praying station."

After attending their weekly gatherings and interviewing the group leaders, I discovered that almost all of the members were recruited into these groups through networks of female relatives and friends. The male believers who had converted to Christianity had also done so with the help of their wives or their wives' sisters. These believers normally met in a leader's home during slack seasons and also engaged in extensive mutual assistance in agricultural production and other forms of cooperation in daily life. From what they told me, the weekly gatherings provided the most important social space for these villagers. Interestingly, preexisting kinship ranks tended to be ignored by these believers, although they were indeed related to one another either by blood or by marriage. Instead it was the spiritual leaders who enjoyed the respect and support of many of the believers. For instance, the mother-in-law of the female leader of the Catholic group always expressed sincere respect for and agreement with her daughter-in-law during religious gatherings. When asked about this new type of interpersonal relations, these believers told me that they were *jiaoyou*—literally "religious friends"—with one another, and they characterized their close ties as *shenqin*, a new term in village public life that might be translated as "spiritual kinship."

As complex as it is, the Xiajia community provides a social stage for individual villagers to fulfill their family duties and to live their personal lives. In such a local moral world, the flow of interpersonal experiences over the period of the past fifty years constitutes the continuing saga of the rise of the private family and the transformation of private life, which will be told in more detail in the chapters that follow.

CHAPTER TWO

Youth Autonomy and Romance in Courtship

In July 1991, I attended a wedding in Xiajia village and was impressed by the public display of affection between the bride and groom. One example of the couple's intimate behavior was their drinking sugar water together during the wedding. According to local custom, this symbolizes that their future life will be as sweet as sugar. When the bride did not want to finish her drink, the groom finished it for her, ignoring the teasing from young onlookers and the gestures of disapproval from his senior relatives in the room (her refusal to finish it was taken as a sign that she might not be a sweet and obedient daughter-in-law). Later I also noticed that the bride did not hesitate to adjust the groom's suit before they began the main ritual performance. They were obviously happy about their marriage and felt free to show their affection in front of more than a hundred people.

I was even more surprised when I learned some details about their story. The bride was 19 years old and the groom was 18. They lived in the same village and had been classmates in both primary and middle school. After graduation from middle school, their friendship continued to develop; or, by their own accounts, they made so many good impressions on each other that they wanted to spend the rest of their lives together. Following the suggestions of the young woman, the young man asked his family to propose marriage in 1990, and the prospective bride's family was happy to accept the proposal. After an engagement ritual at the end of 1990, the young couple went to Ha'erbin, the provincial capital, to take an engagement photo and to buy betrothal gifts for the bride. Over the following several months, they continued to visit each other and developed good relationships with their respective in-laws. Because of their young age (the minimum age for marriage required by Chinese law is 22 for males and 20 for females), neither family considered that the wedding would be held soon, until the bride's mother learned, in June of 1991, that her daughter was pregnant. Then the two families hurriedly went through all the necessary procedures: registering the marriage with the local government and procuring the official certificate, decorating the conjugal room, and preparing for the wedding ritual.[1]

My initial excitement about this case gradually abated, as I learned of many similar circumstances during subsequent field visits to the village in 1993, 1994, and 1997. But I was once again surprised in 1998 when an engagement between a young couple was canceled unexpectedly. Many in Xiajia could not believe this news, having heard rumors that the young couple had been sexually involved after their engagement. In the recent past, public knowledge of sexual intimacy would have definitely secured a marriage proposal, because the young woman would have been considered "loose" if she then broke up with her boyfriend. But in this case the pressures of public opinion did not prevent her from breaking off the engagement. When asked about the potential damage caused by her earlier sexual intimacy, she reportedly said: "It did not change anything; I will find a better boy." Although many villagers considered her statement shameful evidence of her lack of female virtue, they also agreed that she would not have any difficulty securing a proper marriage, because, as a middle-aged man lamented, "Times have changed. The younger generation has different ideas about everything, and some of them don't even care whether a bride is a virgin."

Obviously, by the end of the 1990s, romantic love occupied an important place in courtship and spouse selection, and premarital sex between an engaged man and woman was becoming socially permissible. These changes were revolutionary and constitute a sharp contrast with our knowledge and perception of the intimate lives of Chinese villagers.

In their 1992 study, Jankowiak and Fischer argue that romantic love is a human universal, or at least a near-universal, because it can be found in most non-Western societies where data are available. However, most scholarly inquiries are still confined by the popular idea that romantic love is essentially limited to, or the product of, Western culture (see Jankowiak and Fischer 1992: 154; Jankowiak 1995: 1–6). Such a Eurocentric conception of romantic love influences the field of China studies as well, particularly the study of rural China. As Jankowiak notes, a number of scholars simply assume that the Chinese are uninterested in romantic love, or are incapable of incorporating romantic love into courtship and marriage, because of the their collective social orientation.[2] As Jankowiak observes: "The remarkable continuity of romantic love found in Chinese literature has been little appreciated, and the reality and the meaning behind its continuity and transformation has been underestimated, if not misconceived" (1995: 167). This underestimation persists because there have been few scholarly attempts to explore the emotional world of ordinary Chinese people, except for Jankowiak's own work in a Chinese city (1993, 1995). Rural China remains, to borrow the title of a Chinese novel, the "forgotten corner of love."

This chapter and the next aim to dispel the prevailing myth that Chinese villagers are not interested in or capable of romantic love. I also demonstrate that the emotional world of villagers is as rich as our observational power and analytical tools can comprehend. In this chapter, I begin with the local terms of spouse selection and then examine the development of romantic love and intimacy in spouse selection over the five decades between 1949 and 1999, situating both dramatic cases of romance and routine arrangements of marriage in their specific social and cultural contexts. I conclude by comparing the Xiajia case with an early study conducted in the late 1970s, highlighting both the continuity and the radical changes in spouse selection since the mid-twentieth century.

In Xiajia village, as elsewhere in rural China, everyone is supposed to marry, and courtship (romantic and nonromantic alike) is the bridge to marriage, rather than a prolonged period of youthful indulgence as an end in itself.[3] The romantic love and intimacy discussed in these two chapters are, therefore, confined to the process of courtship and postengagement interactions.

Local Categories of Spouse Selection

During one of my interviews with a 71-year-old informant, the scholarly term "spouse selection" (*zeou* in Chinese) slipped from my mouth. He looked at me with puzzled eyes; repeating the word several times, he asked me my meaning. When I explained the meaning of the word, he shook his head and told me there were two other local terms to describe what I was interested in; that for males is *shuo xifu* and that for females is *zhao pojia*. Intrigued by his insistence on the correct use of these terms, I made further inquiries about local vocabulary and discovered that there are actually three major terms, and the differences among them are noteworthy.

In the first term, shuo xifu, the last two characters, xifu, refer to either one's wife or one's daughter-in-law, depending on the context; and the verb shuo in this context means to obtain the targeted woman by negotiating with her parents through a matchmaker. So, shuo xifu vividly depicts the act of negotiation by parents for a wife for their son (or a daughter-in-law for themselves, depending on how one looks at the issue). In the second term, zhao pojia, pojia literally means the home of a woman's future mother-in-law (her natal family is called *niangjia*, literally the home of one's mother), and the verb zhao means to search or look for, and in this context it refers to the parents' concern and action to find a suitable home for their daughter. Clearly, in both instances, the agents/subjects are the parents, who are supposed to take action and make decisions regarding the search for a spouse for their son or daughter. This is why the old man insisted that I learn the differences and use the terms correctly.

There is, however, a third term, *zhao duixiang*, which in the 1990s was more popular than the first two. According to the *Modern Chinese Dictionary*, duixiang refers exclusively to the other party in a romantic love relationship; with the addition of the verb zhao, the term means avidly searching for a particular one, the beloved other. The word duixiang seems to have first appeared in the literature of the May Fourth Movement in the 1920s and has since been used to refer to one's lover.[4] The agent/subject of searching for a duixiang is the individual instead of the parents. According to some older villagers, this term was first brought into Xiajia village during the land reform campaign by outside Communist cadres, and it took a rather long time for the word to become part of villagers' daily vocabulary; some say it was not until the 1960s, and others claim that it was even later.

In today's Xiajia, villagers use the three terms selectively, depending on the context. When parents are asked about their children's marriage prospects they use the traditional terms; when young people talk among themselves or with others about spouse selection, the term zhao duixiang is more frequently used, an indication that they have some autonomy and are looking for romantic love. During my fieldwork in the 1990s, the modern term zhao duixiang was used much more often when spouse selection was discussed as a general social practice, regardless of the age of my informants. But when the discussion turned to their own family affairs, older villagers tended to use the two traditional terms rather than the modern one.

When discussing marriage patterns with me, Xiajia villagers used the modern term duixiang to distinguish among three types of spouse selection. The first is *ziyou duixiang* (literally meaning free spouse selection), which refers to when a young couple falls in love and becomes engaged without the assistance or interference of a third party. The second type is called *jieshao duixiang*, which refers to finding a mate through the introduction of a relative, friend, or professional matchmaker. The last type is *fumu baoban*, which refers to the situation in which the parents make all major decisions regarding their children's marriage. Hereafter, I will translate these three types as free-choice match, match-by-introduction, and arranged marriage, respectively. Such a tripartite classification also corresponds to ethnographic evidence found elsewhere in rural China (see, e.g., Xu 1997).

During my fieldwork in 1998 and 1999, I surveyed the marriages of male villagers that took place between 1949 and the summer of 1999 and classified each of the 484 cases in one of the three categories used by Xiajia villagers (see Table 2.1).[5]

This investigation clearly indicates a shift toward free-choice matches over the five decades: in the 1960s only 7 percent of marriages were the result of free choice, and in the 1990s the figure was 36 percent. Likewise, the percentage of arranged marriages declined sharply—from a dominant 87 percent in the 1950s to 11 percent in the 1960s and to zero in the 1990s. The majority of Xiajia villagers found their spouses through an introduction by an intermediary; thus matches-by-introduction were dominant for three decades.

TABLE 2.1.

Spouse Selection among Xiajia Men, 1949–1999

Years	Arranged marriages		Matches-by-introduction		Free-choice matches		Total number of marriages
	Number	Percent	Number	Percent	Number	Percent	
1949–59	28	73	9	24	1	3	38
1960–69	8	11	61	82	5	7	74
1970–79	6	5	101	79	21	16	128
1980–89		0	107	81	25	19	132
1990–99		0	72	64	40	36	112
Total	42		350		92		484

The trend toward free-choice matches also raises some questions. For instance, despite the implementation of the 1950 Marriage Law and other state-sponsored efforts at family reform, there was only one case of a free-choice match in Xiajia village during the first decade. This seems to contradict accepted wisdom about radical social reforms in the 1950s. Moreover, their number did not grow in the 1980s (remaining at 16 percent, as in the previous decade), a fact that also requires further explanation.

The numbers themselves cannot solve these puzzles; the real answers lie in the lived experiences of the villagers. Through in-depth interviews during several field visits, I discovered that, if one focused on actual changes in spouse selection, the 484 marriages represent three stages of the trend toward free-choice matches, but these stages do not always correspond to changes in national policy.

The Rise of Youth Autonomy, 1946–1962

Love affairs existed in Xiajia village well before the Communist revolution, and in the 1940s one young couple who fell madly in love even engaged in premarital sex. But the isolated love affair did not prevent the young woman's parents from marrying her out to a total stranger, and she thereafter suffered greatly from an abusive husband who scolded her for being a loose woman. At that time village youth did not have any say about their own marriages, which were arranged according to *fumu zhi ming, meishuo zhi yan* (parental order and matchmaker's advice). An old woman told me that as a little girl she had learned from her mother that she must accept her fate in an arranged marriage. A local adage dictated one's behavior: "To follow the cock if marrying a cock, to follow the dog if marrying a dog; to carry it on your shoulder and walk your life course if you marry a shoulder-carrying pole" (*jiaji suiji, jiagou suigou, jiagei biandan tiao zhe zou*).

Beginning in 1946 the land reform campaign turned Xiajia society and social life upside down. The new marriage law, which was meant to revolutionize marriage customs in China, was implemented officially in the area in 1951–52, and through various study meetings villagers learned about the legal ban on arranged marriages, concubinage, and purchased marriages. Older villagers recalled that a messenger from the local town government brought the printed marriage law to the village and that they were required to attend a meeting to study it.

However, the state-sponsored official campaigns seemed to have little immediate impact on spouse selection and other areas in private life at the grassroots level. According to a number of older villagers, parents were firmly in control of the marriages of their adult children, and the village youth, many of whom actively participated in political activities, did not show a strong desire for marital autonomy. Uncle Lu, who had been a work team member, considered the lack of romance during the land reform period to be evidence of the selflessness of young activists, as demonstrated by his own experience.

> As a 22-year-old, I had endless energy to work and often slept for only three or four hours a day. There were so many exciting new things happening every day, and I only wanted to stay home for meals. When my parents told me that I was to be engaged to a girl from the Xu family, I did not have any opinions about it, except to realize that I was lucky because the girl was considered to be good looking in our village. I told my parents I had no idea [which meant "no objection" in this context], and that was it! By the end of the year I was called back by my parents to get married. I spent only one night at home for the wedding and returned to my work team the very next morning. I was so happy when my leader praised me for being a devoted revolutionary, always putting work ahead of my personal life. It was not until more than half a month when I returned and saw my wife working in the kitchen of my parents' home that I realized I was a married man.

Uncle Lu and several older villagers agreed that women did play a very important role in land reform, but they rejected the idea that women's participation in public life had any impact on young men. "We always worked separately," they recalled.

Aunt Gao, a female activist during the literacy movement in the early 1950s, confirmed this point. According to her, women were mobilized to join mass meetings, participating in night school and sometimes also doing logistical work for the men; but they rarely worked side by side with the men. As a group leader of the night school, Aunt Gao had come up with the idea of teaching middle-aged women to read while they were working at home. In that way they did not have an excuse to avoid the classes, and the teaching was much easier if the newly learned characters could be related to actual objects around the house. Aunt Gao noted: "We also learned about the marriage law and about ideas of free choice [in spouse selection], equality between husband and wife, and other new things. But few of us actually dared to go out to search for a man. We were too young and very shy."

The major change during the 1950s was that most parents began consulting with their children when deciding on a marriage partner, and parents also tried to convince their children that a particular match would be a good one if they disagreed. A technical change allowed the boy and girl to meet briefly under the watchful eyes of parents and matchmaker and then to say what they thought of each other. In this way, most parents were able to exert their power and authority with the consensus of the young people. Matches-by-introduction thus emerged as a new type of spouse selection during the 1950s that was enthusiastically welcomed by village youth. There were several generational conflicts over the selection of a spouse in the late 1950s, but the disagreements were all eventually solved between the parents and their sons.

The first noteworthy case of a love match occurred in 1961–62.[6] It began with parental manipulation and ended with an outraged protest by the young woman against her parents. Mr. Wang, then party secretary in Xiajia village, was fond of Little Zhang, a young man living in a neighboring house, and wanted his daughter, Wang Shuqin, to marry him; but the young man secretly loved another girl. To achieve his goal, Secretary Wang first matched the rival girl to a man from another lineage. Then he arranged for his daughter to marry Little Zhang, his hand-picked son-in-law. Initially, Wang Shuqin accepted the arranged marriage, but she fought with her husband from day one and demanded a divorce shortly thereafter. After a few months Secretary Wang discovered that his daughter really loved Mr. Li, a man she had chosen for herself, and was furious for two reasons. First, he considered it morally wrong and shameful for his daughter to love someone else after she was already married. Second, Mr. Li, his daughter's lover, was not his ideal choice of son-in-law—because the young man was lazy, disobedient, and addicted to gambling. On several occasions when he caught his daughter with her lover at his house, he beat the young man severely and threw him out. He and his wife also tried to change their daughter's mind by alternately punishing her physically and treating her very well materially.

To the surprise of all, Wang Shuqin was very determined and insisted on having her own way. According to several informants and herself, while she was married she had always slept with her clothes on and with a pair of scissors under her pillow. Whenever her husband tried to approach her, she threatened to kill herself. She then went to enlist support from upper-level government agencies—the women's association, the party secretary in the commune, and the local court. As a party member herself, she knew how to get help from these sources and eventually she won her battle: she divorced her husband and married her lover shortly thereafter. But she paid dearly in two ways. First, feeling defeated and ashamed, her father refused to see her for the next two decades; he only forgave her when he was dying in 1993. Second, her strong will and independence led to serious conflicts with her second husband after their marriage, and he frequently beat her because he too was hot-tempered. This was particularly painful for her because, having sacrificed the relationship with her natal family, she had nowhere to go to escape her sometimes violent husband. She had no choice but to relent and become a docile wife, like most other women of her age.

This case is noteworthy for two reasons. First, romantic love during courtship did not necessarily lead to a harmonious and fulfilling conjugal love if the two parties involved still lived in the shadow of patriarchal authority. Driven by their passion and supported by the official ideology, the young couple acted bravely by doing something most of their peers did not dare to do in the early 1960s, namely, to publicize their romantic love and to marry against strong parental objections (and the power of a village leader as well). But once they entered into married life and a husband-wife relationship, male supremacy took center stage; when the husband encountered resistance, he did not hesitate to resort to violence to secure his "rightful place" at home.

Second, despite the state's radical attempts to reform marriage and the family institution in the countryside, overall cultural expectations and the social environment did not change much at the grassroots level in the early 1960s. For instance, when Wang Shuqin was beaten up by her second husband, the community was not on her side. In the early 1960s, wife beating was still regarded as nothing more than a common way by which a husband could make things right at home. Its acceptability was reflected in the popular saying *dadao de laopo, roudao de mian* (roughly translated: "taming a wife by beating, and making dough by kneading"). Like many others in the village, Wang's second husband quoted this old saying while beating her. I first learned of the saying directly from her husband during my interview with him. With his wife by his side, he proudly recalled their romance, marriage, and how he had tamed her. She did not protest at all, but nodded her head in agreement.

It is clear that changes in the private sphere usually do not immediately coincide with or follow changes in the public sphere. Because of its exclusive and protected nature, the private sphere tends to resist outside change. This was so even during the 1950s and early 1960s when the state made bold attempts to transform the Chinese society.

Nevertheless, the state-sponsored program was successful in the ideological realm. The new ideology that supported youth autonomy, free choice in marriage, and gender equality was introduced into village life through political meetings, media coverage, and entertainment. The mobilization of women to participate in agricultural production, irrigation projects, and other collective work during the Great Leap opened a new social outlet for village women, which in turn had some influence on private life. Wang Shuqin, for example, had become acquainted with her lover while working in the public canteen. He had caught her attention because he was a good actor performing in the village troupe, and in several plays he assumed the role of model husband who was caring and loving. Impressed by his handsome appearance and his role on stage, she chatted with him whenever he came to eat in the canteen. The couple's idealization of free love began in the public domain and was reinforced by the idealist political atmosphere of the 1950s, a kind of romantic and radical atmosphere accurately analyzed by Blake in his article on romance and love songs during the Great Leap Forward (see Blake

1979). Inspired by this couple's courage, four other men also found their spouses by free choice during this period; fortunately, they did not encounter as much disapproval from their parents.

The Rise of Romantic Encounters, 1963–1983

As far as spouse selection was concerned, the 1960s were a springtime. The new leadership in Xiajia village in the early 1960s took the lessons of the Great Leap seriously and tried to focus on agricultural production in a pragmatic manner. As a result, collective farming in Xiajia started to improve, and the village enjoyed relative peace and prosperity during the subsequent two decades. The stable collective economy provided a good base for the development of a new style of public life centered on the promotion of collectivism and socialist values, and of a new social space whereby village youth of opposite sexes could socialize together. Movies and basketball games were the most popular activities among young villagers. Many villagers recalled that when a movie started some young men and women always stood at the edge of the audience and paid more attention to each other than to the screen. A similar opportunity for romance was provided by the annual basketball tournament, which always aroused a great deal of excitement. "It was like a holiday season for us," recalled several villagers. Although it was not as convenient to flirt at games as it was during a movie young villagers still enjoyed the spectacle and used it as an opportunity to become familiar with those of the opposite sex.

Labor in the fields offered the most frequent and long-lasting opportunities for young villagers to see, talk, and work among peers of the opposite sex. Young women and men worked side by side during the busy seasons of spring ploughing, summer hoeing, and autumn harvest. For instance, corn planting required the cooperation of two people—one to dig a small hole in the ground and the other to throw seeds into the hole and cover it with dirt. Usually a male did the digging, and a female took care of the other tasks. Although the hoeing and harvesting were done individually, it was common for young men who had finished their chores to help the women and then for the two to take a break together (they had one break in the morning and two breaks in the afternoon, each lasting ten to twenty minutes).

Most often, romance between young people grew out of mutual attraction and idealization that developed while they worked together in the fields. In 1972 a young woman from a cadre family who was fond of a young man in the same production team frequently tried to talk to him while they worked or asked him to help her with her chores. It happened that the young man spoke with a bit of a stutter when he became excited or embarrassed. One day during the harvest season, he stuttered for half a minute to tell the young woman: "Let me help you sharpen your sickle." Fellow team members over-head this and laughed out loud. Within a couple of days, everyone in the village knew the story, and many purposely repeated his words in front of each of them. The public teasing actually made the previously hazy feelings between them much more clear and explicit, and by the end of the harvest season, the young woman told her family that she wanted to marry the young man. Her parents tried to discourage her because the young man's family held the class label of upper-middle peasant, which was considered a very suspicious political status during the early 1970s. But she persuaded her parents and eventually married the young man with her parents' blessing and the provision of a dowry.

In addition to shared work experiences, there were some other channels by which personal contact could develop into romance among young villagers. In the mid-1970s, a high school graduate returned to work in the farm fields. He had hoped to go to university, but at that time, even city-born youths had to leave the urban areas to work in the countryside (a movement known as *xiaxiang*, "up to the mountains and down to the countryside"). He was de-pressed and isolated himself at work and in public gatherings. A number of villagers laughed at his unrealistic dreams, but one of his former female class-mates respected him, listened to his complaints, and openly supported him. He was touched, and the two soon secretly fell in love. "It was on a winter afternoon of 1974," the man recalled during my 1994 interview, "in her house when her parents were not there, I held her hands and asked her to be my *duixiang* [loved one]. She burst into tears, saying nothing but nodding her head." Unfortunately, the girl's father rejected the marriage proposal by the young man's family because he favored marrying his daughter to the son of a cadre in another village. According to the father, allowing his daughter to marry this young man would have been a disaster because the latter was not a good farmer and his family was poor and thus could not offer a respectable betrothal gift. Unable to change her father's mind, the girl adopted a common yet effective strategy—she simply refused to consent to the other marriage proposal. During the following year, she vetoed several proposals by matchmakers, making the point very clear that she would only agree to marry the man she loved. Finally, her father had to give in, and the couple married in 1977, three years after they first promised to become duixiang.

During the 1960s and 1970s, when free-choice matches first began to be acceptable, not a single case led to a breakdown of the parent-child relationship; and in most cases the young people eventually won their parents' approval and blessing. This is because by the late 1960s youth autonomy in spouse selection had increased to the extent that few parents would decide on a spouse for their children without their consent. A good indicator is that the majority of village youth say they were satisfied with their choice of spouse during this period, and only a small number reported that they had not chosen their spouse voluntarily. Also during this period both pre- and postengagement interactions between young men and women expanded and became more intense. Romantic love also occurred in a number of match-by-introduction cases, but my informants did not consider them examples of romantic love because they fell into the category of a good match and thus did not involve any generational conflicts.

New Developments in the Post-Mao Era: 1984 to the Present

My interviews with the Xiajia villagers contained fewer stories of romance during the early 1980s, and a survey confirmed that the number of free-choice matches indeed decreased during the first half of the 1980s, but thereafter steadily climbed back up. Several factors may account for the change. The collectives were officially dismantled by the end of 1983, and the following spring villagers found themselves tending numerous small pieces of farmland, working only with family members. Many villagers recalled that initially it felt odd to work independently. The youths particularly disliked this new type of family farming because it was "boring and cold," as they put it. Another reason that free-choice matches reportedly decreased during this period was that parents became more open-minded about their adult children's marriage choices. Usually the two generations could work things out, either smoothly or with only minor disagreements, which rarely led to direct confrontation between the youth and their parents. As a result, my informants regarded a number of free-choice matches as matches-by-introduction simply because they lacked generational conflicts.

That situation changed quickly. The generation that reached adulthood in the late 1980s and early 1990s did not benefit from the land distribution in 1983 and thus became landless laborers in the village. The best way for them to earn an income was to seek jobs outside the community, which opened a new horizon of social life.

At the same time, television sets became a desirable commodity and quickly entered the list of bridewealth items (see Chapter 6). By the mid-1990s, watching television had become a major part of the everyday life of Xiajia villagers, creating another kind of space for the development of romantic love and intimacy. Unlike political meetings or collective farming, television presented the most up-to-date, fashionable lifestyles to villagers, arousing new aspirations among the young and making the older people regret their lost years. In addition, beginning in the late 1980s, villagers began to remodel their houses to create more rooms for individual activities; they separated the bedrooms from the living room and the parents from the grown-up children. The availability of personal space within one's home also enabled some young villagers to develop a close relationship with the opposite sex (see Chapter 5).

In the summer of 1997, the owner of a small shop in Xiajia village turned the courtyard of his home into an open-air dance hall for ballroom dancing and disco, attracting many young people every evening. The young and open-minded shop owner originally intended to make his shop competitive with another shop in the village, using the dance floor to attract customers. But once the evening dancing became a regular event, and especially after the other shop owner followed suit and created an even better dance floor, dancing became a popular new social activity. Initially the youth danced only with partners of the same sex; but gradually dancing with members of the opposite sex became popular and some youth began to flirt. According to my informants, at least three couples fell in love at these dances. But a year or so later the police called this privately organized social activity immoral and forced the dances to stop during a campaign against the increasing crime rate. But some villagers insisted that the real reason was that the shop owners failed to bribe the policemen.

In the 1990s the scope of socializing among youth became more narrow in some ways and expanded in others. On the one hand, the absence of an overarching collective entity meant that villagers in the 1990s farmed family land and organized their social lives independently. Thus today, people normally interact with those who are already in their existing guanxi networks, and they are rarely brought together by community activities. In the summer of 1999 I accompanied a group of more than eighty villagers to a flood-prevention project; during the trip I repeatedly heard the villagers exchange greetings like "Haven't seen you for quite a long time" and "Where have you been these days?" And the replies were "I haven't seen you for a while too" and "Nowhere, I've just been staying at home." Some older villagers also asked about the unfamiliar faces in the crowd, especially the young women who had recently married into the village. It was obvious that the lack of social activities had created more distance and unfamiliarity among villagers.

On the other hand, more and more villagers regularly began seeking employment outside the village community, often in cities hundreds of miles away, where they have opportunities to interact with strangers in unfamiliar social environments. After thirty years of rural-urban separation and the development of large economic and social gaps, villagers frequently encountered urban prejudices and stereotyping against peasants. To survive in this modern yet hostile urban setting, they relied on support from their own group and guanxi networks. And in daily life, they also sought support from the opposite sex to relieve their loneliness and fears. As a result, a number of young villagers fell in love while working outside Xiajia village, and some brought their partners back to Xiajia to marry. Of the free-choice matches, more than 30 percent were romances developed outside the village.

Eloping is another new development. Decollectivization and the opening up of the urban job market (primarily for low-end jobs) provided the material basis for adventurous young lovers to seek personal happiness beyond the village boundaries. Their elopements and lives together in the outside world inevitably had a further influence on both their own lives and those of village youths in the future. Six couples eloped in Xiajia village during the 1990s. In two of the six cases Xiajia women eloped with their lovers from other villages; the other four couples were all from Xiajia village. Some resorted to eloping when they encountered parental objections or interference, but others eloped for no obvious reason. One young woman from Xiajia told her parents that she had been recruited as a domestic worker in a nearby city, which is the most common form of urban employment arranged through the local women's federation. But four months later she wrote her parents a letter from Guangzhou, telling them that she and her boyfriend, Mr. Xu, were working and living together and that everything was fine. They had fallen in love on their way to search for better employment opportunities in southern China, and the girl had not told her parents because she did not want them to worry about her going so far away from home.

Romantic love in the reform era appears to be more passionate than it was earlier. In 1994 one young couple fell in love after spending time together in the fields taking care of their families' cows. The 17-year-old young man's parents were unhappy when they learned of the love affair because they thought the young woman would not be the right type of wife for their son. To solve the problem they immediately arranged a marriage for their son with someone from another village. Being so young, the son was not completely sure what he wanted and thus accepted his parents' proposal after he met the second young woman. But at the formal engagement ritual, the first young woman, who was only 16 at the time, stormed into the ritual, announced that she was already pregnant, and demanded that the young man's parents cancel the engagement. She won the battle on the spot when the second young woman left the ceremony in a fury.

One dramatic case of romance occurred in 1998. A poor and conservative father was strongly opposed to the young man his daughter had chosen for herself because the father considered the young man's family too poor to pay a handsome bridewealth. This was unusual because by the late 1990s most parents did not object to their children's marriage proposals on such grounds, since the monetary gifts go directly to the young women rather than to her parents. Pressured by financial difficulties, however, this father was interested in the potential profits from his daughter's marriage, and this was obvious to everyone, including the two lovers. It is said that one day the daughter asked her lover if he really loved her and wanted to start a family with her. The young man swore that he did. When the young woman then asked for special proof of his love, saying nothing, the boy found a knife and, before the girl could react, chopped off the tip of his left baby finger. The young woman was deeply touched and left Xiajia with her boyfriend; they worked in two cities successively for nearly a year until she became pregnant. When I was in Xiajia village in the summer of 1999 they had just settled with the young woman's father, paying less than one-fourth of the bridewealth he had demanded, and they had held their wedding in the village. Because of his heroic demonstration of love, the young man not only won absolute devotion from the young woman but also had a moral advantage over her family.

Love and Intimacy in Matches-by-Introduction

An examination of the 484 marriages among Xiajia men reveals that love and affection also have a place in matches-by-introduction, a finding that echoes Victor De Munck's observation of "romantically motivated arranged marriages" in Sri Lanka.[7] This was particularly true during the collective period because the older generation was much less open in expressing their emotions to the opposite sex without the backup of a legitimate engagement. Two trends in emotional development in matches-by-introduction deserve close attention.

In most cases of village endogamy, brides and grooms already knew their prospective mates before they were brought together by an introducer or matchmaker. In this type, the introducer often serves as a middle-person to negotiate the marriage transaction between the two families. Sometimes an introducer is called in only for ritual purposes because the couple has already become engaged in private, and sometimes the families have even already agreed on the amount of the marital gifts. A good friend told me that before his parents asked the matchmaker to make a proposal he had already developed a strong emotional bond with his future wife. They were both active in the village troupe—the woman was an actress and the man played a musical instrument. They were very open and relaxed with each other when they were in the troupe but felt quite awkward when they were alone. According to my friend, his girlfriend was just too old-fashioned to approach him further, and according to his wife, the young man had been too stupid to say anything warm and nice. But during their separation in the busy farming seasons (they belonged to different production teams) they realized how much they missed each other. Hence the request for a matchmaker after the harvest season in 1968. Similarly, many couples became more deeply involved right after their engagement because they felt they were protected and also entitled to indulge in affection.

In another type of match-by-introduction, couples do not know each other before being introduced by the matchmaker, but they somehow fall in love during the engagement period (this contrasts to love that develops after marriage, a pattern I refer to as conjugal love, discussed in Chapter 4). Engagement love usually occurs when the engaged couple come from different villages. In 1975 one young woman from Xiajia was engaged to a man in a village thirty-five kilometers away, and the two were not acquainted before their first meeting, which was arranged by the girl's distant cousin. The young woman later told me that she did not have any special feelings toward the man during their first meeting, except for noting that he was good looking. Because she was under some financial pressure to marry in order to help her family financially (her father had died a few years earlier and her mother single-handedly ran the family with five children), she accepted the marriage proposal after three brief meetings with the young man. During the following year, she visited the man's family on four occasions, staying there for a few days each time, and the man visited her on three occasions. They also went to take an engagement photo in Ha'erbin city. It was clear to the young woman's good friends in Xiajia that her passion toward her future husband increased with each visit, after which she talked about him for days. Evidence frequently cited by the villagers was that she was so eager to join her future husband that on her wedding day she did not even cry during the farewell ritual to her natal family, a tradition for all departing brides. Later she told me that she simply could not make any tears in her eyes, even with some hot pepper on her handkerchief. "I missed him so much and I was just happy to leave," she confessed to her good friends. Rumor also had it that she and her future husband had had sex shortly after their engagement, and that was how the passion had started. Fifteen years later, I asked her about this rumor when I visited her during a reunion of old friends as well as during an interview as part of my 1991 fieldwork. She refused to give me a direct answer but laughed, even when I told her that I would regard the laughing as a "yes." When I teased her for being so romantic, she replied that what she had done was rather common among her contemporaries. This was the first time I realized that premarital sex between engaged couples might have been going on for quite a while, a topic that I return to in the next chapter.

Late development of romance does not only take place among those whose fiancés/fiancées are not in the same village. A large number of engaged couples in Xiajia village had similar experiences. One couple who became engaged in 1976 told me in 1998 that even though they both worked for a special team conducting scientific experiments related to farming, a small and elite institution in the village, they did not talk to each other at any length before a friend suggested the marriage proposal to them; but they became very close after their engagement because they had the advantage of seeing one another daily at work. I then speculated that their experience might fit the pattern of the 1970s when village youth were still shy and avoided peers of the opposite sex. The couple disagreed, and the wife immediately provided me with an example from 1998. She told of an engagement between the son of an ordinary family and the daughter of the party secretary who was also a temporary teacher in the preschool class in the village school. The son's mother favored the engagement because she thought the marriage would produce a powerful kinship alliance, and thus she offered the highest payment of bridewealth. Her son initially was rather passive, merely accepting his mother's aggressive arrangements. But once he and his fiancée became better acquainted, he became a famous suitor who would do anything to please her. He often accompanied the young woman to her class, helping her to maintain classroom order and to collect the homework. Some children became confused and told their parents that they had two teachers in their class, which quickly became a local joke.

Finally, even when the opinions of the parents dominate the spouse selection process, couples are able to develop a romantic attachment after their engagement, and, interestingly, among the young villagers I interviewed, three defended parental interference. In the mid-1990s, a bright young woman who was able to receive further education at a vocational school faced a dilemma after her graduation. She had a boyfriend in her class whom she had come to love deeply. But each had to return to their home counties after graduation in order to take state-allocated jobs. If she were to continue her romance and eventually marry her lover, she would have to move to his county, which was far from her parents' home. More important, her lover was from a poor family and had heavy duties and potential economic difficulties because he needed to support his aging parents. As expected, her parents objected strongly to this romance, and many conflicts developed between the parents and their daughter. Her father finally managed to secure a relatively good job for her in a town close to Xiajia village and also found her a potential spouse through a powerful cadre in the town. After some tough emotional ups and downs, she accepted her parents' wishes, broke off her first love relationship, and developed a new romance with the second man, to whom she eventually was happily married. Years later she told me that she felt lucky that her parents had stepped in and stopped her crazy romance. Otherwise she would not be living so happily with her son and husband. "In the end, it was my own choice, and nobody could have forced me if I had decided to marry my classmate," she said. "My parents only provided me with valuable advice and used their authority to convince me. They were more experienced and thus right in this case."

From Autonomy to Romance

In their 1978 study of rural life in Guangdong province in southern China, Parish and Whyte offer an excellent overview of changes in marriage patterns up to the mid-1970s. They point out that although patriarchal power was still in place, youth autonomy in spouse selection was one of the most obvious and important changes since the 1949 revolution. They attribute the changes mainly to the availability of social space for youth to interact with peers of the opposite sex, not necessarily to the 1950 Marriage Law and the state-sponsored family reforms. They also point out the complexity of youth autonomy in spouse selection, arguing that most marriages were neither the result of free choice nor completely arranged. Even in the middle-ground category of match-by-introduction, youth autonomy and parental assistance and interference were intermingled: "In most cases mate choice involves double approval and a double veto power; both the young people and their respective parents must agree. Few young people are pressured into a match, and few couples marry in defiance of parental wishes" (Parish and Whyte 1978: 173).

The Xiajia evidence echoes Parish and Whyte's conclusion, revealing the continuation of the same trend of youth autonomy since the 1970s, but also demonstrating some new developments. In general, the tripartite division of spouse selection still exists in Xiajia village and the surrounding areas, and youth autonomy in spouse selection continued to grow in the 1980s and 1990s. There was a steady increase in the number of free-choice matches after the 1950s and a decline in the number of arranged marriages by the late 1970s. Given the complexity of matches-by-introduction, where young couples frequently take the initiative, I follow the approach used by Parish and Whyte to divide the 484 Xiajia marriages into two categories. The first, "youth dominance," includes both free-choice matches and matches-by-introduction in which the couple played the dominant role. The second category, "parental dominance," covers both arranged marriages and matches-by-introduction in which the parents played the dominant role. Table 2.2 shows that the trends described by Parish and Whyte in the late 1970s continued in the 1980s and 1990s (see esp. table 33 in Parish and Whyte 1978: 174).

According to Parish and Whyte, parental dominance in mate choice declined from 83 percent in the 1950s to 41 percent by the mid-1960s and to 38 percent by the mid-1970s. Over the same period, youth dominance increased from 17 percent to 59 percent and then to 62 percent. My Xiajia survey here reveals a similar trend of increased youth autonomy during the first three decades, as cases of parental dominance dropped from 87 percent in the 1950s to 28 percent in the 1970s. This trend seemed to stop in the 1970s, however: parents still played a dominant role in nearly a quarter of the marriages during the 1980s and 1990s, almost the same as during the previous decade. Similarly, Parish and Whyte note in their early study: "There has not been much further progress toward free mate-choice since the mid-1960s,

TABLE 2.2.

Dominance in Spouse Selection in Xiajia Village,
1949–1999 (percent)

Years	Parents	Young couple	Total number of marriages
1949–59	87	13	38
1960–69	38	62	74
1970–79	28	72	128
1980–89	25	75	132
1990–99	24	76	112
Total			484

although this ideal has received more stress than usual in the media since the Cutural Revolution" (1978: 180). Does this mean the growth of youth autonomy reached a ceiling by the end of the 1970s?

To understand this phenomenon, we must take two factors into consideration. First, in any society and at any time, there are always dependent children and domineering parents, regardless of the social ideals in spouse selection. In some cases, the high cost of marriage also made the youth dependent on their parents (more on this in Chapter 5). Thus it is unrealistic to expect parental dominance in spouse selection to disappear completely. Given that some village youths will always rely on their parents to take the initiative in spouse selection, the crucial issue here is to determine whether the young people agree to a given mate choice. Some Chinese scholars use a more detailed and case-sensitive standard in their surveys, distinguishing "parents dominate, children dissatisfy" from "parents dominate, children satisfy" (see, e.g., Xu 1997).

Second, and more important, because the distinction between parental and youth dominance in spouse selection depends mostly on who makes the initial proposal, these labels tell us little about the actual discourse and practice of romantic love and intimacy. This is particularly true in the more recent past; virtually all engagements after the 1970s were based on youth consensus, which made the presence or absence of parental involvement in spouse selection less important than before. My survey shows that a couple who fell in love in the 1960s did not enjoy the same kind of romantic love and intimacy that couples did in the 1990s because of differences in prevailing cultural ideals and social norms as well as the availability of social space. In the everyday discourse and practice of romantic courtship today, village youths in Xiajia have gained more freedom and individual power. Consequently, the focus of change in spouse selection has shifted from the growth of autonomy among village youth as a social group from the 1950s to the 1970s to their individual lived experiences of romantic love and intimacy during the 1980s and 1990s.

CHAPTER THREE

Sex, Intimacy, and the Language of Love

By the 1990s, most young couples were able to fully enjoy the joy of romantic love after their engagement because the ritual not only symbolizes the acceptance of a couple's relationship by their respective families but also gives them the legitimacy to interact with each other more frequently and closely. Thanks to the institutionalized time and space of the postengagement period, village youths have been able to cultivate the emotions of love and intimacy, develop new ways of expressing themselves emotionally, and deepen their lived experiences in courtship.

In this chapter I first briefly review the changing content of postengagement interactions and the emergence of premarital sex among engaged couples. How villagers express love to the opposite sex is the focus in the second section, which leads to the third section in which I examine the local discourse on the ideal mate. In this connection, the Xiajia case sheds new light on earlier debates over whether Chinese villagers are capable of expressing and experiencing romantic love. In the fourth section I discuss the expressivity of love and intimacy. I conclude the chapter with a summary of the romantic revolution of spouse selection and courtship.

Postengagement "Dating" and Premarital Sex

During the 1950s and 1960s, local custom allowed an engaged couple to visit each other a few times before their wedding, but unless it was absolutely necessary (for example, because the distance between their homes was too great), a visiting future daughter-in-law had to return to her family on the same day. It was not unusual, however, for a young man to stay in his future wife's home for a few days if his parents-in-law needed his labor or assistance. Given the lack of transportation facilities during that time (few villagers owned bicycles until the late 1970s), a same-day visit meant little more than having a meal at one's future in-laws' house. Indeed, the real purpose of the visit was to reaffirm the newly established affinal ties (and for a visiting son-in-law, to offer free labor). The visitor spent almost all of her or his time with the prospective in-laws, rather than with the future spouse. Several older women said that these visits were unpleasant because they had not liked being observed by so many strangers and had been nervous about making conversation with their future in-laws. Many simply found excuses to skip the scheduled visits.

In the early 1970s, engaged young women began purchasing material goods for their own betrothals, a development that would have scandalized their mothers' generation. The bride and groom made a ritualized trip to the county seat or the provincial capital of Ha'erbin to buy clothes and other personal items on the gift list. They also sat for an engagement picture in a professional photo studio. More important, many couples spent a night or two together either at the home of an urban relative or in a hotel. In the latter case, the production brigade office issued them an official introduction letter indicating that they were a couple from Xiajia village and should be offered assistance if they needed it. This official letter entitled them to rent one room in a hotel as a couple, which a number of village youths did. This new custom was literally called "taking an engagement photo" (*zhao dinghun xiang*), and it quickly became a "must" for all engaged couples in the 1970s.

The effect of this custom has been twofold. First, because the engaged couple stays together in a hotel room, implying sexual activity, it gives the groom's family an opportunity to secure a marriage contract. In public opinion, a de facto marital relationship has been established: as the villagers put it, "raw rice has become cooked" (*shengmi zhu cheng shufan*). Thus the parents from the male side usually welcomed the custom. Second, traveling and living together for a few days gives the couple a feeling of conjugal union and naturally leads them to make plans for their future life after the wedding ceremony. This rather romantic experience is believed to create mutual affection and emotional ties between the two. As one informant recalled: "After the trip [for the engagement photo] my son's heart was stolen [by his bride]; he always defended the young woman when we criticized them for spending too much during the trip." It is clear that the emotional ties between the young couple may develop into strong conjugal solidarity, which generally tends to be against the interests of the groom's family, especially the groom's mother.

A further development in the 1980s and 1990s was for the engaged couple to enjoy intimacy at the home of one of their parents, which may be regarded as the local version of dating. At first, a girl visiting her fiancé's home was allowed to stay for several days, but her time alone with her future husband was limited by family activities during the day, and at night she shared a room with a female in-law. Mutual visits between engaged couples became more frequent, and by the 1990s it was not uncommon for one member of the couple to stay for several weeks in the home of the other party's parents. More important, young couples spent much more time alone thanks to the trend of house remodeling (see Chapter 5), and naturally, intimacy of all sorts developed behind closed doors. This was a remarkable move away from traditional custom, because it occurred right under the eyes of the parents and, as many informants noted, led to the surge of premarital sex among engaged couples.

It should be noted that Chinese villagers tend to have a more open attitude toward sex and sexuality than do the elite and, therefore, during the radical period of Maoism (1958–76), the Communist-style asceticism had much less influence in rural areas.[1] In Xiajia village, as elsewhere, married adults often exchanged anecdotes about sex during socializing, and they enjoyed erotic jokes and using words with sexual implications in conversation with both sexes. The youth, particularly boys, were constantly exposed to erotic jokes and sexual metaphors during socialization, and both boys and girls could obtain some basic knowledge of reproduction from observing domestic animals around the house. Sex, therefore, is neither a dirty secret nor a shameful wrongdoing in peasant culture, but a natural part of one's life experience.[2]

Only married men and women could indulge freely in "horseplay" and jokes with strong sexual implications in public; as they got older they enjoyed more privileges in talking about sex openly. Unmarried youth, particularly young women, had to be more discreet. During the early 1970s I often heard married men and women challenging one another with sex slang and lewd jokes—a popular form of entertainment—when they worked together in the collectives. Metaphors for sexual organs and intercourse constitute the core of most jokes, erotic stories, and slang. Interestingly, middle-aged women enjoyed a special advantage in such verbal contests between the two sexes because they could simply claim to be the mother of their opponents and therefore force the latter into a loser's position—nobody could take sexual advantage of a mother-figure. In one of the more provocative contests that I witnessed in either 1974 or 1975, several women threw a man on the ground who had used a sexual term that was particularly offensive and insulting to the women, literally breast-fed him, and finally put him under the open legs of a woman who was squatting on top of him, symbolizing the birth of this man. The man ended up begging for forgiveness.

Extramarital sex is not socially acceptable in village society, yet those who enter into illicit affairs for purely emotional reasons are often tolerated by many villagers.[3] However, premarital sex was long an absolute social taboo that until recently was strictly observed by generations of young villagers.

The local term for premarital sex is *xianyou houjia* (first have it, and then marry). The phrase "have it" means either to have sex before marriage or to have a premarital pregnancy that is revealed by a birth soon after marriage. Before the post-Mao reform period, the public knew about a couple's premarital sex only if the woman delivered a baby shortly after her wedding; the baby was thus born under the condition of *wuyuexian* (a fresh [fruit] of five months). Premarital sex that did not lead to pregnancy was kept secret by the people involved, and thus the community was usually unaware of it.

According to older villagers, premarital sex was rare during the 1950s and 1960s because of the strong expectation of bridal virginity and because engaged couples had limited space and time to be intimate beyond the watchful eyes of family members. Moreover, the official ideology throughout the first three decades of socialism denounced premarital sex as part of the corrupt lifestyle of rotten capitalist societies.

The sensitivity regarding premarital sex is reflected in both free-choice matches and other types of mate choice. In the 1961 free-choice match between Mr. Li and his wife, Mr. Li was extremely proud that his wife had been able to protect her virginity during her first, short marriage, and he was overly defensive if anyone hinted otherwise. He liked to tell, and also encourage other villagers to tell, the story of how she wore several layers of clothes in bed and kept a pair of scissors under her pillow to protect herself from her first husband's sexual overtures. Other couples whose marriages were based on love also vigorously defended their sexual virginity before marriage. When I lived in the village during the 1970s, I frequently heard my peers, who were of marriage age, discuss the importance of female virginity for a proper marriage.

During my investigation of this topic, several older informants recalled how strict the rules had been when they were young. A 45-year-old man told me that after he secretly developed a close relationship with a young woman who later became his wife in 1967, they were both very nervous and cautious. He said: "We often went to the fields at night and stayed there for a long time. I touched her body many times but did not dare to go further, because we both knew if she were to become pregnant our reputations would be ruined."

Following my usual procedures, I began collecting data on premarital sex from the most contemporary marriages and gradually traced emerging patterns back to their origins. I first stumbled onto the topic of premarital sex at a 1991 wedding and was particularly impressed by some villagers' "no-big-deal" reaction to the bride, who was four months pregnant. Later, in 1997 I was able to reconstruct the frequency of premarital sex by examining the birth planning files that are updated twice a year by the head of the women's federation in Xiajia village. It was not until 1998, however, that I found anyone willing to discuss this topic in detail.

On a hot Sunday morning during the summer of 1998, I was discussing the changes in conjugal life since the 1949 revolution with Mr. Liang, a 50-year-old schoolteacher and one of my key informants over the previous ten years. He recalled that he had never seen his father sleeping with his mother—the old man was never at home except during meals and late at night. Even during the long winter season when villagers had nothing to do in the fields, his father left the house to socialize with his friends. His elder sister had married a mute, and he could not imagine how she spent her life without being able to converse with her husband. Turning to the current young generation, Mr. Liang shook his head and said that sometimes the changes were a bit too much.

It has become common practice after the engagement ritual, according to Mr. Liang, for the young woman to stay at her fiancé's home for a week before going to have the engagement photos taken. The pre-trip visit was something new that emerged in the 1980s. But what surprised me is that often the couple engaged in sexual activity during the home visit as well (Liang estimated about one-fifth of the cases in the mid-1980s, a quarter in the late 1980s, and more than one-third in the late 1990s). This is most likely to occur at the young man's home because his parents perceive this as a way to secure the engagement contract. Mr. Liang continued:

> To be frank with you, this kind of thing happened right here in my own house. On the day that my eldest son became engaged, he asked his mother if it was OK to let his fiancée stay over for a couple of days, because she wanted to help us hoe the fields. We were very happy that the young woman was so considerate. She was indeed a very good laborer, and she worked with my wife and my son in the fields all day long. Everything was fine until the next morning, when I discovered that she had left our room and slept with my son in the storage room. Both my wife and I were upset and ashamed, but my wife changed her mind after a while, telling me that it was really a good thing because the young woman would never want to leave our son. I agreed with my wife because women always understand these kinds of things better than men. So, on the second night, we did not even bother to make up the bed for the young woman in our room, and she simply disappeared with my son after dinner. I was just amazed how energetic these youngsters were! You know, after a whole day of hard labor, they still had the spirit to play! Well, I would have been too ashamed to tell you this before, but it is so common now, and I no longer care.

Liang went on to tell me that the same thing had happened with his second son in 1987 and third son in 1991. "It seemed to become a family tradition here," he said, trying to be humorous, while watching my reactions carefully. I told him that several national surveys showed that premarital sex among the younger generation had increased rapidly throughout China, so his experience was perhaps not unusual. One survey showed that 24 percent of villagers regard premarital sex among engaged young couples as "permissible" or "unimportant" (ZGNCJTDCZ 1993: 53). According to another survey in the late 1980s, "Forty-one percent of the males and 30 percent of the females thought that pre-marital intercourse was not wrong and was entirely a private affairs. When pre-marital intercourse occurs between fiancés, few think it immoral or unchaste" (Zha and Geng 1992: 10).[4] Premarital sex, taboo in the 1960s, became a rather common practice among engaged couples in the 1990s.

Although no one else was as open and interested in the topic as Mr. Liang, other villagers also confirmed that premarital sex had become more and more popular and acceptable among engaged couples. Many older villagers rationalized this with the excuse that the young couple would marry anyway and spend their lives together. And a younger villager argued that, "nowadays, *kaidan* [the engagement ritual] means to be married; so it's fine to sleep together." However, more than in the past, the engagement contract is frequently broken. According to my surveys in 1994 and 1997, among the forty-two engagements that occurred during this three-year period, five were canceled. The female side initiated four of the five cancellations; at least one of these four couples is known to have had sex before breaking the engagement.

To get a sense of how many engaged youths might have had premarital sex, I used the *Records of Birth Control Implementation* in Xiajia village to examine the wedding dates and the dates of the delivery of the first baby for every woman in the village since 1979. Among the forty-nine couples who married between 1991 and 1993, thirteen had babies within eight months after their weddings, and of these thirteen couples ten had babies within seven months. This shows that, conservatively speaking, during this period 20 percent of the newlyweds engaged in premarital sex. The actual percentage was probably larger since not every woman who has premarital sex becomes pregnant.

How do villagers see this change? As Mr. Liang suggested above, most villagers see it as a fact that you have to accept, and many parents actually give a green light to their sons during the postengagement visits. As a result, some weddings had to be performed in a hurry because parents were ashamed of having a "five-months fresh" grandchild. One of the older informants who had fought to suppress his sexual drive when courting his wife told me that when he learned that the fiancée of his elder son had become pregnant in 1990 the only thing to do was to get them married. "It was an emergency but not a disaster. They had to get married as quickly as possible. That was all," the man concluded with a smile.

The increased tolerance of premarital sex among engaged couples also challenges earlier notions that a bride should be a virgin. With more than 10 percent of engagements being canceled, many young women reenter the marriage market after it is known that they have had premarital sex. Does this affect their chances in the marriage market? Not much, according to my informants. Mr. Liang noted that the easy access to abortions and the new scientific knowledge about loss of virginity (that is, that harsh labor or sports may break the hymen) helped to ease the worries of many people, particularly young women. But the most important factor is that, as premarital sex has become so common, the importance of bridal virginity has decreased among the younger generation. Other villagers I consulted on this issue claimed that Mr. Liang's explanation was too idealized or too complicated. Nevertheless, using the amount of bridewealth as a measure, they admitted that women who had lost their virginity were not as disadvantaged in the 1990s marriage market as they would have been in earlier decades because they asked for the same amount of bridewealth that the virgin brides did.

During the summer of 1999, for example, a young man brought his girl-friend back from a city where the two had met while working on the same construction site. They stayed at his parents' home as if they were already an engaged couple. But when the young man's parents refused to pay the bridewealth of 20,000 yuan required by the young woman, she decided to leave him. When she was asked by a female relative how other people would react when they knew she had already slept with a man in Xiajia village, she replied: "So what! Sleeping together changed nothing in me. I am still the same me." In another case in 1998, a young man in Xiajia village became engaged to a young woman who had had sex during her first engagement. The man's parents tried to use this as an excuse to lower the amount of bridewealth from 25,000 yuan to 20,000 yuan, but the young woman refused to accept this. She also told the young man's parents that she wanted to sleep with her lover (*airen*) on the first day of her postengagement visit. In the end, his family relented and provided the couple with exactly 25,000 yuan in the form of converted bridewealth (see more on bridewealth transactions in Chapter 6).

It should be noted that premarital sex among engaged couples is far different from the kind of dating culture that prevails in, say, American society or among trendy urban youths in major Chinese cities, in which sex can be separated from marriage. The young couples in Xiajia are serious about their relationships and committed to each other by the time of engagement. It is this commitment to marriage, together with the social charter of the engagement ritual, that legitimizes the young couples' intimate activities, including premarital sex.[5]

Words and Gestures of Love

Expressivity has long been regarded as a core element in the development of romantic love, and the particular form of emotional expressivity has led to scholarly debate about whether love in particular and emotionality in general play any significant role in rural China (see Kipnis 1997; Kleinman and Kleinman 1991; and Potter and Potter 1990). To better understand this issue, we must start with the specific forms of emotional expressivity—both verbal and nonverbal—that are employed in the everyday life of villagers.

During courtship, village youths tend to use many words to express romantic love and affection. Among the most frequently used are *xihuanni* (like you) and *xiangni* (miss you). A number of young villagers said that they often let their fiancé/fiancée know how much they liked or how much they missed the other party. Sometimes, the word *libukai* (cannot be separated from) is also used to express passionate affection among engaged couples.

The word *love* (*ai*) has also appeared in the discourse of mate choice in recent years, but mostly to refer to another person's experience, such as who loves, or does not love, whom. But somewhat unusually, when one young woman was reprimanded by her parents for having sex with her fiancé, she defended herself by saying "I love him" (*wo ai ta*). I was told that some village youths do use the word in a face-to-face situation, but I did not hear it. According to some informants, young men tend to be bolder and more direct in face-to-face expression and thus tend to use the word *love* more frequently. But during conversations among same-sex peers, women tend to use the word *love* more often than men. A common practice among both sexes is to use the words of pop songs that contain the expression "I love you" or similar messages. Those who can use this strategy skillfully are praised for being *fengliu* (romantic) or *youfengdu* (having an elegant demeanor), and in many cases, pop songs have proven to be a user-friendly and effective means of emotional communication.

For contemporary Xiajia youth, courtship itself has yet to become an independent stage of the life course; rather, it remains a bridge to marriage, although admittedly a much longer and wider bridge by the standards of earlier generations. Consequently, the most frequently used word to describe an engaged couple is *banpei*, which means good match. Banpei is an old word that is also used in ancient books, popular operas, and villagers' conversations. However, the specific elements that make a couple a good match have changed greatly since the 1950s. It used to mean a match of family status and economic standing between the male and female side, but now it focuses more on personality and other individual traits. When I pressed young villagers to explain what constitutes a good match, there was consensus about two elements—*duipiqi* and *youhuashuo*.

The Chinese term *duipiqi*, which literally means "having matching tempers," can be translated as "matching characteristics," such as personal hobbies, tempers, and speaking patterns. The word is also used to describe conjugal relations. In practice it also sometimes refers to the mysterious feeling of mutual attraction between lovers, which is perhaps best described as "chemistry" in colloquial English. For instance, a couple explained their love at first sight during a wedding in 1998 as the result of duipiqi (matching characteristics). When the young woman's parents attempted to tell her that in fact many aspects of their personalities were quite different, such as their tempers, personal habits, and appearance, the young woman told her parents that duipiqi cannot be explained by any of these elements. "I just feel that he suits me, and I fit him. That is it," she claimed. Intrigued by this inexplicable self-claimed "fitness," I tried to discuss the matter with the young woman in terms of the language of romantic love. She said it was fine if I insisted it was romantic love, but again she simply felt that there was a close bond and attraction between her and her boyfriend. "And that is all," she maintained, refusing to accept my characterization of their relationship as an example of romantic love. Because of this mythical notion of duipiqi, it is not unusual for younger villagers, particularly women, to find the absence of duipiqi in their courtship experiences a sufficient reason to call off an engagement.

Similarly, the absence of youhuashuo is another common reason to break an engagement contract. The meaning of youhuashuo is clear and simple; it

means to have a lot to talk about (literally "to have talk to speak"). However, the standard to have something to talk about is subjective and varies
greatly from one individual to another. A young man nicknamed *xiaobailian*
(little white face) is widely praised by young women for being able to speak
interestingly, while older villagers dismiss him as always "talking nonsense."
I discovered that the young man understands contemporary urban life fairly
well because he has worked in several cities and is a great fan of pop songs
from Hong Kong and Taiwan. He has a large collection of cassette tapes (all
by Hong Kong and Taiwan pop stars) and can recite many songs (though he
has a poor voice and rarely sings them) and keeps up on news about the music world. Because most pop songs are love songs, he can carry on a romantic conversation using the songs' lyrics.

There are, I was told by my informants, other kinds of youhuashuo, which
are equally important and can be attractive to potential mates. One man fell
in love with a woman, for instance, because she was a devout Christian and
a capable self-appointed preacher. She was known for being able to tell Bible
stories for hours without a break. Many villagers found her preaching annoy-
ing, yet this young man was interested in Christianity and thus felt that they
had a lot to talk about.

The contemporary emphasis on youhuashuo, to a great extent, derives from
official propaganda regarding marriage reforms during the first three decades
of socialism, in which having "common language" (*gongtong yuyan*) was promoted as one of main criteria in mate choice. The official definition of "common language" varied in accordance with the changing priorities of national
politics, but the stress on shared aspirations and goals remained the core for
the new ideal type of revolutionary couple. The idea was that lovers who share
a common language will always have something to talk about. It is interesting that contemporary youth and their parents may argue for youhuashuo,
but for different reasons. While the former always use the phrase as a reflection of their intimacy and closeness, the latter tend to use it as a marker of
matching social status between two families who are assumed to have a common language. For instance, in the 1970s, when the younger sister of a village cadre fell in love with a young man from a family with a bad-class label,
her family rejected her choice with the blunt comment, "How can you have a
common language with someone from a bad-class family?" Both manipulat-
ing and being influenced by the then dominant official ideology, the young

woman replied cleverly that they shared a common language when they talked about their revolutionary ideals and that she wanted to help him become a revolutionary. By the 1990s, although parents still questioned the existence of a common language whenever they felt a couple was not a good match, young people no longer needed to resort to political rhetoric to defend themselves. Instead they stressed the intimacy and closeness in youhuashuo.

Most older Xiajia residents had been much more subtle than their 1990s counterparts in expressing passionate affection during courtship. Throughout the 1960s and 1970s, recalled many villagers, love and intimacy were hinted at with words, body language, and actions. These older villagers insisted that actions mean more than words and that there are hundreds of ways to express good feelings between the sexes. Some more articulate older villagers criticized contemporary love songs as boring because, as one put it, "All they do is to repeat the same phrase 'I love you' again and again."

One 43-year-old woman said that her future husband had always dealt her good cards when they played poker during work breaks, and after he had done this for a while the other team members began to tease her. "That was how the whole thing [the courtship] started," she said. Another man told me that he and his wife had worked in the same production team and had been good friends for several years without any further development. It was before a political meeting at the production team headquarters that he told his peers that if his children did not do well in school he would throw them out of his house. When his future wife blushed in reaction to this comment, her friends began to tease her. "I realized at that moment that she liked me and wanted to give birth to my children. That was why her face turned red," the man concluded.

One 39-year-old villager recalled that the first time he had special feelings toward his wife, then a pretty and shy girl from the same production team, was during a harvest break in 1979: "I was sharpening my sickle when she called my name from behind, holding a small muskmelon in her hand" the man said. "She asked me if I wanted half of a melon that she had just found in the corn field. I asked why me. Her face got very red, and she said that I was really bad. From that moment I knew she liked me, and I wanted to marry her. And I did. I always teased her that our real matchmaker was that small muskmelon."[6]

Indeed, almost every gesture and act in everyday life can be regarded as a signal of love, although only those who are involved in an interactive context can appreciate it. A daughter of a former landlord told me that she felt extremely grateful when she overheard a boy saying that the discrimination against bad-class people was unfair. She was so touched by his sympathetic words that she developed fond feelings for him and eventually married him in the 1980s. Her decision caused some gossip because, after the class label system was officially removed in the 1980s, she seemed to be in a much better position in the marriage market than the young man, whose family was among the poorest in the village.

Although there is no clear line of evolution, generational differences in expressing one's affections seem to suggest a shift from more symbolic, indirect, and work-related modes of expression (such as shared foods, mutual help, and body language) to more direct forms of expressing love and intimacy. In comparison to their parents and older siblings, village youth of both sexes in the 1990s mastered a wider range of love words and were more open and skillful in communicating their affections. Those who were incapable of communicating love and intimacy encountered increasing difficulty attracting the opposite sex—so much so that, by summer 1999, villagers told me that *huishuohua* (knowing how to speak [about love]) had become an important trait of the ideal spouse.

Changing Discourse on the Ideal Spouse

Strictly speaking, there was hardly any discourse about ideal mates when parents arranged most marriages in the 1950s. The real subjects and agents were the parents on each side who were looking for a good match. The standards for a good marriage, therefore, were first and foremost good affines and then ideal daughters- and sons-in-law; the suitability of mates from the young persons' perspective was not at issue. Discourse on ideal spouses (rather than ideal affines) started during the collective period and changed dramatically in the postcollective era.

According to older villagers, the preferred mate during the collective period (the 1960s and 1970s) was a decent person (*laoshiren*, in local terms) who had a good temper, worked hard, and listened to his or her elders and to the leaders. Physical strength was emphasized for both sexes, because the ability to earn work points was greatly valued at that time. Family background was important but was judged differently by each sex. From the young woman's perspective, it was important to make sure that the young man's family was in good shape financially, but from his side, the moral reputation of the young woman's family was more important because it was believed to determine the woman's personality. Class labeling was another nonpersonal element to be considered in mate choice, but it had more influence on the marriage chances of men than of women (class labels were inherited through the male line, affecting the prospects of future children). But for those who had political ambitions, political standards were even more important than personal ones. During the early 1970s, two of the top youth activists in Xiajia village were not recruited into the Communist Party or appointed as cadres because they had married women from bad-class families. They were criticized by their political opponents for having wives who could be "time bombs" of counterrevolution. As a result, for a period of approximately ten years, class labels were seriously considered when ambitious young villagers chose their spouses.

Here the term *laoshi* deserves a closer look. Depending on the context, it can mean a cluster of personal attributes such as honesty, frankness, good behavior, obedience, and simple-mindedness (cf. Kipnis 1997: 112). Among these, obedience and honesty were emphasized more frequently in everyday life discourse. Until the early 1980s, being laoshi (obedient and honest) was a highly regarded merit in village society, and laoshi boys were normally welcomed as ideal mates (even the local party organizations preferred to recruit laoshi youth). But in the postreform era, laoshi has gradually become a negative term, and anyone so labeled is looked down upon by ambitious young women. When asked why, they commented that laoshi young men can easily be taken advantage of or cheated in today's society and thus are unlikely to be able to support a family well.

In my opinion, laoshi is a good quality for intragroup interactions. When villagers were confined to their close-knit local community and interacted only with people in their existing social networks, laoshi meant trustworthy and reliable, qualities that could reduce transaction costs within the village society. However, the other merits of laoshi, such as naïveté and honesty, could be fatal shortcomings outside the local community, especially during the postreform era when villagers had to deal with strangers in the unregulated market. In the new circumstances, laoshi invites aggression and cheating; a laoshi husband cannot be expected to provide the kind of safety and protection that a prospective bride desires. For almost the same reason, more than half a century ago, Lu Xun, the famous writer and thinker, observed that in Shanghai of the 1930s laoshi was synonymous with uselessness.

The young women of Xiajia, however, did not abandon the merits of laoshi merely for pragmatic reasons. A number of them maintained that laoshi young men had difficulty expressing themselves emotionally (*buhui shuohua*) and lacked attractive manners (*meiyou fengdu*). They thus identified emotional expressivity and behavioral elegance as important traits of an ideal mate, qualities that conflict with obedience and simple-mindedness.

The loss of appeal of laoshi in a mate was first brought to my attention in 1991 by a 27-year-old man who had encountered several failures in his search for a wife because he was labeled a laoshi guy. When he told me that the new favored type was a fengliu (romantic) man or woman, I thought he was just overwhelmed by his bad luck and expressing his anger at some of the new ideals. Subsequently, however, several informants confirmed that fengliu was indeed one of the new standards for an ideal spouse; this surprised me because the word once carried a very negative meaning in local usage.

According to the *Modern Chinese Dictionary*, *fengliu* has three meanings: (1) a person who is celebrated for having both career achievements and literary talents; (2) a person who is talented yet does not stick to social norms; and (3) a person who is loose and lascivious. In village society, however, only the third connotation was widely used in everyday discourse before the 1990s: describing a man as fengliu was the equivalent of saying he was a womanizer, and a fengliu woman was licentious and promiscuous.

When asked what exactly fengliu meant in the 1990s, villagers gave various answers. In general, a young man who was handsome, clean, well dressed, and, more important, knew how to talk (huishuohua) was considered by young women to be fengliu. A woman was regarded as fengliu if she was pretty, knew how to dress and use makeup, and was capable of conversing and socializing.[7] If we understand huishuohua to mean "being articulate," it becomes clear that by the 1990s Xiajia youths had picked up the two positive meanings of fengliu and had transformed fengliu into a positive feature of the ideal mate. Further inquiries with village youth convinced me that the new meaning of being fengliu was derived from contemporary pop culture, primarily love songs and soap operas, rather than from literary sources.

With fengliu as the new feature of an ideal mate, it is easy to understand why being laoshi fell out of favor, and why verbal expressions of love and intimacy are emphasized by contemporary village youth. When asked what kind of speech their grandsons had to master, several older men told me: "Nothing serious. It's all *erpihua* [sex talk]." This echoes the sexual aspect of being fengliu. But when I asked several young women the same question, their answers were much more complicated. One told me that a young man should know how to make his girlfriend happy, and it is the way he speaks, not the exact content of his speech, that matters. A pretty but blunt young woman admitted that she liked to hear her boyfriend praise her beauty and admire her when she dressed up. Disagreeing, a third young woman insisted that huishuohua means a man knows how to express his feelings: "Not like my father who could never say anything other than to scold us. I hope my future husband can say some nice things and also teach me things that I don't know." It is clear that, at least for these women, knowing how to speak meant being appreciative and supportive in conversation.

How serious are these young women? I got an answer when I heard of the fate of an old friend's son. This young man was known for being hardworking and good-tempered, but he was not at all talkative. According to some of his peers, he could work for an entire day without saying more than three sentences; but he was always attentive and liked to listen to others' conversations. A family friend had tried to set up a marriage for him three times by the summer of 1998, and all three attempts had failed. The first time, the young woman said no shortly after meeting with him in a neutral place. The second time, he and a young woman became engaged and had gone on the trip to take an engagement photo; but after one day she called off the engagement, telling his parents that he did not know how to talk. The third time, he was invited to visit the young woman's family after their first meeting and again failed the test for the same reason. By the time I left Xiajia village in 1999, he was still on the marriage market and was even less talkative than before.

Another feature of the discourse on the ideal spouse in the 1990s was its materialist orientation, which was equally obvious among both sexes, although some gender distinctions could be detected. According to young women, the ideal husband should meet the following qualifications. The prospective groom should come from a well-off family because most young women hoped to avoid poverty; they hesitated even when poor families offered a higher bride-wealth. Another important qualification was the young man's ability to work. Physical strength and the ability to farm are no longer the top qualities for an ideal husband. In their stead are the ability to make money through non-agricultural jobs, notably skilled labor. Finally, physical appearance is also important. In the 1990s women favored young men who were handsome, tall, and light-skinned (the latter being a sign that he has avoided farm labor). Male attractiveness also depended to a great extent on communication skills and emotional expressiveness.

For young men, the ideal bride was judged by similar standards, yet in a different order of importance. Beauty was a top priority, which includes a good body shape (i.e., slim, with a good figure and well-developed breasts). Other personal traits considered important were whether the young woman is romantic (fengliu) and knows how to dress and use makeup. It was not important whether she is capable of working in the fields, because nowadays farm work is much less physically demanding. The next concern was a woman's personality: she should have a good temper and be gentle and sweet. Villagers believe that personality traits are inherited through family lines, so the personalities of a young woman's parents were also considered. The last important standard was the economic status of the woman's family.

The Expressivity of Love and Intimacy

The various accounts of love outlined here and the results of my survey on mate choice in the previous chapter conflict with the existing literature on rural China, in which romantic love and intimacy are regarded as nonexistent or unimportant.[8] Why is this so? In my opinion, the major reason is a widely held presumption that Chinese villagers are incapable of expressing their affections and are not interested in the emotional aspects of interpersonal relations. Here let me cite two recent works by China anthropologists.

Sulamith and Jack Potter claim: "Presently, marriage choice is ideally based on what are called 'good feelings,' but the phrase is never used in the sense of a romantic or passionate emotional response" (1990: 191). Given that villagers emphasized work and mutual help in dealing with familial and other relationships, the Potters concluded that emotion is irrelevant to the construction of a social world for Chinese villagers. They argued that, while love is the medium of social relations in American society, it is work that connects people in rural China: "But work is the symbolic medium for the expression of social connection, and work affirms relationship in the most fundamental terms the villagers know" (1990: 195).

In contrast, Andrew Kipnis (1997) has argued that, unlike Americans who emphasize an accurate representation of emotions in honest speech, Chinese villagers share what he calls "nonrepresentational ethics," which center on the propriety of guanxi (social networks). According to Kipnis, *ganqing* (emotion) cannot be separated from guanxi, but it must always be expressed in ways that can serve the normal operation and perpetuation of guanxi. For this purpose, villagers sometimes express their emotions indirectly, such as by emphasizing work and mutual aid, because these are the embodiment of guanxi proprieties. The Western emphasis on the sincerity and authenticity of emotions through accurate representations, therefore, cannot be applied to Chinese villagers (Kipnis 1997: 104–15). Because of his emphasis on the role of emotionality in guanxi culture in general, Kipnis does not explore the specific forms of love expression.

Both the Potters and Kipnis try to understand the absence of a strong expression of emotionality (though they focus on verbal expression only) among Chinese villagers, and they attribute it to the uniqueness of Chinese culture. The Potters take the absence of emotional expressivity as a sign of the insignificance of emotions in the social life of Chinese villagers. In contrast, Kipnis argues that emotionality is so important for the construction of guanxi that it has to be expressed carefully in accordance with guanxi propriety. Thus, from almost every example that the Potters cite to show the irrelevance of emotion to the maintenance of social relations, Kipnis sees the opposite, namely, that the villagers use emotions to manipulate their guanxi networks. This actually brings Kipnis back to the position held by the Potters: that emotionality exists only as means to a utilitarian end, albeit an important means.

The key issue, therefore, is how we should understand the lack of strong verbal expression of emotions in general and of romantic love in particular among Chinese villagers. Both the Potters and Kipnis regard this lack as a fundamental feature of emotional life in rural China and contrast it with an ideal type of emotional expressivity in the West (mostly in contemporary American society). Although they come to different conclusions, both analyses essentialize the exotic features of the other (Chinese villagers in this case). An irony is that the Potters and Kipnis oppose ethnocentrism and try to understand the unique features of Chinese culture from an emic point of view.

Commenting on the Potters' and other works in Chinese psychology, Arthur and Joan Kleinman suggest that a valid theory of psychosocial dynamics of Chinese society "should begin with an historical reconstruction of Chinese cultural categories of personal experience and interpersonal engagement." This is because "emotion means a contextualized response, a response one feels or senses in experiencing the concrete particularity of lived situations" (1991: 286–87). More important, the Kleinmans warn, one should avoid the simple dichotomy of sociocentric non-Western societies and an individual-centered West. In my opinion, like the Potters, Kipnis also falls into the trap of such a dichotomy when he tries to use "nonrepresentational ethics" to explain the contrast between Chinese villagers and contemporary Americans (whoever they might be).

Based on ethnographic evidence from Xiajia village, I argue that, in the first place, it is highly questionable that Chinese villagers are incapable of expressing their emotions, including the most intimate and romantic affection. As Xiajia villagers put it, if one loves another person, there are "hundreds of ways to express one's heart." Work can be used as an idiom of love, as can food, care, or just a few words of comfort. It does not much matter whether the expression is verbal or nonverbal; what counts is whether the two individuals involved have found a way to express their affection to each other. The examples cited here (the woman who offered a muskmelon to her future husband, the man who stuttered in the presence of his loved one, and the woman whose red face betrayed her love) show that—without uttering the phrase "I love you"—villagers successfully conveyed their affections to their loved ones in obvious, easily understood ways. It is true that Xiajia villagers normally did not hug or kiss in public, yet public displays of intimacy between people were not unusual in everyday life contexts, albeit in ways that were often difficult to spot. The Potters miss the significance of love and intimacy in village life because they define the expression of love and other kinds of emotions too narrowly. Similarly, Kipnis's explanation of "nonrepresentational ethics" derives from the assumption that emotions should be expressed vocally and directly. Given that Chinese villagers do not conform to American expectations, a more rational explanation is in order; hence Kipnis's argument that Chinese villagers prioritize social relationships and embed their emotional expressions in guanxi connections.[9]

Moreover, Kipnis's explanation of "nonrepresentational ethics" and the Potters' argument of "social insignificance" assume a static, immutable, and unique Chinese mode of dealing with emotions (and implicitly, a similarly immutable and unique American way, too). This approach underestimates the great potential of rural Chinese to cope with rapid social changes in the wider social context. My longitudinal research in Xiajia shows that contemporary youths have become more vocal and open in expressing their most intimate feelings. The magic word *love* (*ai*) has entered their discourse of romance and intimacy, and young people also include the ability to communicate their affection to the opposite sex as a new standard for the ideal mate. It is true that young people have been heavily influenced by the media and pop culture as well as by urban lifestyles, but this does not prevent them from incorporating some of the most contemporary (and controversial) forms of emotional expression into their local universe, while at the same time developing their own subculture of love and intimacy (see Yan 1999: 79–81). The expression of love and intimacy is a learned behavior, and if it can be learned by American youths it can certainly be learned by their counterparts in rural China or elsewhere— as long as social conditions allow it.[10] Given the increased flow of information and rapid spread of a global pop culture, the earlier lack of strong verbal expressivity of love and subtle modes of expressing intimacy are likely to disappear among the next generation of rural youth. If this happens, will anthropologists and other social scientists argue that this is an example of the globalization of the "American way" of love and intimacy? Or, will it be seen as a case of indigenous change, in response to local conditions? This is a matter that bears close analysis and careful monitoring.[11]

The Romantic Revolution of Spouse Selection

In short, the early trend of youth autonomy in mate choice documented by Parish and Whyte (1978) continued in the subsequent two decades and culminated in what I call a romantic revolution in courtship by the end of the

1990s, characterized by three major developments. The first important change was the obvious increase of intimacy in courtship and postengagement interactions, including the increasing popularity of premarital sex. To a certain extent, premarital sex between engaged couples has evolved into a socially accepted norm of behavior, which in turn has transformed the postengagement time from a preparation for marriage to a passionate and erotic period of romance. More important, parental attitudes toward premarital sex among engaged youths have also changed from opposition to tolerance, as shown by the shift of the venue for sexual intimacy from a brief hotel stay during the engagement photo trip to long-term visits to the homes of the engaged couple's parents.

Second, the discourse on an ideal mate shows that, along with increasingly materialist concerns, contemporary youth also pay more attention to their future spouse's individual characteristics, such as physical appearance, respect and caring, emotional expressivity, and communication skills. This is in sharp contrast to the earlier standards for a good match, which focused on the making of good affines and the selection of a good daughter- or son-in-law from the perspective of the parents.

Third, village youths of the 1990s tended to be more open and vocal than their parents and older siblings in expressing their emotions to their lovers and future spouses. In addition to conventional ways of caring, direct and passionate expressions of love have become a favored form of emotional expression among the youths. Pop culture and mass media seem to be the most obvious and direct influence on the development of the language of love and intimacy, which both enriches and alters the discourse on an ideal mate and the practice of choosing a mate. The new emphasis on communication skills, particularly on whether one is able to speak *fengliu hua* (romantic talk), shows that the imaginative and subjective world of young people is expanding, and the idealization of a romantic partner is also emerging as an important part of mate choice.

These three major changes are all related to the process of subjectivity construction among village youth, a development that was not documented in Parish and Whyte's 1978 study. Unlike their parents and older siblings, Xiajia youths of the 1990s preferred to take their fate into their own hands; they enjoyed making decisions and had a strong sense of entitlement. It is interesting to note that, during both the collective period and the postreform period, village women played a leading role in pursuing romantic love and freedom of mate choice. In most free-choice matches in Xiajia village, females were far more active than males, either directly confronting parental authority or using their veto power to resist parental interference. Similarly, women initiated almost all of the engagement breakups.[12]

As a result of these three changes, many mate choices in Xiajia involve an idealization of the other party, an erotic context, and an expectation of a long-lasting relationship—the three basic components of romantic love (see Lindholm 1988). By the 1990s, romantic love and intimacy had become a cultural ideal widely accepted by villagers. That one should have the right and power to choose one's own spouse is no longer an issue of intergenerational disagreement or social disruption. The truly crucial developments lie in the villagers' individual capacities to implement the new cultural ideals of love and intimacy.

The increasing importance of romantic love and its development in Xiajia village since 1949 provide concrete evidence that Chinese villagers are interested in and capable of romantic love. Although anthropologists long overlooked or denied the existence of romantic love in non-Western societies (Goode 1959; Jankowiak and Fisher 1992; Rosenblatt 1967), more recent literature has shown a positive and promising trend that emphasizes not only the existence but also the varieties of romantic love in non-Western societies.[13] It is now, therefore, the time for students of rural China to pay close attention to this important part of village life. In this connection I would like to borrow a blunt statement that De Munck made based on his careful examination of romantic love in a system of arranged marriage in Sri Lanka: "Romantic love is important to Kutali villagers; to deny its importance is to deny their humanity" (1996: 708).

Romantic love always has a profound impact on the family and society at large, which is why it has been controlled in one way or another in virtually all societies (see Goode 1959: 43–47).[14] The romantic revolution in mate choice results from the rise of youth autonomy and the decline of patriarchal power and in turn speeds up the same process of transformation in other respects of private life, such as family formation, property division, support of the elderly, and fertility culture.

CHAPTER FOUR

Gender Dynamics and the Triumph of Conjugal Power

During a cold night in the winter of 1990, Mr. Li, a 64-year-old man in Xiajia village, took his life by drinking a bottle of pesticide. His suicide was hardly a mystery to the community because he had been having conflicts with his daughter-in-law and his younger son and had threatened to kill himself many times. But what struck his fellow villagers was the irony of his life as it drew to a tragic end.

According to fellow villagers, Mr. Li was an aggressive person in public life and a tyrant at home. He had an exceptional ability to manage his finances, and as a result his family was better off than many neighbors; however Li made virtually every decision at home and never tried to control his bad temper, often beating his wife and children. His wife passed away after the marriage of their elder son, and a family division occurred after the marriage of the younger son a few years later. Following customary practice, Li chose to live with his younger son but showed no intention of giving up his power. The wife of his younger son, however, was an independent woman who refused to listen to the old man's orders. As a result, she quickly changed the power structure in the family. Mr. Li fought fiercely to defend his position, often bringing family disputes to the village office. He did not gain the full support of the village cadres, however, because his daughter-in-law had successfully convinced them that the old man's tyrannical behavior should be held in check.

When I began to investigate this family tragedy during my fieldwork in the spring of 1991, I was particularly interested in the reactions of the older villagers who had children of marriageable age or experience in dealing with married sons. They all agreed that the daughter-in-law had been disobedient and that her husband should have stopped the conflict before it got out of hand. Nevertheless, sixteen out of the twenty-two older informants (average age 48) whom I interviewed also suggested that the late Mr. Li was partly responsible. Eleven informants maintained that the late Mr. Li was ill-tempered and his demands were unreasonable; five informants concurred, commenting that Mr. Li had been unwise to continue living with his son after the disputes. He had accumulated a large amount of cash savings, owned a good house, and could have had a comfortable retired life living alone.

This case reveals several interesting points. First, the rapid shift in inter-generational power relations in Mr. Li's family suggests that the existing stereotype of the patriarchal extended family may no longer hold true in today's Xiajia village. Moreover, in her struggle against patriarchal power, the daughter-in-law had gained moral support from public opinion and from the village government. After the tragedy she was not the only one to be blamed. This indicates that villagers' perceptions about what intergenerational relations ought to be in a stem family may also have changed. It is particularly striking that some villagers believed that economically secure parents should live in separate households if problems arose with their married sons in a stem family. Until the 1980s it would have been disgraceful for parents to live alone in their later years because it would have indicated their failure to raise filial children (see Chapter 6).

Intrigued by this incident, I started to take a closer look at the internal dynamics of family life from the perspective of individual villagers. I was soon convinced that the newly emerged centrality of the husband-wife relationship in the domestic sphere—what I call the rise of conjugality—represents another significant change for rural families since the early 1950s. In the following, I

first examine the changing patterns of family composition and the relationship between family structure and economic stratification. I explore the key
aspects of the husband-wife tie in everyday life, including intimacy and emotionality, division of labor and decision-making, and the perceived gender
roles of the husband and wife. Recent changes in these areas demonstrate
the emergence of a new type of conjugality based on mutual respect, intimacy,
and in many cases, affectionate love. I also explore the obvious shift in the
power balance between the older and younger generations in big families,
especially in terms of family management and the waning of parental power.
I conclude by discussing the theoretical implications of the rise of conjugality in the Chinese family.

Changing Patterns of Family Structure

Let me begin with some numerical indicators generated from a comparison
of three sets of data: 1980 household registration, my 1991 household survey, and a follow-up household survey in 1998 (see Table 4.1). The trend
toward conjugal independence is obvious. In 1980—three years before
decollectivization—there were 1,469 people in the Xiajia collectives, living
in 276 families; eleven years later, there were 1,542 people in 368 families. In
other words, during this period Xiajia village increased by 73 people and 92
new households. The number of households grew much more rapidly than
the population. Accordingly, the size of families became smaller, and the average number of family members dropped from 5.3 in 1980 to 4.2 in 1991.
By the summer of 1998 the total number of households had increased to
381, and the population had shrunk to 1,492. The decrease in the population
is related to the wave of out-migration in the mid-1990s when several dozen
families left the village. Consequently, the average household size was further reduced to 3.9 in 1998.[1] A change of this nature could have been the result of the strict control of population growth by the state, plus the influence
of out-migration (as suggested by Davis and Harrell 1993: 7). But a closer
look at the structural composition of Xiajia families reveals that there has
been a more significant change—that is, a trend toward a simpler, husband-
and-wife-centered form of family organization.

TABLE 4.1.
Family Composition in Xiajia Village, 1980, 1991, and 1998

Family structure	1980		1991		1998	
	Number	Percent	Number	Percent	Number	Percent
Nuclear family	162	59	264	72	308	81
Stem family	88	32	82	22	62	16
Joint family	11	4				
Incomplete family	15	5	22	6	11	3
Total	276	100	368	100	381	100

NOTE: A nuclear family refers to a married couple with unmarried children; a stem family is a married couple or a surviving spouse in each of at least two generations and unmarried children; a joint family is defined by the presence of at least two married brothers, with or without unmarried children. An incomplete family is one that does not fall into any of the first three categories, such as a one-person family or the family of a widower/widow.

Table 4.1 shows that the percentage of conjugal families in Xiajia increased from 59 percent in 1980 to 81 percent in 1998. The number of stem families, however, remained almost the same during the 1980s, but the overall percentage of stem families decreased from 32 percent in 1980 to 22 percent in 1991, resulting from the rapid growth of nuclear families. The persistence of stem families began to take a more radical turn during the 1990s, dropping by 6 percent. The more interesting indicator is that of the joint family (a household with at least two married brothers, with or without children). There were eleven joint families in 1980, 4 percent of the total number of families in the village; but there were no joint families in either 1991 or 1998.

During the 1980s and the 1990s the rapid increase in the number of nuclear families in Xiajia village was accompanied by a slow decrease in the number of stem families. This pattern matches the national trend as reported by large-scale surveys (see ZGNCJTDCZ 1993: 13, 82–83) and has also been found in other parts of rural China (Harrell 1993; Selden 1993). An appropriate study of family change, therefore, should be able to explain both the popularity of the nuclear family and the persistence (and slow decrease) of the stem family.

Given that so many people have chosen to live in nuclear families, one might infer that Xiajia residents consider the nuclear family the best form for developing the household economy in the postreform era. But further analysis of the relationship between family structure and economic stratification reveals the opposite: the extended families (stem and joint families)

enjoyed a significantly higher economic level in the collective and postcollective periods. Based on annual income and family assets, Xiajia households
can be classified into three strata: rich, average, and poor (see Table 4.2).[2] In
1980, 11 percent of the stem families and 36 percent of the joint families
were rich, but only 4 percent of the nuclear families fell into this category. In
1991, 17 percent of the stem families were rich but only 10 percent of the
nuclear families. The nuclear families had done better by 1998, with 16 percent of them falling into the category of the rich, but 21 percent of the stem
families were still in this category. At the other end of the spectrum, in 1980,
32 percent of the nuclear families and only 6 percent of the stem families
were poor. Although the gap became smaller in 1991, the percentage of poor
nuclear families remained 17 percent higher than that of stem families. This
pattern remained almost the same in 1998, when 31 percent of the nuclear
families and less than 14 percent of the stem families were poor.

The Xiajia case clearly presents a challenge to the corporate model of the
Chinese family. If the extended family has proven itself economically more
functional than the nuclear family, why have a growing number of people
chosen to live in nuclear families since the 1980s? Further investigation reveals that it is the ideal of an affectionate, intimate, and more equal conjugal
relationship that attract so many young villagers to the nuclear family, although some others have managed to achieve the same goal in stem families.

TABLE 4.2.

Family Structure and Economic Stratification in Xiajia Village, 1980, 1991, and 1998

Family structure	Percent rich			Percent average			Percent poor			Total number of families		
	1980	1991	1998	1980	1991	1998	1980	1991	1998	1980	1991	1998
Nuclear family	4	10	16	64	53	55	32	37	29	162	264	308
Stem family	11	17	21	83	63	52	6	20	27	88	82	62
Joint family	36			55			9			11		
Incomplete family				53	18	20	47	82	80	15	22	11
Average	7	11	13	69	51	56	24	38	31	276	368	381

Intimacy and Conjugal Love

In Chapter 3, I described a consistent development of intimacy and romantic love in courtship among village youth. The same is true in conjugal relationships. Generally speaking, older villagers found it difficult to verbally express affection to their spouses. While older women usually said it was embarrassing to display conjugal affection and intimacy, many older men considered the lack of communication with their wives to be an integrated part of masculinity, that is, what a man should be. When they encountered the radical changes in courtship and romantic love among contemporary youths, however, some older villagers began to change their opinions, as illustrated in my interview with a 52-year-old schoolteacher during a relaxed evening chat in 1997.

According to this man, couples spent much less time together when he was a schoolboy (i.e., in the early 1950s), and this was not healthy for family harmony. He recalled that his parents rarely spoke at home, except for a few words related to work or during quarrels that often ended in his father beating his mother. His father worked in the fields or elsewhere during the day and rushed out of the house again after each meal. During the long winters when there was nothing to do in the fields, his father still went out every day to socialize with several old friends, who also left their wives working at home.

As one of the most well-educated men in Xiajia village, this schoolteacher is more expressive emotionally toward his wife and other family members than most other men, as evidenced by his many light-hearted comments about how he could not live without his wife. Yet by the late 1990s he had become dissatisfied with his emotional life. He admitted that he had enjoyed much more conjugal intimacy than his parents, but also much less than the youth of the 1990s. "The youngsters now are much more open," he noted. "When my eldest son became engaged in 1986 and invited his fiancée to stay at our home, I was amazed and also felt a bit uncomfortable to see how he spoke with the girl. It seemed as if they could talk endlessly. I asked my wife why we older couples could not communicate in such a way, and guess what? My wife scolded me for becoming shameless in my old age."

The schoolteacher was not the only reflective man dissatisfied with his emotional life. In 1994 a friend confessed to me that he felt it was a pity that he had talked so little to his wife during their thirty-plus years of marriage.

He and his wife are distant cousins and had become engaged when he was only 6 years old and his wife 9. "We know each other so well," he recalled, "that when she opens her mouth I already know what she wants to say. So, I do not feel the need to sit down and talk with her at length. But this does not mean we don't have good feelings toward each other." He confided that in 1967 he had encountered a serious challenge when a female political activist from another village directly expressed her love to him when they were working together on an intervillage job assignment. He had struggled with this for quite a while because the female cadre was lovely and well educated, but each time he was about to succumb he thought of his wife and could not bring himself to accept the other woman's warm overtures. Nothing happened between them, but he never told his wife about it.

When I pointed out that this was a moving love story, he said that people of his generation would never think of it as a love story because they feel a bond with their spouses. He then told another story. After recovering from a fourteen-year struggle with chronic stomach pain in the late 1980s, he learned that his wife had converted to Buddhism and had secretly prayed for him every day while he was ill. She never told him about her prayers until the reform era. He was deeply touched by his wife's action, yet he could not express his affection to her openly, instead telling her that women are always too superstitious. But since then, his children told me, his behavior had changed greatly; he helped their mother with her household chores and expressed concern about her health and comfort.

There seemed to be little difference between couples in their early forties and thirties, both of whom grew up during the collective period. These middle-aged couples tended to spend more time together than the older generation and were also close companions at work and at home. As the beneficiaries of more open and free mate-choice customs, these couples enjoyed a certain degree of intimacy during their engagement, and many established independent households earlier than their parents. As a result, their conjugal relationships were much closer than those of the older couples. During a group interview with several key female informants, I asked them to name the couples in their generation who were in conjugal love (*gangqing hao* in local terms). Without hesitation, they listed thirty-nine couples, telling me various anecdotes about them. One wife, they said, had wanted to have minor cosmetic surgery (to make double-folded eyelids) during the middle of the year when most families, including hers, are short of cash. Unable to persuade her to wait for a few months, her husband borrowed the money from his parents to pay for the plastic surgery. The husband's parents were extremely upset when they found out why he needed the money, scolding him for being a coward who could not control his wife's unreasonable desires. But, according to my informants, among the young couples, this man was praised as a "model husband."

The openness among the current generation of village youths during courtship is also reflected in their pursuit of intimacy after marriage. It is very common to see young couples in their twenties walking side by side in the local marketplace, playing cards together at home gatherings, and sharing a relaxed after-dinner chat in a courtyard during the summer. The most common activity shared by young couples, however, is watching TV. Those who enjoy pop music also occasionally sing karaoke together. It is interesting to note that the karaoke machine has become a necessary item in bridewealth and is requested by many young woman, a clear sign that they expect to spend leisure time with their husbands. Like courtship and mate choice, television and other forms of pop culture have had a tremendous impact on married life. When young couples watch TV or sing pop songs together, they also incorporate the values and behavioral norms transmitted by the contemporary culture. Romantic love is one major new value that has spread quickly among young couples. To underscore this point, a 32-year-old female schoolteacher told me that her young daughter and son, ages 10 and 6 respectively, had early on learned to kiss because of the influence of television. "When they grow up, they certainly will know how to *zhao duixiang* [date and search for a spouse]," concluded this young mother.

Christian beliefs have also played a role in shaping the conjugal relationship of some villagers. During my interviews with two converted men, they frequently used the word *love* (*ai*) to describe their experience. The group leader's husband told me that his wife said the more he read the Bible and prayed, the more she loved him. Another man also fondly recalled their conjugal relationship after he and his wife converted to Christianity, and he repeated several times that thereafter his wife loved him much more. The group leader appeared to know more about theology: she talked to me about the different kinds of love—conjugal love, parental love, and universal love; but the love of God, she said, is the highest kind of love. I was impressed to hear these villagers speak of love in such a natural manner, as if they had been using the word for many years.

I described in Chapter 3 the emerging phenomenon of premarital sex between engaged couples. As might be expected, many young villagers who had engaged in premarital sex found conjugal love and intimacy to be much easier after marriage. To illustrate this point, suffice it to cite a counterexample from the early 1970s.

An old friend of mine married in 1974 through a rather traditional type of mate choice. He had been introduced to his wife and had had few interactions with her during their engagement period. When he visited my home on the day after his wedding, a group of us urged him to tell us how he had spent his wedding night (I was a single 20-year-old living alone in the village, and thus a small group of young men often hung around my place). He told us some funny stories about drunken guests, spilled foods, and other incidents. But our real intention was to get him to tell us about his first sexual experience, because none of us was married and thus we were all naturally very curious. Finally, he told us that the experience had not been very good because his wife had not responded to his gestures of intimacy; instead, she wrapped herself tightly in the comforter and did not move. He twice tried to get into her comforter but she rejected him. He then got angry and forced himself on her, but he had a premature ejaculation before he could do anything further. This was repeated when he tried again later during the night. "It was really messy, not good at all," he said as he told us of his frustrations. However, things must have worked out later on, because his wife soon became pregnant, and he gradually retreated from our small circle of young bachelors. Such stories were not uncommon about the 1970s and before, but were quite rare in the 1990s. Premarriage interactions seem to contribute to couples' development of better and more intimate conjugal relationships.

Education seems to be another important element in the development of conjugal love and intimacy. My survey shows that more than 90 percent of the couples age 30 and older (N = 52) who were listed by my informants as having intimate and/or romantic conjugal relationships had a middle-school or high school education. In more than 60 percent of these marriages, the wives had more education than their husbands, and the conjugal relationships of these couples were also ranked as the best by the other villagers. Some older villagers, who also noted the correlation between education and the quality of married life, said that better-educated daughters-in-law tend to treat their parents-in-law better. It should be noted that nine years of mandatory and free education was fully implemented during the late 1970s and early 1980s, a period during which most village girls had the chance to attend middle school. These girls reached marriage age in the late 1980s and 1990s. But when free education ended in the 1990s, many village girls were forced to drop out of school. It is hard to predict what impact this change in educational opportunity will have on the married lives of the next generation.

Division of Labor and the Decision-Making Process

To better understand the internal dynamics of the conjugal relationship, I conducted two separate structured group interviews with female and male informants in the summer of 1999. I asked them to go through the household registers with me household by household and answer six questions about each one. I also asked them to rank all the households on a 100-point scale. The questions were: (1) Who is in charge in a given household—husband or wife? (2) Who does the household chores? (3) Does the couple have good feelings (conjugal love) toward each other? (4) Does the husband beat his wife? (5) Does the couple treat the husband's parents well (are they filial or unfilial)? (6) Does the couple spoil their young child(ren)?[3] The information I received from these interviews is by no means comprehensive, but it is nevertheless illuminating and enlightening for our understanding of conjugal life among Xiajia villagers. Now let us take a closer look at the first two issues.

Although my original question asked who was in charge of family affairs (either the man or the woman, or both of them), most villager informants answered the question as if it were "whether the woman of the household is in charge," or, in their words, whether the wife has the final say (*shuo le suan*). Informants debated among themselves what it meant for a wife to have the final say. According to some, a wife is regarded as having the final say when she also makes decisions regarding extradomestic issues, such as what kind of crops to plant or whether the family should remodel its house. They argued that a wife automatically has the final say about purely domestic affairs, such as cooking or clothing or child-rearing, because her husband usually has no opinion or knowledge about these issues, and that it is the extrado-mestic issues that reveal whether a wife has power over her husband. Dis-agreeing with this view, some others suggested that one should consider only domestic affairs (*jiawushi*); judged by this standard, they claimed that more than 90 percent of the wives were in charge. Yet a third group of informants pointed out that cultivating guanxi networks can be seen as both a domestic and an extradomestic affair, and it is usually a wife's job to keep track of and take care of gift exchange, the most important way of cultivating networks. Deciding with whom to exchange gifts can reflect who is in charge: a power-ful wife tends to bring more relatives from her natal family into the network and leave out some of the patrilineal/patrilateral relatives of her husband.

We finally agreed to use gift-giving and guanxi network-building as the primary determinants of whether a wife has the final say in family affairs; in-evitably, though, in the actual ranking process some informants used what-ever standards they preferred. Thus, although I do not consider the numer-ical indicators from these interviews to be completely accurate, I believe that they indicate current trends.

Of the 308 nuclear families, 109 (35 percent) were regarded as wife-led, and only 57 of them (19 percent) as husband-led; the remaining 46 percent were considered to be "equal status" marriages, meaning the wife and the husband had equal power in decision-making. There are, of course, differ-ences in degree within each category, because I included all those who were given 60 points or more on a 100-point scale in a given category. If we con-sider only those wives who scored 80 points or more, only 28 of the families are wife-led. Further open-ended interviews indeed confirmed that these 28 wives make decisions about almost everything in their respective families, ranging from purchasing budgets to farming plans. Interestingly, 41 of the 57 powerful husbands scored more than 80 points, with many having a full score of 100. These men were known to be tyrants at home, and some were also wife-beaters.

It seemed to be easier for villagers to conclude that a wife is in charge rather than a husband. This is because the traditional type of conjugal rela-tionship was dominated by the husband; when this changed, villagers shifted to the other extreme in emphasizing the dominance of the wife. My specula-tions were confirmed indirectly through further interviews and casual chats with other villagers, many of whom told me that among the couples younger than 40 more than 80 percent of the wives had the final say. Among couples younger than 30, they said, all the families were wife-led. These villagers may have exaggerated the situation to a certain degree, but their impression of the changing husband-wife relationship in decision-making was largely consistent with the structured group interviews: the group said that more than 30 percent of the nuclear families were led by wives, and that another 46 percent of the marriages were equal-status. Their impression of gender and power is nonetheless interesting and important, because it is likely to become the ideal type of the next generation.

The group's impressions of the division of labor in household chores, however, was not so dramatically different from conventional wisdom, because in most families it is still the wife who does the household chores. During my interviews, I again asked the informants to rank a wife or husband's share of household chores on a 100-point scale, and I classified those who scored 60 points or higher into the category of heavily burdened. The survey results show that 188 wives (61 percent) were regarded as having major responsibility for household chores. In contrast, only 6 husbands (2 percent) received 60 points or more. The remaining 34 percent of couples were considered to share household responsibilities.

Again cultural bias and customary standards must be taken into consideration. For instance, of the 188 women who were regarded as doing most of the household chores, most scored 75, 85, 90, or 100 points; in contrast, the six husbands considered to have major responsibility for household chores received only 60 points each. Moreover, among the equal-status couples, the wives still performed more household chores than their husbands, the only difference being that their husbands were willing to share the household chores when they were home. Given that many young husbands spend at least three months every year working on temporary jobs in cities or other regions, how much help they can give their wives with household chores is indeed questionable.

Nevertheless, both male and female informants insisted that more husbands are now willing to share some household chores at home. This represents a significant change from the late 1970s and early 1980s, when husbands in Xiajia village rarely helped with household chores, except by carrying water home from the village well. Villagers, especially young wives, also frequently mentioned that more husbands had learned to cook and take care of their

TABLE 4.3.

Decision-Making and Household Chores in Nuclear Families, 1998–1999

	Wife-dominance[a]		Husband-dominance[b]		Equal status		Total number of families
	Number	Percent	Number	Percent	Number	Percent	
Decision-making	109	35	57	19	142	46	308
Household chores	6	2	187	61	115	37	308

[a] In wife-dominant families, wives do most of the decision-making and their husbands help with many of the household chores.
[b] In husband-dominant families, husbands do most of the decision-making and their wives do most of the household chores.

young children. To test this response, I asked some men whether they could make dumplings, and to my surprise more than 80 percent of the men age 40 or younger had mastered the skill and frequently participated in the preparation of the special food. Because the making of dumplings requires somewhat more complicated preparations and skills than usual meals, it has long been considered a woman's job. The fact that so many young men could perform this task indicates a subtle yet important change in attitudes toward gender roles at home.

Table 4.3 summarizes my survey results. In the category of household chores, I classify those marriages where the wives take major responsibility for household chores as husband-dominant, and vice versa for marriages where the husbands do so. Unfortunately, I do not have enough historical data to trace precisely when and how the dominance on these issues changed. It should be reiterated, however, that what is most important for our understanding of villagers' private lives is the trend of change; and the numbers in Table 4.3 may be sufficient for this purpose.

Redefining Gender Relationships at Home

In the summer of 1997, on the fifteenth day of the seventh month of the Chinese lunar calendar, the date for the traditional Ghost Festival, I sat with a group of men at the central intersection in Xiajia village, watching villagers chat on their way to and from the family graveyards. Suddenly Uncle Lu, a 74-year-old man, called out my name and challenged me to review the most important social changes in a few words. Having caught me unprepared, he went on to comment that there had really been only two social changes over the previous five decades. One was "grandfather is turned into a grandson" (*yeye bian sunzi*), and the other is "women have gone up to the sky" (*funü shang le tian*). The first refers to the loss of parental authority and power and the rise of youth autonomy. In this context, the kinship terms "grandfather" and "grandson" connote different positions of status and power; a powerless person is said to look like a *sunzi* (grandson). The second phrase is derived from the Communist slogan "women uphold half of the sky" and was meant to complain that the status of women has dramatically improved.

Uncle Lu then challenged the men: "Tell me, do any one of you not take orders from your wife? When facing your wife, you all act like mice meeting a cat. Isn't that right?" His anger aroused both laughter and intense discussion among the audience, who offered more anecdotes and various jokes. One man said that one day the men in Xiajia had been assembled at a meeting to answer a simple question: "Are you afraid of your wife [your wife's authority]?" All the men admitted that they were afraid of their wives' authority, except for one. When asked why he did not say yes, the exceptional man responded: "Well, my case is different. You are all afraid of your wives, but my wife is not afraid of me." The joke provoked more discussion of the husband-wife relationship, and again, many villagers expressed the belief that in most families it is the wife who has the final say.

Such a discussion of gender role and intergenerational relations was by no means the only one I encountered during my numerous trips to Xiajia village over the decade; often without any encouragement or inquiry, villagers themselves raised these issues. Their deep concern and keen interest in them convinced me that a redefinition of family relations and gender roles is perhaps the most significant change in the sphere of private life since 1949. The rising status of the wife in the domestic sphere, which is a key aspect of conjugality, deserves our close attention.

Although my data do not allow me to chart the improvement of the wife's status in a detailed manner, various ethnographic pieces of evidence support such an observation. According to older villagers, during the 1950s and 1960s the father was the indisputable leader in his family, and he controlled all the resources. There were households in which the wife performed the role of manager, but she never interfered with the husband's decisions on important issues.

Moreover, more than a dozen villagers, both men and women, used domestic violence as a measurement of the rising status of the wife. Wife-beating used to be common in Xiajia and the surrounding areas because it was believed to be an indicator of masculinity and a husband's leadership at home. The local saying "tame a wife through beating; make dough through kneading" is still frequently cited by older men when they lament the loss of male power in the home during the 1990s. Middle-aged women said that more than half of the women had been beaten by their husbands, but that most such incidents occurred before the 1990s. In my structured group interviews on family relations, villagers said that nineteen households had been the scene of domestic violence, including two where the wife physically attacked the husband more than once. Given that domestic violence tends to be underreported everywhere in the world, the reality may be a lot harsher than what was reported. Nevertheless, in comparison to previous patterns, it seems that wife-beating had greatly diminished by the end of the 1990s.

Like the changing patterns of mate choice and romantic love described in previous chapters, no family change can occur abruptly; nor can it be separated from what occurs in the public sphere. I reiterate this point from time to time throughout the book; here I examine how villagers link family changes with social changes in larger settings.

Let us return to my discussion with the villagers during the Ghost Festival in 1997. When asked why nowadays so many wives have the final say at home, Uncle Lu replied that it was the *gongjia* (the government, officials, and/or the state) that has spoiled women, enabling them to threaten men with divorce. According to Uncle Lu, once women could freely ask for divorce, their husbands were transformed into weak cowards; after a divorce a man could not afford to remarry because of the high financial costs. Uncle Lu dismissed my suggestion that the Cultural Revolution might have had a great influence on women's status; instead he insisted that this all started in the 1950s. He then told the story of a struggle meeting in the late 1950s, a famous event in local history known as "the night trial of Wang Kun."

Mr. Wang Kun, who was accused of abusing his wife, was an ordinary villager from a neighboring village in the same administrative district as Xiajia village. He was 1.8 meters tall and well built, but he was also ill-tempered and was much older than his wife, who, according to the memory of several elderly villagers, was a soft-spoken, petite woman named Kong Xianlan. The evening struggle meeting was held in the village school in late 1958. Wang was forced to stand in the center of the stage and listen to his wife's tearful complaints, which were followed by supportive testimony from several other women from the same village. The wife told the masses that Wang frequently beat her up; sometimes one slap across her face would knock her out of the room because he was so big and strong. Wang also forced her to have sex with him during menstruation, and when she refused Wang hit her and raped her in the corn-field. The audience became really angry and continued to shout "Down with Wang Kun" throughout the evening. At the end of the struggle meeting, a government official denounced Wang for having feudal thoughts, for wife-beating, and for the crime of disturbing the Great Leap Forward campaign. Then Wang was taken away in handcuffs by the local police. No one in Xiajia village, including Uncle Lu, knows what then happened to Wang, but many said that shortly thereafter his wife divorced him and remarried.

Although this was not the first time I heard this story, Uncle Lu's narra-tive surprises several of the younger men in the audience. They had heard older villagers talk about the "night trial of Wang Kun" before, but they had thought it was a local opera. They regarded Wang's behavior as abnormal and sick; yet Uncle Lu reminded audiences that in the old days many hus-bands had really bad tempers and held all the power in the home. He then concluded that the second reason for women's higher status today was that few men dared to tame their wives, and, as I expected, he nostalgically re-cited the old saying about taming a wife through beating.[4]

The men taking part in our discussion on that day, and some other male informants in my subsequent interviews, confirmed that the high cost of mar-riage, which amounts to at least a five-year household income, and a wife's threats of divorce are indeed the main reasons the husband-wife relationship has been redefined. Yet many younger villagers added that conjugal love is an even more important reason. A 29-year-old man who had had extensive experience working in cities and was also known for loving his wife, elabo-rated on this view:

> I always feel a bit guilty because I cannot give my wife a better life. When I saw those urban girls in fashionable dresses and high heels walking in and out of the tall buildings I thought of my wife. She would have been more

beautiful if we had been urban residents and she worked in an office building. A man is afraid of his wife if he loves her very much but cannot satisfy her needs. So, we should blame no one other than ourselves because we don't have the ability to make more money.

This view was shared by many young men his age and slightly older, but those in their late thirties and forties tended to emphasize the importance of family harmony as the reason for allowing the wife to be in charge of family affairs. However, listening to their views carefully, I realized that what they really meant is that, in the postreform era, women actually contribute more to the proper functioning of the family both economically and socially, and it is therefore natural that a wife should have the final say. This view was better elaborated upon by the women I interviewed, because they did not need to hide the fact that they work harder now than during the collective period. Because the men now have to leave the village to seek temporary work in cities, all the farm work, plus the routine household chores and child-rearing, is left to their wives at home. As a 29-year-old woman noted: "Every March my husband leaves home to work in the city, and he only comes home when the weather is too cold for construction work. You can figure out yourself how busy I am during this period, taking care of everything on my own. I sometimes think that I am at least one and a half people" (referring to her work load).

When I brought the women's views back to my male informants, most of them agreed that the women's claims were reasonable. Three men admitted to me on three different occasions that it is possible for a woman to support a family on her own, but not for a man. They all emphasized that a household without a wife is not a real family.

It is clear that in the 1990s the husband-wife relationship was redefined in all major respects: intimacy and affection in conjugal life increased; a wife's indispensable contribution to the family economy and her power to be in charge of family affairs were recognized; domestic violence declined significantly; and many husbands began to share in the household chores. It is within the context of these changes that conjugal independence has become so important and attractive for the younger villagers.

The Democratization of Stem Families

Thus far my analysis has focused on nuclear families, trying to show that many villagers have pursued conjugal independence, regardless of its disadvantages with respect to economic performance. Then what about the persistence of the stem family? The total number of stem families remained stable during the 1980s (there were eighty-eight in 1980, eighty-two in 1991) but declined to sixty-two in 1998. Are the villagers who have chosen to live in stem families less enthusiastic about conjugality than their counterparts in nuclear families? Or have they simply been overwhelmed by their parents' authority and power? Either of these speculations may be valid for individual cases. Nonetheless, my focused survey on stem families in Xiajia village reveals that a shift in power and authority from the senior to the junior generation has occurred in most stem families as well. As a result, conjugality has assumed a central role in family relations, and family life in stem families has become more democratic.

In order to understand the exercise of parental power and authority in stem families, I focus on the following three questions: (1) Who is the recognized family head in official documents and important daily life ceremonies—the father or the son? (2) Who controls the family resources and makes the decisions—the parents or the young couple? (3) What is the position of the married son when his wife has conflicts with his parents?

The first two questions are designed to examine the changing power relations in family life in both nominal and practical terms. There are two leadership roles in Chinese family life: that of the family head (*jiazhang*), who represents the family to the outside world, and that of the family manager (*dangjia*), who is in charge of the overall management of the family as an enterprise (Cohen 1976; Levy 1949; C. K. Yang 1965). These two roles are usually filled by the senior male—the father—in a nuclear or extended family. However, when seniority and managerial capability do not coincide, a more competent yet less senior person may play the role of family manager. As Cohen points out, the distinction between these two terms is far more important than semantics, because it also "provides for the family the cultural basis of the coexistence and reconciliation of ultimate aspirations and practical management" (1992: 363). Whether a father remains as family head, therefore, may tell us much about the image that the family wishes to present to the outside world, while the question about decision-making may reveal the actual power balance between senior and junior generations in a stem family.

Of the eighty-two stem families in Xiajia village in 1991, thirty-three (40 percent) were headed by fathers, mostly in their late fifties, and the remaining forty-nine households were headed by married sons. By contrast, fifty-four (61 percent) out of the eighty-eight stem families in 1980 were headed by parents.[5] This means that the power shift to the younger generation in stem families had become obvious by the early 1990s. This trend continued throughout the 1990s, when forty-eight of the sixty-two stem families (77 percent) were headed by married sons in 1998. The change can be seen in both official documents, such as household registrations and house certificates, as well as important everyday rituals. For instance, on a number of occasions I witnessed older men presenting gifts to the hosts at weddings or funerals and asking the bookkeeper to enter their son's name into the gift record—clearly demonstrating who was the real family head.

Owing to the increased importance of building family networks and keeping up with the fast-changing trends in the market-oriented economy of the 1990s, a family head must be more "presentable" to the outside world than in the recent past (see Yan 1996: 74–97, 229–38); as the family representative he or she must dress properly, talk skillfully, and make connections efficiently. The old-fashioned, conservative fathers in stem families, therefore, are not well qualified for such tasks; many have also found their knowledge to be out of date. As a 56-year-old man put it, "I am good at growing crops, but farming won't make much money. I know how to offer sacrifices to our ancestors [he is a local ritual specialist], but this is superstition and not allowed in our new society. The last thing I want to do is to talk with policemen or officials, but someone has to deal with these people every day. It is better to let my son do it [as the family head]."

With respect to control over resources and decision-making, I found that in 1991 only twenty-six (32 percent) of the eighty-two stem families were actually run by parents. Though my 1980 data do not reveal exactly how many fathers were actually in charge of the eighty-eight stem families at that time, all my informants confirmed that more fathers were family managers during that period. Given the much higher number of parental family heads in 1980, it is safe to speculate that more parents were in charge of stem families in the 1980s than in the 1990s. Looking at the data from another angle, younger couples were in charge of fifty-six (68 percent) of the eighty-two stem families in 1991. In these fifty-six families the young members enjoyed almost the same conjugal independence and power as their counterparts in nuclear families, plus they had the advantage of parental support for household chores and resource allocation; their elderly parents were their dependents and had little influence in decision-making or resource allocation. A follow-up survey of the sixty-two stem families in 1998 shows a similar pattern by the late 1990s, when nineteen of the sixty-two stem families (31 percent) were run by parents, and forty-three (69 percent) were led by young couples.

Furthermore, my earlier survey found that in the twenty-six stem families that were both headed and managed by parents in 1991, most parents could hardly be described as patriarchal tyrants; instead, parental power was expressed in moderate terms because of both the self-restraint of the parents and the strong resistance from the young people. During my fieldwork in 1991, five older villagers who acted as both family head and family manager explained how difficult it was to run a stem family. For instance, a father had to talk with his son and daughter-in-law on eight separate occasions in order to convince them that it was too early for the family to purchase a motorcycle. When I returned to Xiajia specifically to investigate family relations in 1993 and 1994, I found more parents complaining about the difficulties of running a stem family. One older woman said: "You cannot imagine how smart they [the young people] have become nowadays. They want me to be in charge; but I have to do everything, cook for the family, raise the chickens and pigs, keep the family savings, and baby-sit for their children. What do they do? They do nothing except watch television and complain. I am an old servant in the family." Later I discovered that the young couple in this particular family worked in a local factory and indeed rarely helped with the household chores when they returned home from work. What really bothered the mother was that only her son handed over his salary to her while her daughter-in-law kept all of her salary as her private money (*sifangqian*), special savings available only to the daughter-in-law or her husband. This is why the mother saw herself as a family servant instead of a family manager. When I revisited the old woman in 1999, she was living separately from her two sons, although still in the house of one of them. She told me that she was happier and that it was much easier to live alone because she no longer had to work as a servant and did not have to be careful not to upset her daughter-in-law.

Many parents in stem families have to make special efforts to communicate with their adult children and to meet the latter's demands in order to keep the family together. During my fieldwork, more than half of the parents who were supposedly in charge of the twenty-six stem families admitted that they could not impose their will on their married sons and daughters-in-law; instead, they discussed important issues in formal or informal family meetings where the young members' opinions were seriously considered. The parents all stressed that family harmony could only be achieved by agreement among all family members.[6]

Another important issue concerns a married son's loyalty and support when his wife quarrels or has a conflict with his mother. From this we can determine whether the parent-son relationship is more important than the conjugal tie. According to older villagers, in the past a man always firmly stood on his mother's (or parents') side, whether his mother or parents were right or wrong. Filial piety is the primary reason for taking such a position: children are supposed to show respect and obedience to their parents in all circumstances, and a daughter-in-law is always in the wrong if she disagrees with her mother-in-law. Another reason is that the wife always remains an outsider in the home of her husband's parents; by conventional reasoning it is wrong for a man to make an alliance with an outsider against his own parents. These ideas are nothing new (see, e.g., Freedman 1979; Levy 1949; M. Wolf 1972), but they reconfirm the notion that when the patrilineal ideology prevails and when the parent-son relationship remains the central axis of family relations, the married son can hardly defend his own wife. Did this tradition change in the 1990s?

When asked, the majority of parents stated that their sons never took their side. This accusation, however, was denied by almost all of the thirty-two married sons I interviewed, although their explanations varied. Nearly two-thirds of the sons told me that sometimes their parents were right and sometimes their wives were right. "We just support the person who is right," many said. Interestingly, when I brought this explanation back to the parents, they dismissed it without hesitation. One elderly woman commented: "This is all bullshit. They just try to make excuses for themselves. Each and every time they can find a reason for their wives to be right and for their parents to be wrong. This is true, and I can speak for all parents." The remaining one-third of the married sons, however, preferred to remain neutral when their wives were involved in conflicts with their parents. Some said that they simply left the house for a while, thus avoiding the need to take sides in an argument.

I soon discovered that my informants were answering my questions at different levels. Most parents based their answers on the facts—referring to the family quarrels and disputes that had actually occurred in the past—and they thus emphasized that their married sons always sided with their wives instead of with their parents. Some parents pointed out that staying neutral in a family quarrel is nothing more than a married son's strategy to support his wife. By contrast, most married sons gave me an "ought to be" answer, namely, the socially accepted attitude toward this issue rather than their actual experiences and behavior patterns. The "ought-to-be" type of answer, nevertheless, is enlightening in and of itself, for it reveals the place of conjugality in the current family ideology. My informants' responses demonstrated that the previous centrality of the parent-son relationship is waning; in its stead the conjugal tie has attained at least equally important weight as the parent-son relationship in contemporary family ideology.

To clarify the issue further, I returned to the married sons and asked them to give me real examples of family quarrels or disputes and to tell me where they stood in such cases. To avoid embarrassing my informants, I did not ask about their own experiences; instead we discussed disputes that had occurred in other families. In these instances the married sons gave me answers that were very close to their parents'; that is, in most or even all cases of family conflict, married sons supported their wives either directly or indirectly. In comparing their responses, I found that, in general, those who claimed that they supported whoever was right tended openly to support their wives against their parents, and those who wanted to be neutral tended to support their wives indirectly, such as by offering moral support in private.

Married sons living in nuclear families had much the same attitude toward the issue of family quarrels as the majority of those living in stem families—namely, that a man should support whoever is right, either his mother or his wife. Again, when confronted with real disagreements, these married sons tended to support their wives unconditionally; the very fact that they lived in nuclear families already provided some evidence of this point since most family divisions result from unresolved family conflicts.

In 1999 I conducted another follow-up survey of the stem families, focusing on the conditions that make people choose to stay in a stem family. It is clear that political power, social capital for networking, and economic prosperity are the major factors in sustaining a stem family. The married sons in two cadre families decided to live together with their parents because they benefited from the fathers' broader networks and political power. Four of the ten richest households were stem families because the parents could afford to provide good housing, fancy consumer durables, and free food to their married sons, allowing the latter and their wives to keep their own income as their private money. There were, however, more than a dozen stem families in which the parents had neither political power nor economic resources, and these were among the poorest families in Xiajia. Ironically, it was family poverty that kept these stem families intact. Villagers in these poor households could not afford to have a family division: there was inadequate housing and/or the younger generation depended financially on their parents. There were indeed stem families in which the need for a better division of labor bound family members together. But, as suggested by many informants, if the parents did not offer additional economic incentives to attract their married sons, the latter would want to set up their own conjugal families. The key determinant again was whether the younger generation felt happy in a stem family.

The Structural Transformation of Family Relations

In his classic work on rural China, Fei Xiaotong compares the Chinese family to its counterpart in Western societies. In the West, Fei notes, "Husband and wife are the central players around whom everything else moves, and the force that holds them together as a couple is their emotional attachment" ([1947] 1992: 85). In contrast, he notes, the main axis of family relations in Chinese society is that of father and son, and mother and daughter-in-law; consequently, the husband-wife relationship plays a minor role in family life. Fei also maintains that because the Chinese family functions like an enterprise that emphasizes order and efficiency, emotionality is suppressed and stripped of significant meaning: "These family attachments have been stripped of 'ordinary emotions' by the demands of a family's practical activities. . . . In order to obtain efficiency, one must have strict discipline. But discipline does not tolerate personal feelings" (Fei [1947] 1992: 85; see also Goode 1963 for a comparison of traditional and modern families in this respect). Although other scholars have not noted such a sharp contrast, most students of the Chinese family agree with Fei, and few would dispute the centrality of the parent-son relationship and its dominance over all other family relations (see, e.g., Baker 1979; Cohen 1976; Freedman 1966; Levy 1949; C. K. Yang 1965). To a great extent, this generalization can be applied to patterns of family relations in Xiajia village up to the 1950s. However, I am suspicious of the characterization of peasant family life as emotionless and highly disciplined (more on this in the concluding chapter).

The examples cited in the previous sections demonstrate that by the early 1990s conjugal independence had become an accepted feature of family ideology for the majority of Xiajia residents. Similarly, the horizontal conjugal tie has replaced the vertical parent-son relationship as the central axis of family relations in most households—nuclear and stem households alike. As a result, parental authority and power have been challenged, and a shift in the balance of power has occurred in favor of the younger generation in all types of families, regardless of the specific structural composition of the household. In light of the existing work by Fei and others, it is clear that what has occurred in Xiajia families represents the triumph of conjugality over patriarchy—an important structural transformation of family relations in terms of both ideology and institutional arrangement. The significant meaning of such a transformation is embodied in the changing nature of the family and the new aspects of personal life within the family, rather than in the patterns of family composition.

The Xiajia case is relevant to William Goode's (1963) classic thesis that industrialization and urbanization lead to a shift from an extended family system to a conjugal family system, that is, "toward fewer kinship ties with distant relatives and a greater emphasis on the 'nuclear' family unit of couple and children" (1963: 1). Goode's argument has been challenged by a series of historical studies demonstrating that nuclear families prevailed long before industrialization in Western Europe (P. Laslett 1971; P. Laslett and Wall 1972; Mitterauer and Sieder 1982; and Stone 1975). Evidence from developing countries reveals that extended families may fit well in market economies undergoing industrialization (Chekki 1988; Conklin 1988; Dasgupta,

Weatherbie, and Mukhopadhyay 1993; and Gallin and Gallin 1982). However, the most important part of Goode's thesis is his interpretation of the
worldwide trend toward the centrality of conjugality in family life, rather
than the dualism of extended families versus nuclear families. In this connection, my case study shows that there has indeed been a shift toward conjugal independence along with the development of the rural economy, although the rise of conjugality does not always show a correlation with
changes in family structure and postmarital residence.

Both Fei's comparative framework and Goode's sociological model of family change, however, do not pay sufficient attention to an important dimension of the same transformation process—that is, that the rise of conjugality
also implies a changing dynamics of gender relations in private life. Several
generations of women in Xiajia experienced a fundamental change in their
role as a wife—from subordinate domestic worker to equal partner in companionate marriage. Again, this change resulted from women's active role in
developing new patterns of spouse selection and romantic love. Women were
the most effective agents of change, through their efforts to win the freedom
of mate choice, equal status in everyday family life, and acceptance of conjugal love. It is true that negotiation and contestation between women and their
parents-in-law or other representatives of the patriarchal order had been going on throughout Chinese history, but the prolonged struggle only took a
dramatic turn in the second half of the twentieth century.

As mentioned at the beginning of this chapter, Mr. Li's daughter-in-law
played a crucial role in transforming the power structure in his household,
which finally ended in the tragedy of his suicide. One detail I would like to
add here is that the daughter-in-law was particularly angry about Mr. Li's
early abusive behavior toward his wife, whom she had never met. She was reported to have shouted at her father-in-law, Mr. Li, on several occasions
during their quarrels: "I know you treated my mother[-in-law] like a hired
maid and you beat her as often as you ate your meals. What kind of person
are you! Don't ever think you can play the tyrant at home any more. Let me
tell you, I am a capable person with a middle-school education. I was sent to
this family by the ghost of my mother-in-law to fight you."

Here I am not implying that the daughter-in-law fought Mr. Li in the
name of all battered women; nor can we take her self-claimed mission of
avenging her mother-in-law too seriously. Yet it is clear that she had her own

views regarding the proper patterns of personal relations at home and was aware of her right to fight an abusive patriarch in the late 1980s. She used this to her advantage when Mr. Li brought their family dispute to the village office, which helped her to win moral support from the cadres, fellow villagers, and her husband. The important implication here is that, because of the changes in ideology and the larger society, these women were able not only to triumph over their parents-in-law but also to redefine the gender dynamics and family ideals as well.

An old-style house, of the sort that are gradually being replaced by new-style houses.

A small group of women chatting in the courtyard of a new-style house.

The multiple functions of the heated bed (*kang*): A girl playing in the front, her mother working in the background, and another heated bed behind it.

The newlyweds' living room (1998); note the changes in furnishings and décor, and the separation of the living room from the bedroom.

The transfer of dowry from the bride's family to the groom's; the bicycle and other goods are wrapped with celebratory red cloth.

A newly married couple is offering wine and cigarettes to the guests at their 1991 wedding; the man standing behind them is the specialist directing the ritual act.

At a 1998 wedding, the groom is symbolically fixing the bride's eyebrows, a new practice emphasizing conjugal intimacy that took hold in the late 1990s.

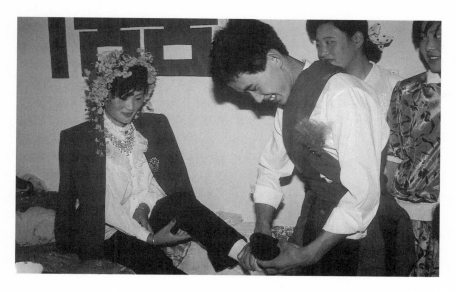

In another recently added wedding ritual, the groom helps the bride change to a new pair of shoes (1991).

A ritual detail from a traditional wedding, in which the bride and groom bow to each other. Compare this with the next photograph, which shows the same ritual act in a more recent version.

The newlyweds exchange bows. Note the influence of Western wedding customs: the bride is in a Western wedding gown, and the whole ritual appears to be westernized and urbanized in comparison with the wedding shown in the previous photograph.

In this region the ancestors are recorded on a scroll and worshiped during ritual occasions. The scroll is rolled up and hung on the wall most of the time. Note the posters on the wall.

A groom makes offerings at the ancestors' graves shortly before his wedding, informing them of the happy event.

Children watching television while the adults are having dinner in 1991. It was impossible in the past for children to ignore dinner. In this picture, the children are watching the American cartoon series "The Transformers," a big hit in China. Television has played a major role in changing people's life aspirations and family ideals.

A teenaged girl; note the poster beside the mirror. Urban
fashion trends have been introduced into village society
through various forms of mass media, including posters.

As a large number of rural men have left for temporary work in the cities, farming is now largely done by women and elderly men who remain home. In the picture two sisters-in-law are harvesting.

Making dinner at home after a day in the fields.

CHAPTER FIVE

Domestic Space and the Quest for Privacy

I have long been interested in the place of personal space (and implicitly, the local notion of privacy) in Xiajia families, first because of its unavailability and then because of the recent radical changes. In Heilongjiang province where Xiajia village is located, the winter season normally lasts more than five months, and for a substantial part of the season the temperature often falls to twenty or thirty degrees below zero centigrade. Because of the severe winters and widespread economic shortages, villagers in Xiajia and the surrounding areas have generally lived in crowded housing conditions since the beginning of the settlement in the early nineteenth century. Until the early 1980s it was not uncommon for a big family—men and women of two or more generations—to sleep in the same room and often in the same heated bed (locally called a *kang*). The traditional dwellings and spatial arrangements, however, were swept away during a wave of house construction and remodeling that started in the mid-1980s. By the 1990s, villagers were competing with one another to design new and functional houses.

In the following, I first review previous patterns of spatial arrangements in the typical village house and the wave of house remodeling since the mid-1980s, focusing on how villagers defined and were defined by the spatial relations in various house plans. The next two sections discuss the changes brought about by house remodeling; they examine the emergence of family privacy and individual privacy within the family. I then discuss the impact of new house designs on intrafamilial relations and conclude with an analysis of the implications of the Xiajia case in comparative perspective.

Spatial Arrangements in the Old House

Before the land reform campaign, as senior residents recalled, people lived in three types of houses. The few rich and powerful landlord families lived in big houses encircled by high walls, which were locally referred as *dayuan-tao*, meaning "big compound." To prevent possible raids by local bandits, which were not uncommon during the first half of the twentieth century, landlord families usually kept their courtyard gates closed. One of the Wang families even built several embrasurelike posts along the walls so that they could defend themselves during bandit attacks.[1] The typical main house in this kind of big compound consisted of six rooms, plus detached rooms for hired laborers, draft animals, and storage. At the other end of village society were the poor peasants who were landless laborers; they typically lived in small huts called *majiazi* (literally "horse stand"). Such huts consisted of several logs leaning toward the center of the frame, and its walls were made of grass mats and small twigs covered with thick mud on the outside. But the poorest, who were mostly new migrants to the area, could not even afford such a modest hut; they just dug a hole in the ground and covered the top with small logs, grass mats, and mud. In the middle of the local housing hierarchy, self-reliant peasants typically lived in small houses with two (or one and one-half) rooms—one was the bedroom for the whole family and the other served as the kitchen, storage space, and entrance. Concerns about saving energy were important for these mid-level peasants; but even those who were much better off and thus were classified as rich peasants during the land reform campaign also lived in similar conditions before the 1949 revolution. "This is just our custom," a 71-year-old man claimed. Class differences in housing and domestic spatiality, therefore, were physically recognizable but only drew a line between the local elite and the rest.

According to these older villagers, the best thing the Chinese Communist Party did for the poor people after the revolution was to help everyone marry and build a house.[2] From the 1950s to the early 1980s, Xiajia villagers lived in houses that resembled one another both inside and out, with small variations in size. Because most houses were built in the 1950s and 1960s and the house plots were allocated by the village office according to certain standards, the village expanded in a planned manner, growing from the original two-street hamlet to the current seven-street community.

During the collective period, a common house consisted of three rooms, with the windows facing south and the entrance in the middle; the three rooms were called the east room (*dongwu*), the outer (central) room (*waiwu*), and the west room (*xiwu*) (see Figure 5.1). It is interesting to note that the room in the center where the entrance was located was called the outer room. Many poor families, however, had only a two-room house, usually the east room and the outer room (like the majority of villagers before the revolution).

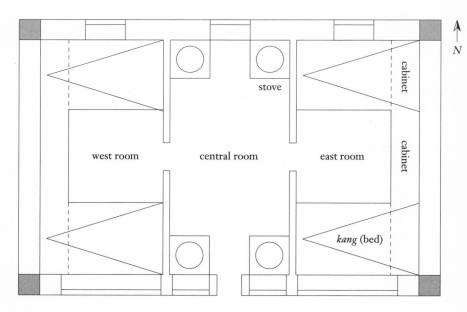

Figure 5.1 Floor Plan of a Pre-1980 House

Functionally, the outer (central) room was used as a kitchen, hallway, and temporary storage space. But some families also kept their pigs in this room during the winter season. Two (and sometimes three or four) stoves for cooking occupied the corners of the outer room, leaving only limited space in the center for people to walk about and work. Unless absolutely necessary, many families used the west room only for storage, or as a bedroom during the summer season. To keep warm during the winter, villagers packed themselves into the east room, which was considered the best of all the rooms.

As shown in Figure 5.1, the beds (locally called *kang* or *huokang*) were built along the walls of the room and were heated by the stove, which was attached to them. When the stove was on, the smoke moved through several zigzagged tunnels under the bed, eventually exiting through a chimney located in a back corner along the northern wall of the house. The two heated beds or *kang* were called the south bed (*nankang*) and the north bed (*beikang*), according to their locations in the room. (Note that all houses faced south in order to absorb the maximum amount of sunshine and light.) And the smaller bed that connected the two larger beds was called a *yaokang* (literally, "waist bed").

Such a house could accommodate the needs of a family throughout its development cycle. The entire family usually stayed in the east room, and when the children were still young they usually used only the south bed for most of their activities. The sleeping arrangement was hierarchical. The end position in the bed closest to the stove is called the bed head (*kangtou*), a privileged place reserved for the most senior male in the household; his spouse occupied the next position. Other members went down the row according to their generational rank, age, and sex. Usually, a daughter (or a granddaughter) slept either at the other end of the south bed or in the north bed because she was ranked low and also had a special need for privacy.

Until the 1970s, newly married young couples also shared a room with the rest of the groom's family (sometimes eight to ten people) and slept in the north bed, with a hanging curtain in front of their bed that separated them from the others.[3] When family division occurred, each of the newly established nuclear families got a stove and a heated bed attached to the stove. A house therefore could include four separate families, as shown in Figure 5.1. The more common practice among young couples in the 1960s and 1970s, however, was to move into another family's house, occupying either the west room or only the north bed of the east room where the host family lived. It was therefore not unusual for two unrelated families to live in the same house. When I first moved to Xiajia village in 1971, I lived in the north bed of a family's east room for nearly a year, and then I lived in the west room in another family's house for six years.

From a contemporary urban perspective, there is not much privacy or personal space in such conditions. Everyone can be observed by everyone else, twenty-four hours a day and seven days a week, including at night. When I first moved into the north bed in my landlord's room during a winter season there were six other people in the same room, including two girls, one my age and one older (I was 17). At first I did not know how to undress myself at bedtime, but I soon learned, copying the example of the girls, to undress underneath my comforter after the light had been turned off. I also became accustomed to doing a lot of things in front of the members of my host family and had no problem following local customs. Once I got used to it, nothing was uncomfortable. Therefore, when I got my own room a year later, I did not feel the need to lock the door when I was away, except to make sure that the pigs did not enter the room. In retrospect, I realize that, under such conditions, most people are not curious to watch or peep at another individual's "private business," and conversely, one does not have much to hide from the domestic "public gaze."

The outer (central) room (see Figure 5.1) was not supposed to be used as a family function space, other than for cooking and storage. The entire family used the east room as an all-purpose space, which was anything but spacious. The beds took up most of the floor space in the room, leaving only a small square in the center, normally forty to sixty square feet. Most activities took place on the beds, primarily the south bed that was the center of the family's private life. Food processing (e.g., corn husking) and food preparation were done on the heated bed; family meals were served on a short-legged table placed on the bed; women did their sewing on the bed; small children also played on the bed on cold days; and visiting friends gathered and chatted on the bed. Thus, when a guest visited, the welcome gesture was to invite him or her onto the bed. Such a limited and crowded space usually could only accommodate one center of attention, and in most cases this was the father. It was very difficult for the less powerful and unprivileged members of a family (the women and the youngsters) to take center stage unless the father was not at home.[4]

The lack of space for family activities was actually one of the major reasons why villagers were so fond of visiting one another, a daily leisure activity locally called *chuanmenzi* (to drop in). During these purposeless and routine visits people socialized in small groups according to their age, sex, and personal characteristics, and the end result was the maximum use of limited domestic space. In each family there was a specific type of gathering, of fathers, mothers, girls, or boys, for example. In a sense, one could find one's personal space among peer gatherings in someone else's home, but not necessarily in one's own home.

This type of socializing is especially relevant to the discussion of conjugality in Chapter 4, because without spending much time together in private, it was difficult for couples to develop stronger bonds and pursue their mutual attraction. As many old and middle-aged villagers recalled, when they were young and newly married, they were discouraged by their parents from spending time with their wives at home. "A man should go out and hang out with the men," one villager told me. It was not accidental that during the collective period the headquarters of the production teams all had huge heated beds that could accommodate several dozen people at the same time. The favorite places for village men during that period, therefore, were the headquarters of the collectives where they could chat with fellow team members or play poker. Young wives either stayed home with their in-laws in their limited space or met their peers in other homes. The only time for a young couple to be together was at bedtime, but this was not quality time because of the communal sleeping arrangements.

House Remodeling Since the 1980s

Significant change occurred in the early 1980s, shortly after the rural economic reforms and decollectivization. The initial success of household farming and the diversified economy increased peasant incomes rapidly, which led to a surge in house construction in Xiajia during the second half of the 1980s. My 1991 survey shows that 102 new houses were built after 1983 (mostly between 1985 and 1988), and 121 houses were rebuilt or enlarged. Traditionally, villagers had built their houses with clay walls and grass roofs; but most of the new houses were built with brick walls and tile roofs. The availability of cement and other modern construction materials enabled villagers to build larger houses or to enlarge their old ones. They also developed new aspirations after observing and even experiencing an urban lifestyle while working on temporary jobs in the cities.

The first wave of change was moderate and experimental. Figure 5.2 shows the floor plan of a house built in 1985 by a man with extensive experience doing construction work in cities, one of the first attempts to build a new-style house. The most obvious change was to divide the outer (central) room into two rooms, with the one in the back to be used as an extra bedroom or a private retreat. In this house the elderly mother in this stem family lived in the small bedroom in the back, a design that was copied by many other families thereafter. A direct result of this design was that many elderly parents moved out of the east room, which was traditionally regarded as the best room in the house, and into the small bedroom in the central part of the house. The second change was to designate the west room as the bedroom for the grown-up children, instead of using it as storage space or for a separate family. This new design feature benefited the middle-aged couple in this family by giving them the very spacious east room all to themselves. However, their room was still filled with the heated beds leaving little open space in the center.

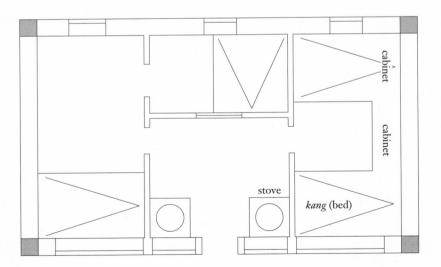

Figure 5.2   Floor Plan of a 1985 House

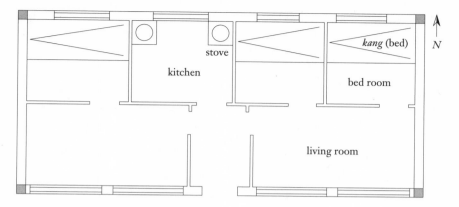

Figure 5.3   Floor Plan of a 1986 House

Figure 5.3 represents a house built in late 1986 by the then village head; it was regarded as the most advanced design at the time. Many villagers copied this model in the following years in a new wave of house remodeling. The internal space of this house measures 740–780 square feet, quite large by 1980 standards. The owner made a revolutionary change in house design by dividing the house into three functional areas (even though it is a four-room structure), separating the areas with walls and doors. The entire southern half of the house is made up of two large rooms without heated beds, plus an entrance door in the center. This was the first time in Xiajia village that the notion of a separate room without the heated bed was put into practice. Following urban usage the room was referred to as *keting* or simply as *ting*, literally guest lounge or lounge, but I will hereafter translate it as the living room. In this design there are actually two living rooms, one for the village head and his wife and the other for their grown children. At the time the house was built, they had an unmarried daughter and an unmarried son, and the mother of the village head also lived with them. To accommodate each individual's needs, the northern half of the house was divided into four equal-sized rooms. The village head and his wife slept in the east room, and his mother and daughter used the adjacent room. Their son was given the far west room because he was older than the daughter and of marriage age. The kitchen was moved to the back and also used to separate the son's room from his parents' room, creating more privacy for both. Through interviews I learned that when the father was not at home, which was most of the time, the daughter and her friends usually occupied the east living room, and the son and his friends used the west living room. The mother spent a lot of time in her own bedroom either alone or with her own friends and sometimes shared the room with her daughter and other young girls. Both living rooms were furnished with sofas and coffee/tea tables—another new development in Xiajia village in the late 1980s. The east room, however, was better decorated because the father sometimes used it to entertain cadres from the town government or other villages.

In another interesting development, the size of the beds in this 1987 house was reduced so that there was more unused floor space in the bedrooms, despite the fact that the rooms were also much smaller. When the door was closed, the bedroom could function as an independent room, instead of merely as a huge bed. For instance, grooming, a daily task that was previously done in either the kitchen/outer room (by men) or the old-style east room (by women), was now performed in one's bedroom and became a more private activity. When the door was closed, people could also wash their bodies inside the bedroom, a new development most appreciated by young women.

The availability of heating resources made the reduction of the bed size in the bedroom and its removal from the living room possible. Thanks to the high-yield seeds and the heavy use of chemical fertilizers, villagers can harvest not only more grain but also more corn stems and corncobs—the major source of cooking and heating fuel. Many villagers built a homemade separate heating system in their houses, using the corn stems and corncobs to heat up the water-tube boiler; yet the more affluent families prefer to use coal purchased from the market for winter heating, leaving their extra corn stems and corncobs unused in the field.

The latest and perhaps potentially most important change has been to add a bathroom in the house, as shown in Figure 5.4. This house was built in 1997 and, although it is a three-room structure, it is 150 square feet larger than the 1987 model. Improvements in construction materials in the 1990s made it possible for villagers to further increase the square footage of the new houses. Comparing the 1997 house with the 1987 house, we can see that in the 1997 house the couple's bedroom is larger than the other rooms, imitating the urban design that boasts a stylish master bedroom in each unit. And in this particular house the main bedroom is separated by a central hallway from the

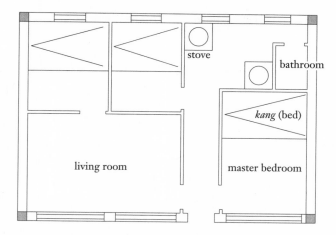

Figure 5.4   Floor Plan of a 1997 House

other two rooms used by the couple's three children. The hallway serves as a transit area that links the bedrooms to the kitchen, and when bedroom doors are closed, the hallway also separates the inner space from visitors. According to my informants, most new houses in the late 1990s had similar features.

A major new feature of the 1997 house, however, is the bathroom at the upper right corner of the house, next to the kitchen. The bathroom boasts a full-size bathtub with a shower above it, and both the walls and ground are covered with white tiles. There is no running water in Xiajia and the surrounding area, so having a bathroom is really quite a luxury. In order to make the bathroom work, the owner of the house dug a well in the backyard and then used pipes to drain water from the bathtub to the well. Because the operation consumes both time and energy, the family only used the bathroom during the summer.[5] This house was not the first to have an indoor bathroom and certainly not the last—virtually all new houses built in the late 1990s added this feature. Although several families found the new fashion useless and ended up using the bathroom for storage instead, more and more villagers had begun to use it during summer season. The most happy beneficiaries were the women who, unlike the men who could bathe naked in the nearby small river and ponds, now finally had a secured sanctuary in which to wash their bodies.[6]

In addition to redesigning the interior of the house, villagers also redesigned the exterior environment—the land where the house sits. The house plot, which varies from 6,000 to 8,000 square feet, is locally called *yuanzi* (the first character bears a second tone), literally "garden." Because peasant houses were never collectivized, the house plot, although originally allocated through the village collectives, was regarded as private property in practice. A family could sell its house plot as well as its house.[7] A house plot was commonly divided into front and back parts, separated by the house in the middle; Xiajia villagers referred to them as the front and the back gardens (yuanzi). From the 1950s to the early 1980s the house garden, together with the officially allocated "private plot land" (*ziliudi*), provided a crucial resource for villagers to supplement their daily necessities.[8] They grew potatoes and corn in the back garden and vegetables in the front (often much smaller) garden. During the spring the production teams helped its members to plough the house plot— usually one or two team members were assigned to do the job for all families. To make the house plot accessible to ploughing machines, no permanent fences or walls were built around the house; instead, the house was situated on open land, only concealed from the public eye by crops and vegetables during growing seasons. Because visitors could easily enter a house from the street without having to cross a clear physical barrier, such as a gate or a fence, villagers freely passed through another family's garden as a short cut from one street to another.[9]

Along with the waves of house construction and remodeling, many villagers stopped growing vegetables in the front garden and turned it into either a courtyard paved with bricks or a work ground for family sidelines, such as running a chicken farm or a grain-processing factory. They had plenty of farmland to grow grain since the reform of household farming in the late 1970s, so they no longer needed the back garden to supplement their diets and turned it into a vegetable garden instead. Many built brick walls to enclose the front yard and the house and installed a gate at the entrance. A new trend in the 1990s was to build a formal entrance with a wooden or iron gate wide enough to allow the tractor-pulled wagon to enter the courtyard; several dozen families had done this by 1999. To match the larger gate, these families had to increase the height of the courtyard walls as well. As a result, many houses were hidden behind walls or encircled by permanent fences.

Although deteriorating public security was listed as a major reason for building walls and gates, the fact that most families did not lock their courtyard gates at night indicates some other motivations. When probed further, many informants admitted that they wanted to match the newly remodeled house interior with a beautiful courtyard or to create a more enclosed feeling of home space.

Almost all of those who remodeled their houses first were cadres or elite villagers who had extensive contacts with the outside world. Because all houses were built by their owners rather than by professional developers, an owner's tolerance for or willingness to accept new ideas was as important as the ideas themselves. This is why ordinary villagers tended to be reluctant to try out new ideas. In addition, there was some competitiveness among elite villagers (cadres and no cadres) to build the best family house and secure their own status. However, once a new design was tried and seemed to work, ordinary villagers quickly followed suit, and the new design soon became standard. This contrasts sharply with the pre-1949 situation when elite families lived in big compounds and the rest of the village lived in very simple small houses or huts. The egalitarian ideal promoted during the collective period still influenced the mentality of Xiajia villagers in the 1990s. The leveling effect of the land reform and collectivization campaigns gave villagers a sense of entitlement and a desire to be like everyone else, and, in the realm of family consumption, to have whatever others had. Few villagers wanted or dared to be left behind the current trends.[10]

Economic prosperity was certainly one reason villagers were able to improve their dwellings; the wave of house construction in the early 1980s resulted directly from the rapid increase in peasant income in Xiajia and the rest of rural China. But they could have just built better and larger houses in the old style, instead of experimenting with new interior designs. But because domestic space is both a physical and a social construct, underlying the specific house forms are principles by which people categorize their relationships and organize their everyday life in spatial terms. Spatial change in Xiajia families thus should not be regarded as merely a one-on-one response to the improvement in economic conditions. Instead it should be understood as part of the transformation of private life, which is characterized by the rise of youth autonomy, the decline of patriarchal power, and at a deeper level, the rising awareness of the individual. In other words, house remodeling should also be viewed as an effort on the part of villagers to accommodate the demands for conjugal independence and individual freedom, which can be examined at two levels—the family and the individual.

Family Privacy and the Notion of Interiority

The aforementioned changes in house form are by no means arbitrary. They are influenced by and in turn reshape the changing ways in which families interact with one another as well with officials and the public. By reducing the size of the heated beds and putting them in separate, enclosed bedrooms, a family created a transitional space with the living room where the family members could receive visitors and entertain guests. The living room also serves as the center of family activities, since the television set, the hanging clock, and sofa or chairs are all placed there. The most obvious reason to have such a space is to protect the privacy of the family: people can literally put on a "public face" in the living room when dealing with visitors, while reserving their private lives for the bedroom(s).

I first noticed the difference during my 1989 fieldwork, when some villagers had separate living rooms and others did not. In the new houses I was invited to sit on a bench, a chair, or a sofa in the living room, chatting with my informants as one would normally do either in urban China or in the United States. But when I visited those who still lived in traditional-style houses, I reverted to earlier customs: going straight to the heated bed, taking off my shoes, jumping onto the bed, and sitting at the inner corner, the position reserved for family guests. This was all done, of course, after a warm invitation from the host (if there was no such invitation, then I knew I was not welcome). As time passed, I found myself increasingly directed to people's living rooms (some of which were quite fancy), because only the poorest families still lived in traditional houses at the end of the 1990s.

As a visiting anthropologist I could sense the inner-outer boundaries. I could no longer be certain of the economic standing of the family by taking a quick look around the house because in the new houses the private rooms are hidden from the public gaze. More important, I could no longer keep the entire family together during my interviews. Previously when I visited and talked with one member of a family, the other members were also present (if they were at home) because there was no other place for them to be. In the new houses, if they wished they could stay in their own bedrooms and not deal with me. On the other hand, because of the new house design, I was able to have a small room of my own inside my host family's house when I conducted my fieldwork, thus making both my life and my work more convenient and pleasant. My own experience in this connection allowed me to understand and appreciate the meaning of the changing spatial arrangement for interpersonal relations within a family house.

The separation of the bedrooms from the living room is not as rigid as that in contemporary American homes; rather, where one is entertained depends on the social distance between a visitor and the host. More often than not, close friends or relatives are invited into the host's bedroom; some can even take off their shoes and climb onto the heated bed (which is much smaller than before).[11] But the main difference in the remodeled house is that the host or hostess can determine which part of the house is to be open to the visitor in accordance with the social distance between the two sides. The new walls, permanent fences, and courtyard gate also help them to control access to their home by nonfamily members. In other words, a by-product of the fashion of house remodeling was the emergence of a physical-social code in the house that separated the inside and the insiders from the outside and outsiders, reduced the accessibility of the family to the public, and created a sense of interiority at home.

When I discussed the new spatial divide between the inside and outside with two village cadres and one government official from the township, they said they shared similar experiences when they visited peasant families to implement policies, such as to collect levies or to enforce the birth control regulations. It became common for the housewife simply to tell the cadres that the household head (her husband) was not at home; in the new-style homes the cadres had no way to check whether this was true, and it became more difficult for them to do their jobs.

Ms. Wang, the head of the village Women's Association, did not have this kind of problem, but she did say that it was more difficult for her simply to walk into the inner part of the house without an invitation from the hostess: "You never know what can happen if you are careless; you could be accused of stealing things, or even worse if you were a man facing a housewife." She then told me about an incident that had occurred in the fall of 1998. Two young men, who worked as village security guards at night, were suspicious that a third man had stolen some crops, so they followed the latter to the gate of his courtyard. When the two guards entered the house, however, they met only the suspect's wife, who said her husband was not home. They insisted that they had seen her husband stealing; the wife then started to cry and accused the two young men of sexual misconduct. Although the two guards left the house as quickly as possible, she filed a complaint against them until they agreed to pay her 500 yuan as a gesture of apology. The investigation of her husband was also dropped.

In contrast, when the entire family lived in a single multipurpose room, cadres seemingly had the right to enter any home without notifying the host in advance. A cadre who worked as the head of a production team during the collective period said that during busy seasons he often changed the scheduled laborer's assignment and sometimes went to a team member's home late at night or in the early morning to reassign the individual. "I sometimes saw a couple still holding one another in sleep and I simply woke them up from their beautiful dreams," he recalled with an obvious tone of satisfaction (remember that villagers did not lock their houses at night during the collective period). He reminded me that when I lived in Xiajia I had hated being awakened at 3:30 A.M. during the busy summer hoeing seasons. The person who did this in our production team was a crippled night guard. He always used his cane to bang on the window above my bed (and others' too) and shout: "Time to get up, get up!" But he performed his duty from outside, never attempting to enter the house, probably because he was not a cadre and thus did not feel he was entitled to do so.

At the same time that the family house has become less accessible to the public and more private, social intimacy among neighbors has declined. Visits between neighbors (chuanmenzi) occur much less often, for two reasons: the improved housing conditions and the more complicated etiquette of visiting. Watching television at a neighbor's home was common when television ownership was not yet widespread. But by the end of 1990s virtually every household in Xiajia owned a TV set (although only a quarter of the families had a color TV set). Many villagers told me that they felt it was inconvenient (bufangbian) or uncomfortable either to watch TV at a neighbor's home or to have a regular guest from outside. More than once I saw parents watching a black-and-white thirteen-inch television set in one room while their married son and his wife watched a twenty-inch color TV in the other room. When asked why they didn't join the young couple, the parents explained that they might want to watch different programs and that they felt more comfortable in their own room.

Another reason the number of mutual visits declined, according to villagers, were the new physical barriers and etiquette. Earlier, one could simply walk into a house without greeting the host in advance, and there were no physical barriers: one could walk straight into the only function room in the house and find the person to be visited right there (unless he or she was not at home). Nowadays, a visitor usually asks "Anybody at home?" while walking through the new courtyard gate or deliberately makes some noise to inform the host that a visitor is arriving. Once inside the house, the host greets the visitor in the outer (central) room and invites the latter into the living room. The physical barriers of the courtyard and the transitional space inside the house remind the visitor to avoid making the host feel uncomfortable. Certainly not everyone observes these new rules, and some are even not fully aware of them because the rules are evolving, as is the house remodeling. However, once some villagers began to restrain themselves and show concern for family privacy, new ways of appropriate behavior were established silently. The comforts of home and the added difficulties of visiting thus work together to prevent many villagers from continuing the former practice of casual mutual visits. The fewer mutual visits there are, the less the villagers know about their neighbors' families, and the less interested they are in visiting. Hence the decrease in social intimacy.

I must add two points to paint a complete picture of the changing village atmosphere. First, what has happened in the villages cannot be compared to what has happened in urban neighborhoods. Villagers still visit one another more often than do their urban counterparts. Still it is the beginning of a significant change. Second, I was probably more sensitive to the change because I too was a "victim" of the new trend of decreasing social intimacy. To verify the data I collected in open-ended interviews and chats with informants, I often cross-checked the data again with others, such as the friends and neighbors of the first group. During my last three trips to Xiajia in 1997, 1998, and 1999, however, I found that many individuals did not know what had happened in a neighbor's home down the street. When I discussed this change with a key informant, he smiled and referred to the phenomenon with a local phrase: *qijia buzhi bajia shi*, which can be translated as, "The seventh family [on the street] does not know the eighth family's affairs."

The Privacy of the Individual

In addition to fencing off outsiders, the recent changes in domestic spatiality enable individuals to have their own personal space inside the house. The direct result of house remodeling was to give a couple (and often elderly parents and grown children) their own bedroom. This alone has increased conjugal privacy to a great extent and improved the bonding and affection between husband and wife in many families, as illustrated by the personal experience of an old friend.

During an informal interview in 1997, I started to talk about the implications of having a separate bedroom for the intimate life of married couples with a friend, a 41-year-old man who had worked in the same production team as I during the 1970s. With no hesitation, he jumped up and said: "No need to hem and haw. It's straightforward. Let me tell you a simple thing. I never slept naked with my wife until we had our own house, and that was ten years after we married! For two years we were living in the north bed of my uncle's home, and we always had to be quiet—you know what I mean? It was awful!"[12]

This man's experience was by no means unique; couples normally wore their clothes to bed. Occasionally, it was rumored that a couple had been accidentally seen naked by other people, and that couple became the target of public teasing and criticism for their carelessness. Although my data do not provide any systematic account, the villagers suggested that by the 1990s it was rather common for young couples to make love fully undressed. A separate bedroom obviously increased their sense of safety.

When asked their reasons for choosing to live in a nuclear family, most Xiajia residents answered with two words: *shunxin* (satisfaction/happiness) and *fangbian* (convenience). The former is not difficult to understand, as many villagers asserted: "Life is always happier when you can manage family life yourself" (*rizi zong shi ziji guozhe shunxin*). In other words, the power to make decisions and the joy of conjugal independence can make one feel happy. The second term, fangbian, however, is more complicated and can only be understood in relation to shunxin. When villagers explain that one may feel more fangbian in a nuclear family, this does not merely mean that they are more convenient or easier, as the term usually implies. In most newly established nuclear households, the couples frequently encounter "inconveniences" such as needing an extra hand for household chores, money for household expenses, or someone to take care of newborns. In this context fangbian actually refers to the notion of conjugal privacy, and a couple's demand for fangbian represents an effort to reduce the accessibility of the conjugal space to others (see B. Laslett 1973).

In a nuclear family a couple may find it more "convenient" to develop conjugal intimacy, to be left alone, and to make decisions without parental intervention. Because of these special kinds of fangbian (convenience) life in a nuclear family is considered to be more shunxin, namely, happier. It is easy to understand why young villagers, especially young wives, welcome such radical changes in house design; they used to complain that they could not spend much time alone with their spouses when they lived with their parents-in-law and unmarried siblings-in-law in the old-style houses. As one young woman put it: "You always feel as though you are being watched; there are eyes around the house all the time."

The pursuit of conjugal privacy as reflected in the local notions of shunxin and fangbian goes beyond the daily appropriation of domestic space; young couples also defend their personal freedom and independence in terms of *sishi* (personal matters/business). One of the most common complaints from the young villagers is that their parents are too nosy and interfere in their personal business. When the younger generation is defensive about their personal business, an uncompromising position can trigger serious intergenerational conflicts in stem families. In 1994 a 32-year-old wife in a stem family liked to play poker and sometimes gamble with several women from her neighborhood. Her mother-in-law regarded this behavior as scandalous and immoral and tried various means to stop the daughter-in-law from playing. When the old lady's discontent escalated into arguments and mutual reproof between the two women in the house, the mother sought support from her son. To her surprise, the son made a three-point statement in defense of his wife. First, the son said, since he himself also liked to gamble it would be unfair to prohibit his wife from playing poker; second, his wife never played until she finished all her household chores; and third, his wife had made a lot of friends in this way because she was an able gambler, and she thus helped the family to build a larger guanxi network. The son then blamed his mother for mindlessly interfering in other people's personal business (*xiaguan bieren de sishi*). Angered and humiliated by her son's accusation, the mother moved out of the house shortly thereafter and has lived alone ever since.

House remodeling provides privacy and freedom not only to the couple but also to the other members in a family, although it may not be perceived and received in the same way across generational lines. When I discussed this issue with middle-aged villagers who had married sons, they said that they too felt the convenience (fangbian) of living either in a new-style house or in their own house alone. As parents of married children, they had to set good, respectable examples in everyday life and thus had to remain self-disciplined at all times. One man provided a simple example: during hot summer days he liked to wear only his shorts when at home, but after his son married (and brought in a daughter-in-law), this man had to dress more formally, no matter how hot it was. Thus when his son moved out he felt happy that he had recovered his freedom (to wear shorts at home).[13] However, elderly parents (defined as those age 60 or older) generally showed little enthusiasm for the new house designs because they were accustomed to the physical proximity in the old house, and more important, they felt (with good reason) left behind by the rapid changes.

Elsewhere I examine the development of a youth subculture in village society and mention an event that occurred during my fieldwork in a village in Hebei province in 1989. When a fellow fieldworker and I were sent by the village party secretary to his son's room to sleep, the 17-year-old son refused to cooperate, angry at our intrusion into his privacy.[14] As he explained to me the next day: "My father is stupid. He doesn't realize that I have already grown up and I want to be left alone. He should have asked me before sending anybody to sleep in my room" (Yan 1999: 78). I encountered similar reactions in Xiajia in 1991, 1994, and 1998, when young people either refused to obey their parents' order to come out of their rooms to talk to me or were reluctant to let me enter their rooms. The new house design also provides opportunities for village youth gatherings; in many families the grown children can develop social worlds with their peers inside a separate bedroom. The availability of such a private space for the youths to interact with peers of the opposite sex facilitates the development of romantic love and intimacy in mate choice, and in some cases also premarital sex.

Reconfiguring Domestic Spatial Relations

The changing spatiality in villagers' homes is replacing old physical markers of proper behavior with new ones. Family members must renegotiate with one another regarding not only the use of space but also the maintenance of intrafamily relations. Take sleeping patterns as an example. During the slack season or the long winter, young couples tend to stay in bed very late in the mornings, a practice that makes many parents very uncomfortable. From the parents' perspective, the most important characteristic of a good farmer is industriousness. Getting up early has been a sign of being hard-working for as long as these parents can remember, regardless of whether there is work to do. The younger villagers, on the other hand, see rising early as stupid and senseless. To them, staying in bed late is their personal business, their moment of happiness, with which their parents have no right to interfere. The tension between parents and married children over this issue did not exist before the wave of house remodeling; young couples could hardly stay in bed too long when they were sharing the bed with the entire family in an all-purpose room and a visitor might arrive at any moment. After the separation of the bedrooms from the living room, however, young couples could and did sleep behind closed doors in their own bedrooms for long hours into the morning. Oversleeping became a common source of intergenerational quarrels in stem families. Most young couples eventually won the argument, but it took the parents time and a lot of effort to adjust to the change.

The reconfiguration of spatial relations in the family has gone far beyond basic living habits to many other aspects of everyday life; as a result, the senior generation, particularly the elderly parents, have lost many previous privileges in the appropriation of domestic space. Gone with the old house design and its underlying principles are the previous hierarchical spatial arrangements; also gone is the kinship hierarchy based on generational seniority and age as well as the superiority of the male gender. The most obvious and significant change is the rise of the centrality of the conjugal relationship, accompanied by the displacement of the previous saliency of parental power and authority, a change that has, unfortunately, led to poorer living conditions for elderly parents.

According to traditional custom, in a three-room house with its door and windows facing south, the room at the east end was regarded as superior and thus was reserved for the ancestral shrine and the residence of the older parents. And, as indicated above, the elders normally slept closest to the cooking stove, the source of heat, and they sat at the inner side of the table that was placed on the heated bed during meals. It was also customary for the elders to enjoy the most comfortable seating (normally the warmest part of the heated bed) both at home and when visiting.[15]

After the wave of house construction and remodeling began, elderly parents lost many of their traditional privileges because most of the new houses were built for young couples or for those who were about to marry. When I first systematically surveyed the living conditions of the elders in 1991, I discovered that many older parents were living in their old clay houses with grass roofs; their newly married sons had moved out to new houses with brick walls and tile roofs. Where both the older parents and their married son lived together in the same old house, the son typically occupied the best room, furnished with new furniture and a TV set, which have been a typical part of the bridewealth since the 1980s. Having spent their savings on the son's marriage, the old parents normally stayed in the other room, with little, if any, furniture. A coal-fueled stove or heater was often installed in the married son's room (or house) instead of in the parents' room. When asked, the parents told me that they were used to the cold winters and did not mind living in a room without a heater, unlike the younger people who could not endure the cold. Given the fact that winter temperatures in this region often drop to twenty or thirty degrees below zero (centigrade), I doubt the elders were telling the truth.

By the time I conducted a second investigation of the elderly in the summer of 1999, less than 10 percent of the older parents were living in conditions better than those of their married sons. I also modified my second survey by removing furniture as one of the variables, because, as my informants told me, a set of new furniture was a must for the marriage of every young couple, and it is extremely rare for older parents to refurnish their own rooms. Only three older couples had done so, and in all three households the father remained the family head with the final say about family affairs. By the end of the 1990s it was rather common to find older parents living in the smallest and darkest room in the house, or, when the parents lived independently, in the old house, having given the new house to their married son(s).

The situation for the poorer elderly was even worse. In many poor families, the parents lived in a small bedroom behind the kitchen in the center of the house, and the two married sons and their wives lived in the two full-sized rooms at the two ends of the house (see the 1985 house in Figure 5.2). This is called *liangtoutiao* by the villagers, meaning the parents are carrying the two married sons as if they were carrying two buckets of water on their shoulders. I visited several houses with such living arrangements and found the living conditions of the older parents almost unbearable. Behind the kitchen, the parents' room was normally one-third the size of a standard room and, with no windows, it was quite dark. The room was hot and humid during the warm seasons because it absorbed all the steam and smoke from the kitchen, and it was the coldest room during the winter because it had no additional source of heat.

Although the new patterns of spatial relations punished some of the elderly, they benefited the previously unprivileged members of a family, namely the youth and women. As Sayer notes, the use of space cannot be separated from the objects in a given physical environment (1985: 30–31). The new house designs required new furnishings or new arrangements of the old furniture, which in turn influenced people's interactions in the new space. Again, take the living room as an example. By the 1990s living room furniture ranged from simple wooden stools and benches to fancy chairs and sofas, depending on the economic status of the family. Beginning in the late 1980s, a set of modern cabinets and a sofa set (normally two chairs and a couch) were a standard part of the bridewealth requested by the bride, thus quickly popularizing the new-style living room furniture. The most important consequence of this change was the disappearance of the old spatial hierarchy. According to my observations, family members can sit anywhere that is comfortable and available, a practice that contrasts with the old custom whereby rank determined people's assigned seating position on the heated bed. And because watching television has become the new focus of family entertainment, the scattered seats provide a more relaxed, equal, and comfortable environment.

Moreover, the new furniture, such as a wardrobe and cabinets, allows family members to put their clothes and other personal belongings in a more permanent, personalized place; earlier it was not uncommon for an entire family to share one cabinet or chest (though people had fewer personal belongings at that time). During my household visits, I frequently heard family members (mostly girls) complaining that someone had taken their space in the wardrobe or cabinet. Window curtains are also a new feature of house decoration, and, needless to say, they also increase privacy.

The dining table is another important new piece of furniture that has changed the gender dynamics in family relations. Until the 1980s, villagers ate their meals at a small, short-legged table that was placed on the heated bed. The usual seating arrangement put the family head, the father, in the upper seat, which was opposite the edge of the heated bed, and the grandparents on the sides but also away from the edge of the bed, where the children were supposed to sit (in other words, the edge of the heated bed was the lowest-ranked seating position). During the entire meal, the wife (or daughter-in-law in a stem family) stood or sat at the very edge of the heated bed, always making herself available to refill the rice bowls or perform other services for the entire family.[16] In a big family, the woman often did not have time to eat because she was busy serving the others. Usually she ate later in the kitchen. But when villagers began to conduct more activities on the floor rather than on the heated bed, and when a table and other pieces of furniture were introduced into daily life, the old seating pattern disappeared. I first noticed the change in 1989, and by the end of the 1990s all villagers used a dining table. Wives no longer served in the old fashion, except at more elaborate meals to entertain guests (women still did not dine at the table with important guests). More interestingly, on several occasions I saw the husband preparing the dining table and serving rice and other foods while the wife was busy caring for their child. Here it is difficult to determine whether the changes in spatial arrangements and changes in the gender dynamics at home were causes or consequences of each other.

Spatial Privacy in the History of Family Life

It should be noted that Xiajia villagers do not use the term *privacy* per se and are unfamiliar with the trendy term *yinsi*, which is the Chinese translation of the Western notion of privacy. Actually, I doubt Chinese villagers in other regions are familiar with the term either, even though it became popular in the 1990s in urban areas.[17] As indicated above, villagers often gave fangbian (convenience) as their reason for house remodeling, and some used the word *freedom* (*ziyou*) to describe their experience of having more personal space. When pressed further about the meaning of convenience and freedom, several used a similar image: "You can sleep on the bed during daytime without worrying about being seen or gossiped about by anyone." To make themselves understood, some villagers also told me that the feeling of freedom meant being able to do whatever you want (*xiang gansha jiu gansha*).[18] Less frequently yet probably equally important, villagers maintained that they liked the new house design because it made one's home *guijü* (well organized) and *youli youwai* (literally, "having an inside and an outside"). One of the first reformers of house design in Xiajia, for instance, told me that he had long dreamed of building a new house similar to an urban apartment, because urban dwellings had a distinction between inside and outside (he used the phrase *youli youwai*) and therefore were convenient (fangbian) to live in. Putting these pieces together, I am convinced that, without resorting to the urban notion of yinsi (privacy), Xiajia villagers actually have begun to pursue and protect their privacy at both the family and individual levels.

According to the legal-liberal approach in the West, privacy as a legal right plays an important role in fostering intimacy, equality, political freedom, and individual autonomy; as a social practice, privacy is crucial to individual development and the formation of diverse social relationships. Autonomy and intimacy are what is at stake in one's life, which are protected by the notion of privacy through depriving personal matters of public significance and protecting the private space from public intrusion (see Boling 1996: 19–31; Moore 1984; Warren and Laslett 1977). With regard to private space, Patricia Boling suggests: "We might expand on the spatial sense of private places, and think more metaphorically about the 'territories of the self' we all carry around with us" (Boling 1996: 27).[19] Here we can see clearly the close links between Xiajia villagers' notions of fangbian, ziyou, guijü, and youli youwai on the one hand and the scholarly discourse of privacy in the West on the other hand.

How can Xiajia villagers pursue and obtain the ideal of privacy in family life without actually understanding the Western notion of privacy? The answer lies in the indigenous notion of privacy in Chinese culture. Throughout

Chinese history a certain degree of privacy has always been carefully protected for some people. Suffice it to note that the elite and the rich have always enjoyed some privacy in family life. Spatially, the private houses of elite
and well-to-do families all drew a clear line between the exteriority of the
community and the interiority of the home and between the outer and inner
parts within the home, regardless of specific architectural styles or regional
differences. The courtyard house (*siheyuan*) in Beijing and the famous garden house in Suzhou, for instance, feature different kinds of physical barriers to control the accessibility of the interiority of the family to the outside
world. In one way or another, they all had an outer part to accommodate
public interactions at home and a keting (guest lounge) to receive visitors
and entertain friends (see Knapp 1986). Female members of an elite family
were generally confined within the inner half of the domestic space; hence
an upper-class man referred to his wife as *neiren* (literally, the inside person).
In pre-1949 Xiajia village, the landlords similarly protected family privacy
inside courtyard walls, closed gates, and armed guards, thus providing living
examples of a house that was fangbian, guiju, and youli youwai.

In this connection, Francesca Bray's study of domestic space and gender
polity in late imperial China is particularly noteworthy. According to Bray,
the Chinese house forms a political and moral continuum with community
and state, instead of a separate, private domain as in the West. One key feature of the traditional Chinese house was the spatial marking of distinctions
within the family, including the seclusion of women in the inner circles (1997:
52–58, 91–150). The physical boundaries within the house, however, are re-
lational and fluid, because women play an active role in the production of
the social space at home through their economic, social, and moral contributions to family life. The secluded space actually offers women a degree of
dignity, freedom, and security that would often be impossible in mixed com-
pany (Bray 1997: 54). As Bray notes: "When considering the significance of
female seclusion in late imperial China we also should remember that it does
not translate into a simple gender polarity in which women were controlled
and men were free. . . . On the one hand the institution of seclusion allowed
the family to contain and control this threat [of wives' unsure loyalty], on the
other it constructed spaces where alternatives to the strict patriarchal order
could flourish" (1997: 171). In other words, at least among the elite in late
imperial China, women played the key role in constructing the private end

of the continuum of the family, community, and state, and thus it was women who turned a multifunctional house into a private home.

Nevertheless, Xiajia villagers' practice of house remodeling in the 1980s and 1990s cannot be viewed as a simple replication of the traditional ideal, for two reasons. First, in the past, privacy was the privilege of the elite and the rich, out of reach by the rank and file, as exemplified by the contrast between the big compounds (dayuantao) and small shacks or "horse stands" (majiazi) in pre-1949 Xiajia village. This is by no means a uniquely Chinese phenomenon. In France, for instance, "For the first half of the twentieth century private life was in most respects subject to communal controls. The wall that was supposed to protect individual privacy was a privilege of the bourgeoisie" (Prost 1991: 67). As Warren and Laslett note: "The use of privacy is most likely for those whose behavior is not suspect and who have financial and other resources sufficient to draw boundaries around their activities" (1977: 48).

Moreover, individual privacy in traditional Chinese culture existed in a hierarchical context: social superiors could enjoy privacy in relation to those who were ranked lower socially and economically, but not vice versa. This is because privacy was not a legal right but a flexible privilege, the boundary of which varied according to one's social status in specific contexts. For instance, a landlord in a rural community could enter a poor tenant's home without any concern for the latter's privacy; but the opposite was unthinkable. However, when facing more powerful local gentry or a magistrate in another context, the landlord's privilege of privacy was less or even nonexistent, depending on the degree of status difference between the two parties. This is like the operation of social face in everyday life, and the actor normally knows how "big" the other party's face is.[20] So, for the reasons described, the head of a production team in Xiajia village was able to go directly to the bed of a sleeping couple and wake up the husband, and no one complained about the cadre's rude behavior. But the crippled night guard had to complete a similar task by knocking on the window from the outside because he had no bigger face and no more privilege of privacy than the other members of the production team.

Through their house remodeling efforts Xiajia villagers actually revolutionized the cultural tradition, turning previously elitist spatial notions into an everyday life necessity of ordinary people. Nowadays most families want to remodel their houses according to the latest floor plan, build a courtyard and a gate, and protect their family privacy from the outside world. Inside the new houses, multiple bedrooms give individual members of a family their own personal space (or territories of the self). The previous class- and status-based social differentiation in spatial privacy in particular and in private life in general has disappeared, and the previous hierarchy of spatial relations based on generational rank and gender has also been undermined. The villagers' efforts to remodel their houses, therefore, represent the democratization of domestic space in a dual sense.

Xiajia villagers are also inspired by their urban counterparts and imitate urban lifestyles in many respects, from house design to the use of domestic space to furniture style. The mass media, television in particular, have brought villagers in touch with a wide range of contemporary values and ideals that have also contributed to changing their mentality and behavior. One of the most important new values is the notion of ziyou (freedom), which is closely related to autonomy and intimacy—the core values that sustain the notion of privacy. We cannot understand the villagers' concern for individual space and autonomy without fully considering the influences of the new cultural values, as exemplified by a son's defending his wife's gambling and blaming his mother for interfering in their personal affairs.

What has occurred in Xiajia village, again, is by no means unique. There are reports of similar practices in other areas of Heilongjiang province.[21] House remodeling and interior decorating have been one of the hot consumer expenditures in urban China for years, and urban residents have made similar efforts to redefine spatial relations at home (see Davis et al. 1995; and Fraser 2000). In France, workers and peasants often lived in extremely crowded housing conditions until the turn of the twentieth century. Many rural homes consisted of a single room used for both cooking and sleeping; privacy and intimacy were nonexistent. Thus Prost calls the improvement in French housing since the 1950s a true "revolution" in the history of private life (1991: 51–67). In the United States, it was not until the late eighteenth century that people began to divide their homes into three functional areas: the kitchen, the dining and drawing room, and the bedroom. A separate living room that screens public interactions from the inner and private life of the family, however, was a much later invention (see Braudel 1967; Rybczynski 1986). It was during the first half of the twentieth century that American families began to enjoy a family room in suburban dwellings and a master bedroom with its own bathroom. In her study of domestic space in Mexican families, Ellen Pader examines both the family-oriented principles of domestic spatiality in Mexican houses and the recent changes that resulted from remodeling, separating public interactions from the bedrooms and creating more personal space for individual use (Pader 1993).

The Xiajia case, therefore, reflects the historical trend in the evolution of private life, whereby the family has become more privatized, family life revolves around the husband-wife union, and family members have become more aware of their individual rights, hence their demands for personal space and privacy. In Xiajia, ordinary villagers' quest for privacy has led to the reconstruction of domestic spatiality. At a deeper level, this reflects a growing sense of entitlement to individual rights in private life.

CHAPTER SIX

The Politics of Family Property

On a windless and hot summer morning in 1999, I returned to Xiajia village for the seventh time in ten years. Within a few minutes of my arrival I was showered by my host family and neighbors with local news and stories about what had occurred since I left a year earlier. "You must remember my elder brother," a neighbor said; "he and his wife have just moved out of the village." "Teacher Liu? Really?" I was surprised. "Yes, I helped them moved out just the other day" another woman added. "They took so few things with them; and Teacher Liu's wife was in tears. They were kicked out by their daughter-in-law." Others nodded, as they lamented that this couple should not have ended up in such a situation.

I was surprised by this news because I had had several long chats with Teacher Liu and his wife and did not believe they would have problems living with their only son. As early as 1994, Teacher Liu, who had taught in the village school since the 1970s, told me that he was preparing a lavish wedding for his only son. Although the bride's family did not make any specific request for bridewealth (a sign that the bride and her family fully trusted the economic status of the groom's family), Teacher Liu insisted on offering them the most valuable betrothal gifts at the time and told his future daughter-in-law that if she and her husband wished they could set up their own conjugal family right after the wedding. Teacher Liu would allow the young couple to have equal shares of everything in his household. He claimed that to offer these options beforehand would prevent potential fights between the two generations and would also make it possible for himself and his wife to live a freer life at home. However, Teacher Liu also told me that by making these generous offers he and his wife were hoping to deliver a message to the young couple, that is: "Everything in the household will belong to you, and your parents will not hide anything from you. So, just be relaxed and enjoy living together with your parents." He referred to his approach by the name of a traditional military strategy, *yuqin guzong*, meaning "to leave the subject at large in order to finally apprehend the subject." Although we laughed heartily at his witty way of using a classical Chinese phrase, I could sense the helplessness of the parents in trying to cope with the ever-increasing demands of their married children.

When I revisited Xiajia in the summer of 1997, I learned that only the downside of Teacher Liu's plan had been realized—his son had married a year earlier and indeed had established a conjugal family with his young wife, enjoying everything that the parents had prepared for the early family division. The young couple lived in the same courtyard with the older couple, eating almost daily with the parents but never contributing anything to the household budget. When asked why, the mother-in-law replied that she and her husband were still young (in their late forties) and still could earn much more than the young couple, so it was perfectly natural to share their resources with them. After all, they still were living together and eating together, despite the fact that the household had been divided in two. More important, they had only one son, and eventually they would rely on him for old-age support. "Family members should not clear the balance sheet" (*zijiaren bu neng suan tai qing*), she concluded. Obviously, their original strategy had not worked well, but they still clung to their original hope that by being generous they could win over the hearts of their son and daughter-in-law and thereby keep them within the old household.

In 1998, three years after the family division that separated this couple from their married son, I learned that the event that had triggered the family division was the celebration ritual of Teacher Liu's grandson, the young couple's baby. Following local custom, the grandparents hosted the ceremony and provided a banquet for all the guests, and as the hosts of the ritual they took the monetary gifts from the ceremony, as was customary in the village.[1] This upset the daughter-in-law, who thought that because the ceremony was held for her baby she should be the recipient of the gifts. When she quarreled about this with her mother-in-law, the natural next step was to ask for a family division. Struggling to keep his face, Teacher Liu told his fellow villagers (and me too, when we met in the summer of 1998) that he had long predicted the conflict and thus had prepared for the family division. "Nowadays, parents should celebrate their good luck if they are not kicked out by their children," he reportedly told his friends.

Teacher Liu and his wife were widely regarded as capable and wise individuals, and they were also known for making extra efforts in raising their only son, so their failure to maintain a stem family was a heavy blow to other parents in similar situations. Moreover, many villagers worried that the Lius' involuntary departure from the old house could start another radical change in the distribution of family property.

Family division and marriage are arguably the two most important turning points for property transactions in a family. In this chapter I look at the changes in those traditions over the five decades after 1949 as evidenced by the shortened duration of patrilocal residence and the resulting multiple fissions of the family and the transformation of bridewealth from intergenerational gifts to a new form of family inheritance. I conclude by analyzing the reasons for the growing number of individual claims over family property, which, together with the new ways of accumulating wealth, contribute to the collapse of patriarchal power in the politics of family property.

Early Family Division and the Decline of Patrilocal Coresidence

Two changes in the custom of family division during the post-Mao era are particularly noteworthy. First, family division happens earlier and, correspondingly, the duration of patrilocal coresidence is shorter (see, e.g., Lavely and Ren 1992; Selden 1993). That is, married sons and their new wives live with their parents for a shorter period of time. Second, instead of dividing family property equally among brothers, the new form of family division divides family property in a series of events, during which each departing son takes away only a part of the family property. These changes, however, have not been studied in their own right and are largely regarded as isolated evidence of family change. In my opinion, though, they are interrelated elements of a significant development in the family institution and therefore must be examined in relation to one another. Let us begin with the first change.

Beginning in the 1980s family division began happening much earlier after a son's marriage, and by the 1990s the customary coresidence of newlyweds with the groom's parents began to lose its significance. According to older villagers, before the 1949 revolution most people tried to delay family division as long as possible, usually until after the death of the father or after his retirement as household head. The 1949 revolution did not undermine this pattern of family division in the 1950s; on the contrary, it strengthened it in the sense that the redistribution of wealth during the land reform campaign enabled many poor men to marry earlier (some of whom might otherwise have remained permanent bachelors). Enriched and empowered by their newly acquired family property, many villagers realized their dream of an extended family within a few years. As a retired local shopkeeper recalled in 1998, when he had conducted a survey for the government-sponsored co-ops in 1956 he was impressed by the number of big families that he found. In one, the family head did not know precisely how many family members he had, and after a careful count it was determined that thirty-six people lived together in this big household. Of the thirteen villagers age 65 or older whom I interviewed during 1997 and 1998, eleven said that they had lived in either a stem family or a joint family during the 1950s.

From the early 1960s to the early 1980s, although families were gradually divided earlier and earlier, almost all couples still lived with the husband's parents for several years. The socially accepted time of division was after the marriage of the first son's younger brother; thus there were usually three to five years of coresidence with the groom's parents, or at least until after the birth of the first-married couple's first child (after at least one or two years of coresidence). In contrast, my 1991 survey shows that nearly one-third of the newly married couples in Xiajia village established their own households before they had a child, and more than 40 percent did so right after the birth of their first child.

The trend has continued to accelerate. By 1994 more than 40 percent of the newlywed couples had established an independent household before the birth of a child, and nearly 80 percent of the family divisions had occurred before the younger brother's marriage. In 1991 the earliest family division occurred seven days after the wedding; in 1994 two couples did not bother to observe the traditional custom of patrilocal coresidence at all—immediately after their weddings they moved into new houses and established independent households.

As a result of earlier family divisions, a growing number of newly established conjugal families consist of young couples who have not yet had a child. I refer to these as "husband-wife families," as opposed to the more conventional nuclear families, which emerged from delayed family division after the birth of a child (see Selden 1993: 148–49). During my 1994 visit to Xiajia, I found that twelve newlyweds had established husband-wife households, two of which included men who were the only sons in their families. Such a phenomenon would have been unheard of in the recent past.

These figures alone do not reflect the actual impact of early family division or of an only son's departure on the parents. A concrete example may be more illuminating. Mr. Fang has four sons; he named his eldest son Gold (*jin*), the second son Silver (*yin*), the third son Full (*man*), and the youngest Storehouse (*ku*). Taken together the four names signify "a storehouse full of gold and silver." This expresses the most common wish of Chinese villagers, that is, to have many sons in order to have more wealth and thus more security late in life. For Mr. Fang, however, things did not work out as he had planned. During the 1980s and early 1990s, he and his wife had to work hard to finance their four sons' marriages—which during the reform era became more and more costly. When their youngest son became engaged in 1990, the older couple thought they had finally reached the end of a dark tunnel. They were soon greatly disappointed when the prospective youngest daughter-in-law demanded a separate new house before marriage and an early family division thereafter. Less than two months after their youngest son's wedding, Mr. Fang and his wife were living alone in their old house, back at the starting point from which they had first established their own household more than thirty years earlier. When I discussed the situation with him, Mr. Fang replied: "All the gold and silver have been taken away by my sons. What is left is only a shaky, empty storehouse, guarded by an old man and an old woman. It has been like a dream, a bad dream."

The most important implication of early family division is the smaller commitment to the custom by both the senior and junior generations. As large-scale surveys have shown, patrilocal coresidence has gradually become a ritual rather than a long-term domestic arrangement in many parts of rural China (Lavely and Ren 1992: 391). In Xiajia village, until the late 1980s young people's demands for an early division frequently resulted in family disputes because parents were reluctant to agree to it. Many parents regarded early family division as a sign of their failure to raise filial sons and thus were upset with any attempt to shorten the duration of coresidence. Some parents even threatened to cut off the parent-child relationship if their sons insisted on moving out early. But over time parents began to deal with this issue more positively, by helping their married sons to relocate or by choosing to live in their own conjugal household after family division. Ironically, by the late 1980s and early 1990s, prolonged coresidence was sometimes associated with parents who were unable to help their married sons set up independent households (see Potter and Potter 1990: 219). Thus social acceptance of early family division actually indicates a change in the family ideal; the best example of this is that some older villagers now prefer to live in their own independent households—the "empty nest."

In Xiajia village a tailor set the precedent by making arrangements for all of his four sons and asking them to move out after their marriages. With a good house, cash savings, and his skills as a tailor that continued to generate an income, he and his wife lived comfortably in an empty nest. Many villagers admired his decision, and others followed his example. In 1991 eight families in the village consisted only of senior couples; by 1993 the number had increased to seventeen. Among them, nine elderly couples claimed that they had made the choice voluntarily (yet, according to some informants, only six had done so willingly). In any case, by the end of the 1990s, empty nest families were no longer regarded as a symbol of misfortune in old age; instead they have become a viable option for some villagers. In 1998 there were then forty-seven empty nest families, suggesting that the empty nest family may have become a new norm, a new phase in the family developmental cycle among villagers.

In this connection a demographic transition is also noteworthy. Life expectancy for both men and women in China increased from 40.8 years in the early 1950s to 69.4 years in the early 1990s (United Nations 1993: 234). With the improvement in living standards and medical care, villagers are much healthier and can work much longer. Moreover, rural youth tend to marry earlier than during the collective era, in part because of their newly attained prosperity and in part because the 1980 Marriage Law lowered the legal marriage age (Ocko 1991; Palmer 1995). As a result, many parents are in their forties when their eldest son gets married; this is more common among well-to-do families. During my 1993 fieldwork, I found the youngest father-in-law to be only 39 years old and the youngest grandfather 42, and newly married couples were in their late teens and early twenties. These middle-aged, healthy, and vigorous parents (even grandparents) are unlikely to retire from family management and thus are more likely to develop conflicts with the younger generation should they all live together (see Davis-Friedmann 1991: 82). A possible solution for both generations, therefore, is to live separately and to respect the other household's independence.

Serial Family Division and Its Impact

Another contributor to the rise of husband-wife families has been the development of a new form of family division. Traditionally, family division (*fen-jia*) occurred after all the sons in a family had married. At that time, the parents divided the family estate equally among the sons and then they lived with one married son in a stem family or rotated their residence among all the married sons (see Hsieh 1985). This form of family division, however, has been gradually replaced; now the first married son moves out soon after his marriage to set up a separate household with his wife. The family estate remains undivided in his parents' home because there are still unmarried siblings who need financial support from the family. Usually a young couple who wishes to live separately is entitled only to their share of the family grain stock and cooking fuel and their own personal belongings. This is locally called *jingshen chuhu*, which literally means "to leave the old household naked" (with no family property). The second son does the same, and the process continues until all sons are married. Xiajia villagers distinguish this new type of family partition from the traditional division by calling it *danguo* (to live independently) as opposed to fenjia (to divide up the family). Following Cohen's characterization of this new practice I hereafter refer to it as "serial family division" (1992: 370).

In Xiajia village, serial family division first emerged during the 1970s, when labor replaced land as the primary source of family income and young couples could set up independent households based on their own income from the collectives (provided that they had a place to stay).[2] By the 1990s it had become the dominant form of family division. Similar practices have been reported in other parts of rural China as well (see, e.g., Cohen 1992; Harrell 1993: 100; S. Huang 1992: 30; and Selden 1993: 148–49).

By the end of the 1990s, the redistribution of family property proceeded as follows. The family-owned grain stock was divided on a per capita basis, and the young couple received their own share, along with their personal belongings. Major family estates, including draft animals, tractors, and dairy cows, were usually kept in the parents' house if unmarried sons still resided there. Cash savings were never divided, even in the last round of serial family division because, as some villagers put it, the parents needed to retain their own "financial security." In the case of debts resulting from the young couple's marriage, the groom's parents (and their unmarried sons) took responsibility to repay them. The family house was retained by the parents and given to whichever son agreed to remain with the parents; but this rule did not apply to the new houses built exclusively for newlyweds. In short, in the 1990s a married couple was entitled to keep whatever they received from their marriage (clothing, furniture, cash, new house, etc.) and their share of the husband's family grain stock. Thus the amount of bridewealth and dowry were highly important for young couples and led to a significant change in the nature of marriage transactions.

A new issue for family division in the postcollective era is how to divide up the farmland, which is legally owned by the state and allocated to individuals as users. Land redistribution in 1983 was based on an egalitarian principle (but was gender-biased, because women received only subsistence-grain land) that gave each qualified individual, instead of the family, an equal share of farmland. Younger villagers invariably insist on maintaining their rights to the land that was granted in 1983 and, as a result, families that divided after that date have adopted a simple solution: land belongs to and will pass on to the person to whom it was allocated in 1983. In other words, the family recognizes and follows the official arrangement of individual rights to land, including women's rights to a share of subsistence-grain land. This solution works perfectly well for the young because it enables them to start their conjugal households with adequate land resources (they still need to pay taxes and grain procurements to the state, which are based on the contract land). In the case of intravillage marriages, the bride also brings her own share of subsistence-grain land, and this becomes a part of the land of the new conjugal household (land is not alienable between villages).[3]

Because the main body of the family estate remains undivided in the serial form of family division, newlywed couples have fewer incentives to remain in their parents' family. The earlier they leave to set up their own conjugal households, the more chance they will have to take advantage of outside opportunities. The younger sons tend to follow the examples of their elder brothers in demanding more from their parents for their own marriages (the most obvious indicator of this is their demand for new houses, which have become a necessary part of the bridewealth in recent years) and then leaving the family as soon as possible. Moreover, for security reasons parents tend to retain control over all their cash savings, and it is common for parents to hold on to their house until they decide to live with a married son in old age (the son then inherits the house). This marks a significant difference from the traditional practice whereby the parents were only the trustees or managers of the family property; with family division they merely gave up their power of management and retained no property of their own. Parents' current retention of property for old-age security indicates that a more individualized perception of family property is being promoted and developed among family members of all generations.

Another important impact of serial family division on family life is the complication of the family development cycle. Traditionally, family division occurred only once in a household, and it was seen as a turning point in a linear process of family development. The nuclear family consisting of parents and unmarried children developed into a stem family when the first son married; it then became a joint family when the second son married. At some point (most commonly upon the death of the father), this joint family divided again, resulting in several nuclear families. Hence a full cycle of family development (see Cohen 1976; Baker 1979).

In contrast, the serial form of family division requires a household to undergo multiple unifications and divisions. A family develops from a nuclear to a stem family with the first son's marriage, and it again becomes a nuclear family when the son and his wife leave the old household in the serial form of family division. This process repeats itself as many times as there are sons. In a well-known case involving seven sons, such a developmental cycle of "nuclear family to stem family and back to nuclear family" was repeated seven times over twenty-one years: it began in 1972 when the eldest son married and it ended in 1993 when the seventh son and his wife finally left the house, leaving the parents in an empty nest. In other words, the cycle of family development has been both accelerated (owing to earlier family division) and repeated or duplicated in each household. The impact of this change on the perception of the family and on behavior within the family remains an interesting topic in its own right.[4]

Bridewealth and Pre-Mortem Inheritance

The serial form of family division allows a young couple to take away from the husband's parents' family whatever marital gifts they receive (bridewealth and dowry), plus their own share of land, which was distributed to them during decollectivization. The efforts of rural youths to increase the standard amounts of bridewealth and dowry have rapidly escalated marriage costs and changed the traditional generational gifts given at marriage to a form of pre-mortem inheritance.[5]

In anthropological literature, the term *bridewealth* commonly refers to the property transferred from the groom's family to the bride's family.[6] It serves to validate a marriage agreement and the transfer of the rights over women from one family to another family. Bridewealth is often used by senior men to establish future marriages for the male siblings of the bride. In contrast, "dowry" is often considered to be the bride's share of her inheritance from the family of her birth, which is taken with her upon marriage. In highly stratified societies in Europe and Asia, a substantial dowry is part of an important strategy to advance family status or build prestige.[7] In Chinese societies dowries are often subsidized by the bridewealth paid by the groom's family to the bride's family (Cohen 1976; McCreery 1976; Ocko 1991; and R. Watson 1985a), a complicated practice characterized by Goody as "indirect dowry" (1973, 1990). The dowry represents only a small proportion of marriage transactions in local practice, so my inquiry here focuses on bridewealth.[8]

In Xiajia village and the surrounding areas, bridewealth is called *caili*, which can be translated as "marital gifts." When I asked what constituted caili, villagers always came up with a short, quick answer: money and goods. Until the mid-1980s, monetary gifts were presented by the groom's family to the bride's family. To follow established scholarly usage, I hereafter call this part of the marital gift the "bridewealth."

Material gifts that constitute another part of the caili include a great variety of goods that can be grouped into three subsets: (1) furniture; (2) bedding items; and (3) major appliances (*dajian*, literally "big items"), such as bicycles and television sets. It is the responsibility of the groom's family to purchase all material gifts. It should be noted that these material gifts are offered by the groom's parents to the newlywed couple as a conjugal unit, or subunit, within the larger family. Thus it might be proper to refer to these items as the "direct endowment" of the new conjugal unit.

Changing Practices of Bridewealth

From the recipient's point of view, both monetary and material gifts (namely bridewealth and direct endowment) can be regarded as marriage finances offered by the groom's family. Table 6.1 summarizes the changes in bridewealth over the five decades after 1949.

The first category of monetary gifts (bridewealth) in Table 6.1 is locally called *liqian*, literally "ritual money." But I prefer to translate it as "betrothal money" since the term *ritual* in this context refers to the engagement ceremony. Ideally, the economic function of the betrothal money is to subsidize the bride's parents in their preparation of the dowry for their daughter. Nevertheless, in the 1950s and 1960s it was not unusual for parents to use a daughter's betrothal money to pay for a son's marriage. Intriguingly, between 1950 and 1964 marriage finances provided by the groom's family consisted of only

TABLE 6.1.

Marriage Financing Provided by the Groom's Family, 1950–1999

Years	Betrothal money	Trousseau	Payment for ritual service	Converted bridewealth	Furniture	Bedding	Major appliances	Converted endowment	Total expenses	No. of marriages
1950–54	200[a]								200	3
1955–59	280								280	5
1960–64	300	100	20						450	4
1965–69	200	300	20			50	120		740	6
1970–74	300	300	50		70	100	150		970	6
1975–79	400	400	200		200	100	300		1,700	8
1980–84	400	700	300		500	200	500		2,700	6
1985–89				4,500	1,000	300	1,000		7,300	7
1990–94				7,200		800		4,000	11,200	9
1995–99				20,000				8,500	28,500	12

[a] The amounts are in RMB yuan and represent the average amount provided by the groom's family in the five-year period.

one category: betrothal money. Thus, until the mid-1960s, all resources were under the control of the bride's parents, and it was very likely that a higher bridewealth benefited the bride's parents rather than the bride.[9]

The second category, "trousseau money," emerged in the mid-1960s. It refers to monetary gifts offered by the groom's family to the bride's family for the purpose of purchasing clothes, shoes, and other minor items for the bride. In local usage, the trousseau money is called *mai dongxi qian*, literally "money for purchasing goods." The trousseau money, however, was not given to the bride's parents. Instead the groom's family used the money in this category to buy trousseau items that were then sent to the bride's family to give to the bride. Later, on the wedding day, the bride took those items, along with her dowry, to the groom's family where they remained her personal property. This category represents a significant change because the goods are specifically for the bride herself.[10]

During the late 1960s a third category, called "money for filling the pipe" (*zhuang yan qian*), began to be a factor in marriage negotiations. Unlike the trousseau money, this monetary gift was given directly to the bride for the ritual service of filling the tobacco pipes of her senior in-laws during the wedding. In Table 6.1 I refer to this as "payment for the ritual service" and regard it as the first basic change in the practice of bridewealth. Although its monetary value was relatively insignificant (twenty to fifty yuan between 1960 and 1969), it constituted, for the first time, a category of gifts that was given by the groom's family to the bride herself—directly and exclusively. The amount of payment for the ritual service increased considerably during the late 1970s and early 1980s, along with the value of the trousseau. It was also during this period that the groom's family relinquished its control over the purchase of the trousseau and allowed the young couple to buy the trousseau items on their own. These developments reflect the growing importance of the bride and groom in marriage transactions.

Beginning in the mid-1980s, however, all monetary gifts were subsumed under a new category, *ganzhe*, which refers to the conversion of material goods into monetary terms.[11] In the context of marriage transactions, the term *ganzhe* implies the conversion of all kinds of betrothal gifts given to the bride's side into a sum of cash. Hereafter I refer to this new category of ganzhe as "converted bridewealth." The total amount of the converted bridewealth is recorded on the bridewealth list and, more important, since the mid-1980s it has been given directly to the bride herself during the engagement ritual. This distinguishes the converted bridewealth from all other forms of monetary gifts that are given to the bride's parents.

According to Xiajia villagers, the first year that ganzhe money became popular was 1985, because it was rumored that after 1985 there would be no extra land allocated for the purpose of house construction. Those planning marriages at that time worried about losing the opportunity to acquire land, so many grooms suggested that their brides ask only for cash as betrothal gifts. This money was then used to buy materials for the construction of a house. The standard amount of ganzhe increased at this time, and in the following years it continued to climb.

Similar changes occurred in the provision of material gifts by the groom's family, namely, the direct endowment to the new couple as a conjugal unit. Direct endowment, as noted earlier, includes three subsets: furniture, bedding items, and major appliances. None of these material goods were part of the marriage transactions during the 1950s. They only began to appear in a small proportion in the 1960s. The demands for material goods for the conjugal unit grew rapidly in the 1970s. Furniture was added as a necessary part of marriage expenses, and demands for the well-known "four big items" (bicycle, sewing machine, wristwatch, and radio) and luxury bedding soon emerged. Although these gift items, as indicated above, were formally written into the bridewealth list, they were not gifts to the bride as an individual; instead, they constituted property owned by the bride and groom together as a conjugal unit.[12]

More radical changes took place during the 1980s. While the "four big items" remained popular, new items appeared on the gift lists, including television sets, tape recorders, washing machines, and motorcycles. Earlier demands for good furniture developed into desires for more modern styles, including a set of sofas that were typical of urban tastes yet also had begun to be popular in farming communities. Some requirements, such as four sets of luxury bedding, exceeded the practical needs of the new couple. This trend reached a new high by the early 1990s when a new form of ganzhe began to emerge. Under this new arrangement, all of the expenses to buy material gifts were also converted into cash and, following the example of the ganzhe money (converted bridewealth), the cash was given to the bride who, as understood by both families, represented the new conjugal unit. Here, direct endowment (material gifts) was finally transformed into what I call "converted endowment." By the end of the 1990s this converted endowment regularly included housing—either a newly built or a purchased house and sometimes even the means of production, such as a share of the contracted farmland or a small tractor.[13]

To sum up, over the five decades marital gifts provided by the groom's family evolved from a simple, single category of betrothal money into six categories of monetary and material gifts. This, in turn, has recently been transformed into a simple, one-category form, namely, the new category of ganzhe (converted bridewealth and converted endowment). These changes are summarized in Table 6.2.

The creation of each new category indicates the emergence of a new relationship in marriage transactions and thus constitutes an important step in the ongoing process of change. Moreover, despite the party-state's severe criticism of marriage payments, the average expenditure per marriage jumped from 200 yuan in 1950 to 28,500 yuan in 1999. However, the practice of high bridewealth does not always imply "marriage by purchase," as party cadres and the official media claim. The bride's parents do not necessarily benefit from the rise in marriage payments provided by the groom's family. In fact, the rise in

TABLE 6.2.
Bridewealth Provided by the Groom's Family, 1950–1999

1950–59	1960–69	1970–79	1980–89	1990–99
Betrothal money	Betrothal money	Betrothal money		
	Trousseau	Trousseau	*Ganzhe[a]*	
	Payment for ritual service	Payment for ritual service		
	Furniture	Furniture	Furniture	*Ganzhe[b]*
	Bedding	Bedding	Bedding	
		Major appliances	Major appliances	

[a] Here *ganzhe* refers to what I call "converted bridewealth," namely, the conversion of the three categories of monetary gifts (betrothal money, trousseau, and payment for ritual service) into a sum of cash. The cash is given directly to the bride by the groom's family.

[b] This ganzhe includes both the "converted bridewealth" and the "converted endowment." The latter refers to furniture, bedding, and major appliances, which are converted into a sum of cash in the form of ganzhe. The cash from these two kinds of ganzhe (converted bridewealth and converted endowment) is given to the bride by the groom's family.

marriage payments resulted mainly from the creation of new categories that privileged the bride and groom as a conjugal unit. Furthermore, the recent innovation of ganzhe has completely altered the structure of marriage transfers: it is now the bride (and the groom, whose role is hidden in public) who has final control over the marriage finances provided by the groom's family.

New Agents in Marriage Transactions

From the early 1950s to late 1970s, engaged young women were not directly involved in purchasing betrothal gifts, but they adopted many strategies to protect their interests. To ensure that the groom's family kept their part of the bargain, some sent an inspector to check the gifts before the wedding day. During the late 1980s and the 1990s, the new form of ganzhe (converted bridewealth and converted endowment) has enabled the bride to take control over most of the marriage finances, and consequently she has became more "greedy" and more active. Before one wedding in July 1991, the toughest negotiator at the engagement table was the prospective bride. She insisted on a ganzhe gift of 5,500 yuan even though the groom's family had originally only offered 4,000 yuan. Ultimately, the two sides agreed on 5,000 yuan, plus 500 yuan to be paid to the bride for performing her duty of serving cigarettes and wine during the wedding ritual. When she returned from the engagement ceremony she had pocketed 3,000 yuan and expected to receive the remaining 2,500 yuan before the wedding.

The deeper motivation for young women to pursue costly bridewealth is to prepare for the prosperity of the conjugal family. My interest in the role of the groom in marriage transactions was inspired in 1989, when my informants told me about a young man who had encouraged his fiancée to demand a large amount of bridewealth from his own family. According to some informants, he told the young woman: "Just be tough. Ask for 4,000 yuan in ganzhe, and don't bargain. Otherwise, you won't be able to extract money from my mother's pocket." Meanwhile, he firmly stated that he would only marry that particular young woman. As can be expected, the prospective bride got everything she demanded. A few months after their wedding, they left the groom's family and established their own home. Some villagers gossiped that he had planned this split from his parents even before the engagement. My informants told me that this case was not as extraordinary as it seemed, and that in recent years many young men had acted similarly without openly declaring their intentions. The significance of these examples is that young villagers may now begin planning their conjugal families during courtship.

In one unusual case in 1990, a bride wanted the grain-processing factory of the groom's family to be included as part of her bridewealth. But because the groom had an unmarried brother, in the end the factory was divided in two, with each son receiving half. New and unconventional items continued to be added to the list of betrothal gifts throughout the 1990s, such as a plot of farmland, a dairy cow, or a family-size tractor. Many of these new bridewealth items are means of production and thus can generate more wealth, further indicating that the ultimate intention of the bride and groom is to accumulate a productive fund for their conjugal family.[14]

From Gifts to Pre-Mortem Inheritance

Tradition in earlier marriage transactions called for the groom's family to give bridewealth to the bride's family in order to endow a bride whose (indirect) dowry would eventually become the conjugal fund for her husband and herself. This conjugal unit did not gain independent status until the end of the natural cycle of family development, which was at the time of family partition. It is true that in traditional Chinese society women could exercise control over their dowries both before and after the marriage.[15] Nevertheless, because the bridewealth went to the bride via the bride's parents, the bride's parents decided what portion of the received bridewealth would be given to the bride as indirect dowry. When a family's economic situation was not good, it was not uncommon for the bride's parents to use the money for other purposes, turning the Chinese system of indirect dowry into something close to the African bridewealth system (see Goody 1973).

In contrast, by the 1990s in Xiajia village marital gifts were transferred from the groom's family directly to the bride herself under the new form of ganzhe transactions. The bride, with the cooperation of the groom, now has full control over her betrothal gifts from the beginning of the marriage negotiations and, due to the serial form of family division, she can use them to establish an independent conjugal family immediately following her marriage. The primary difference between the two patterns is that in the former conjugality was not the goal of either the older or the younger generation, and the individuality of the bride and groom was overshadowed by parental power and family interests. In the latter, conjugal independence has become the motivation for the young people to demand costly bridewealth and dowries, and both the bride and groom (whose role remains largely hidden) have become active agents in marriage transactions.[16]

As a result, it is no longer sufficient or accurate to view the transfer of bridewealth as a family strategy employed by the parents to secure the bride or to establish an affinal alliance. Instead, the new form of converted bridewealth (ganzhe) might be considered a form of wealth devolution for the groom who seeks to claim his inheritance rights.[17] In other words, the bridewealth is no longer a ritualized gift (or payment in some cases) by one family to another; instead it has become a way of distributing wealth from one generation to the next.

Individual Rights and the Collapse of Patriarchal Power

Although property itself is important in the marriage transaction, the *control* of the family property often matters more in the politics of family division and marriage. In many cases, an early family division hurts the economic performance of both the old and the new households. Young couples in newly established nuclear families tend to encounter more financial difficulties than those who stay in a stem family, as shown in my survey on the links between family structure and economic status (see Chapter 4, especially Table 4.2). Nevertheless, the popularity of early family division in the serial form of partition (danguo) continues to grow because family division can solve the issue of who controls the money, regardless of how much money a family may have. As a young woman who just established her own conjugal household explained to me in 1994: "It is true that there are a lot of things in the old house; but they are not ours. Those things belong to his [her husband's] parents and brothers. Look around this small house. Every single item is ours! I can do whatever I want to do with them. I am so happy."

Family division is one of the most important events in family politics for control, because it redistributes family property and redefines the power structure in a household. Similarly, marriage transactions have long been used by parents to control adult children and to prolong their power and authority in the domestic sphere (see Meillassoux 1981). Over several decades, negotiations between the senior and younger generations have led to parents' losing their control over family property on two fronts. This is a further indication of the collapse of patriarchy and the rising power of village youths of both sexes.

One wonders why the young people have been so successful in their negotiations for family property and resources with their parents. Social changes at the macro level, such as the socialist practice of collectivization, the influence of state policies, and the market-oriented reforms, are certainly relevant (I will return to them in the concluding chapter). Yet they did not directly cause parents to lose control over family property, which is probably the basis of patriarchal power. Looking at the issue at a micro level, I find the new ways of wealth accumulation and the changing perception of property rights particularly noteworthy.[18]

In his study of family division in rural Taiwan, Lung-sheng Sung suggests a distinction between inherited property and acquired property in a family. Inherited property, such as land and buildings, is passed from one generation to another through the male line so that men can fulfill their duty of perpetuating their descent lines. Equal rights to inherited property are shared by living members of a descent line on a per stirpes basis. In contrast, new property can be acquired through the efforts of living family members. Rights to such property are shared by all family members on a per capita basis (Sung 1981: 366). With regard to a father's power and authority over the time of family division, Sung maintains: "A father is better able to control his son if he has inherited his estate than if he has acquired it with his sons' help. His position as father is then reinforced by his position as the head of the line that holds the estate" (1981: 377). The father's power would be undermined significantly if the family property were acquired through the joint efforts of all adult members.

Applying this distinction between inherited and acquired property to family wealth in Xiajia village, we can see that the bargaining power of young people in demanding early family division and lavish bridewealth/dowry derives mostly from their awareness of their own contributions to the accumulation of family wealth. Radical social changes brought about by the 1949 revolution completely altered the traditional patterns of property accumulation. The land reform campaign leveled villagers' economic status; the collectivization campaign in the mid-1950s stripped the peasant families of their inherited property, including farmland, draft animals, and other important means of production. Since then, family wealth has been acquired mainly through the contributions of individual laborers. It is true that officially the family remained the basic unit for redistribution during the collective era; however, at the same time, the individual contribution to family wealth was recognized and emphasized through the work-point system and other institutions in the collectives.

Under the accounting system in the collectives, one's daily contribution was recorded as work points, which were converted into cash after the harvest (see Cohen 1999; Parish and Whyte 1978). The work-point records were open to the public and were posted annually on the walls of the team headquarters, thus making one's income and contribution to one's family a matter of public record. Fathers could no longer deny or understate the contributions made by other members, particularly younger members, to the family economy, as they had done in traditional family farming. Because younger people adapted easily to collective farming and learned new skills, many could earn more work points than their fathers could. As they became aware of their important contribution to the family economy, the young people became less respectful of parental authority at home. As an old villager put it, "The young kids quickly developed bad tempers once they could earn their own rice."

Decollectivization in 1983 did not change this trend, even though the household has been restored as the unit of production. As noted in Chapter 1, subsistence-grain land was redistributed equally to each person, and contract land was divided equally among all adult male laborers. Rights to land (users' rights, to be more precise) were granted by the state to individual villagers rather than to families. Accordingly, rural families are operating units in agricultural production, not owners of farmland. In a family, the father and his adult sons receive equal shares from the state. Thus, when family division occurs, the father has no right to prevent his sons from taking possession of their own land and their share of the income from family farming.

Moreover, in the majority of Xiajia families, almost all property of value, such as new housing, tractors, cows, and cash savings, was acquired during the 1980s and 1990s through the joint efforts of parents and adult children. Although farmland remains important in securing a family's subsistence needs, it is hardly a major means of accumulating family wealth. During an average harvest year, the gross income generated from farming can only meet a family's basic needs, including living expenses, replacement funds, and taxes and local levies. Therefore, in addition to farming, most families in Xiajia must engage in various forms of petty commodity production, such as growing cash crops or dairy farming, and many young villagers seek temporary city jobs. In family businesses, petty commodity production, and wage labor, young family members play at least as important a role as their parents and, more important, can likely make cash contributions that their parents cannot.

As family wealth has been accumulated mainly through individual contributions rather than through inheritance over the past five decades, a more individualized perception of family property has emerged. Village youths have developed a much stronger sense of entitlement to a share of jointly acquired family wealth, especially during the 1980s and 1990s. This sense of entitlement manifests itself in marriage transactions in particular. I frequently asked young informants why they were so aggressive in demanding a lavish bridewealth and dowry. Without exception they said that they had worked hard and made important contributions to their families and wanted no more than what they had contributed over the years. The young villagers did not perceive the property that they claimed through the marriage transaction and family division to be a share of the family's property. Instead, they insisted that it was their individual property to begin with. This mentality of withdrawing one's own deposit can be traced back to the collective era. Here let me cite a less formal yet perhaps more interesting example from the 1970s.

Each year in the slack season between the summer weeding and the autumn harvest (from late August to mid-September), collectives organized a lot of public activities such as movies, basketball games, village troupe performances, and banquets. The production teams customarily lent young men money to buy new T-shirts and young women money to have their photos taken at a photo studio, both of which involved group trips to the county seat. The Youth League and the Women's Association organized these activities respectively, but all expenses were shared by the young participants (about ten yuan per person), and the collectives then deducted their expenses from their annual income at the end of the year.

Before the market-oriented reforms, villagers did not see much cash until the end of a year, and they lived simple lives just above the subsistence level.

The youths thus naturally welcomed the opportunity to buy new clothes, have photos taken, and visit the county seat. But most parents considered such expenditures wasteful. The parents could not stop these activities, though, because the youths claimed that they were spending their own money and, after a season of hard work, they deserved a break. And because the activities were organized by the Youth League and the Women's Association, even the most conservative patriarch knew that he could not openly oppose these party-sponsored organizations. In fact, the pooling of the family income gave the young people an extra motivation to participate in these activities. When I lived in Xiajia during the 1970s, I frequently heard from my peers that if they did not buy the T-shirt or have their photos taken the small amount of money would just be lost in the family budget.[19]

I am tempted to speculate that activities like these during the collective era planted the seeds for the next generation of village youths to squeeze higher bridewealth and dowries out of their parents and choose an early family division with a full sense of entitlement. The new combination of entitlement, individual rights in the family estate, and desire to control one's own family life may help explain why, despite the self-sacrificing efforts of Teacher Liu and his wife to maintain their stem family, their son and his wife chose to establish their own nuclear family.

Nevertheless, it should also be noted that the awareness of individual rights to family property emerged, ironically, from the larger context of the collective ownership of the means of production and thus was confined to the private sphere (even in the postcollective era, villagers still do not own the farmland). More important, the young villagers' claim to family property was backed up by state-sponsored ideological attacks on parental power and the general discourse on modernization, which placed the senior generation at a disadvantage. The two generations were not on an equal footing in the intergenerational negotiations over the control of family property. As a result, the village youth began placing more emphasis on their rights and entitlements to family property, while downplaying their duties and obligations. This unbalanced development of individual rights also led to radical changes in the support of the elderly, another important area of family life where patriarchal power has collapsed.

CHAPTER SEVEN

Support for the Elderly and the Crisis of Filial Piety

In Chapter 4, I begin my account of the structural transformation of family relations with a 1990 family tragedy, in which a previously powerful patriarch took his life because he could not stand losing power to his son and daughter-in-law. At that time, public opinion regarding his death was divided; a number of villagers thought that the victim himself was partly at fault for being an unreasonable tyrant at home. A similar tragedy occurred in 1995 when a 71-year-old, soft-spoken man hung himself. But this aged father was a kind and quiet person who had tried to get along with his son and daughter-in-law. On the day of this man's suicide, his son had entertained an important visiting relative of his wife's with meat dishes, dumplings, and liquor. The old man had not dared to participate in the family banquet because he had long been excluded from eating at the dining table. He always took simple foods or left-overs from the kitchen and had his meals alone in his own room. On this occasion, however, he had asked for some of the meat dishes and dumplings, but his daughter-in-law bluntly refused. Then his son, who was already drunk, scolded him for being a shameless glutton, which, as some villagers analyzed afterward, was the last straw in this old man's bitter life. The villagers were outraged by the death of this old man; some openly criticized the son and his wife for their unfilial behavior, and some threatened to report it as a case of parent abuse to the local court. The pressure of public opinion forced the couple to avoid public life for a while, but nothing else happened to them, and their life soon returned to normal.

Unfortunately, the deaths of these two elderly men did not reverse the trend in support for the elderly. By the end of the 1990s the living conditions of some elderly parents had worsened, and the family status of elders continued to decline. Elders trembled to speak of their fate, the middle-aged were worried about their immediate future, and young couples were confused by the storm of complaints from their parents and grandparents.

In this chapter, I address these issues in four sections. First, I examine the current living conditions of elders age 60 and older, focusing on their living arrangements and their interactions with the younger generation. I also examine the living conditions of middle-aged parents age 45 and older and compare the circumstances of the two groups. Next I explore the different generational views of villagers regarding the issue of old-age security. The traditional mechanism of intergenerational reciprocity has broken down, mainly in response to the introduction of values associated with the market economy. I then discuss the strategies of parental investment for old age, focusing on parents' efforts to improve the emotional bonds with both their sons and their married daughters. The last section concerns the decline of the notion of filial piety, which is a major cause of the current social problem of support for the elderly.[1]

Living Arrangements

The first critical issue that middle-aged parents face is whether to live with a married son. Because many young couples want independence and leave their parents' homes when they marry, their elderly parents end up living in a nuclear or empty nest family. In Xiajia, however, villagers simply refer to it as *danguo* (living alone), the same word that is used to describe the serial form of family division; yet in this context the term conveys the loneliness of the elderly. To live with a married son is described locally as *gen erzi guo*, which might be translated as "following a [married] son to live one's life." Here, the character *gen* carries a passive tone (as in "to follow") and is the same character that is used to describe a woman's married life with her husband, indicating powerlessness and submissiveness. The use of that character in the context of elderly support thus clearly implies the vulnerable dependent position of the aged.

From my household survey in 1998 and a follow-up check up in the summer of 1999, I gathered information about the living arrangements of elderly and late-middle-aged parents at the end of 1990s. Table 7.1 summarizes the survey data regarding the former, the parents who were 60 or older in 1998; the results are astonishing in several respects.

In 1998 119 people were age 60 or older, 8 percent of the total population (1,492) of Xiajia village. Eighty-three households contained one or two elders,

TABLE 7.1.
Living Arrangements of Elderly Parents in 1998

Living arrangements	Age 60–64	Age 65–69	Age 70–74	Age 75 or older	Total number of households
Couple lives in nuclear household	5	4	5	3	17
Elderly man lives alone	1		1	1	3
Elderly woman lives alone	1	3	1		5
Couple lives with married son	4	7	5	3	19
Elderly man lives with a married son	1	1	3	4	9
Elderly woman lives with a married son	4	5	8	6	23
Elderly man lives with a married daughter			1		1
Elderly woman lives with a married daughter		1			1
Elderly man lives with an unmarried son	1				1
Elderly woman lives with an unmarried son	2		1	1	4
Total number of households	19	21	25	18	83

about 22 percent of the village households. Seventeen elderly couples constituted empty nest families, and eight single elderly lived alone, including two
men and one woman over 70 years old. Altogether they constituted 30 percent of the households with elderly. This is the other side of the current trend
toward nuclearization of the family, but its meaning for the elderly cannot be
fully reflected in survey figures alone. In addition to the expected difficulties in
their material life, rural elders face more inconveniences and troubles in their
daily routines than their urban counterparts, ranging from the lack of running
water to the absence of indoor toilets. And their situation can only get worse
as they become older. Each of these seventeen couples and eight single elderly,
therefore, had made the difficult decision to live apart from their married sons.
Most of them told a sad story about old age.

The fact that seventeen couples (half of the village's thirty-six older couples) lived in empty nests suggests that when both husband and wife are alive
in old age they either choose or are forced to live alone as a nuclear family.
Of those who lived with their married children in stem families, the majority were either widows or widowers who became lonely dependents after
their spouses died.

Finally, there were seven older people living in unusual situations, and, interestingly, most of them enjoyed a much better life than the other elders. One
older man had lived with his married daughter for more than two decades,
and he remained the family head until the early 1990s. He did not have children of his own but he adopted a girl in the early 1960s; when she married,
his new son-in-law married into Xiajia uxorilocally. This elderly man was one
of the very few who still enjoyed respect even after he could no longer engage
in manual work. An old woman living with her married daughter in Xiajia was
also having a good life in her old age; her daughter was firmly in charge of family affairs and her son-in-law was well known as a good husband in the village.
Four other older people (one man and three women) lived in incomplete
families because their sons were bachelors, divorced, or widowed. Although the
lack of a complete family (namely, having a daughter-in-law) is indicative of
the family's poverty and low status, the older people in three of the four families enjoyed a relatively high status. Many of the villagers found it ironic that
these six older people were living better lives than many of those who had
several sons but no one to rely upon.

TABLE 7.2.
Living Arrangements of Middle-Aged Parents in 1998

Living arrangements	Age 45–49	Age 50–54	Age 55–59	Total number of households
Couple lives in nuclear household	3	11	7	21
Man lives alone			1	1
Woman lives alone		1	1	2
Couple lives with unmarried child(ren)	28	13	9	50
Couple lives with married son		7	2	9
Man lives with a married son		1	2	3
Woman lives with a married son		2		2
Woman lives with an unmarried son	1	1		2
Total number of households	32	36	22	90

Now let us take a close look at the living arrangements of another group of villagers, those between the ages of 45 and 59, whom I refer to as middle-aged parents (see Table 7.2). Most villagers have at least one married son by the age of 45 (some also have a grandchild); and most people in this group are still physically strong and earning their own incomes, mainly through farming. But they all have begun to deal with the same issues the older parents did when their sons married and moved out. In fact, these middle-aged villagers seemed the most concerned about this issue and were the most vocal in my interviews with them.

There were 161 people in this group, living in ninety households; they constituted a little less than 10 percent of the village population and 23 percent of the total households. Thus 18 percent of the village population were elderly and middle-aged parents, and 45 percent of the households had one or two elderly or middle-aged parents. Xiajia village, like the rest of China, was quickly becoming a society of the elderly.[2]

Two features are particularly noteworthy here. Fifty households fell into the category of "couples living with unmarried children," which is the result of the relatively young age of many parents in the middle-aged group. Yet within a few years it is likely that a large portion of these fifty couples will need to choose between an empty nest family and a stem family. If the current patterns continue, most of them will end up living in empty nests.

Second, in the ninety households, only fourteen couples or individuals chose to live with a married son in a stem family, 16 percent of the households in this group. This contrasts sharply with older parents, of whom fifty-four couples or individuals lived with a married son (or daughter), about 64 percent of the total households. This confirms the villagers' testimony that more and more able-bodied parents preferred to live apart from their married sons, unless their age and deteriorating health forced them to do otherwise.

According to my informants, most parents still hoped to keep one married son in their household. Because newlywed young couples typically demand family divisions and leave the old family on a "first married, first out" basis, most parents hope eventually to live with their youngest son. So, in their late forties, most parents still live with one or two unmarried children, while their elder son(s) have married and moved out. This is why only three middle-aged couples lived in nuclear households and none lived with a married son. By the time the parents had reached age 50–54, one-third had abandoned their ideal and were living in empty nests, and another one-third still had unmarried children with them; only ten households (28 percent) in this age cohort tried out the extended family ideal by establishing a stem family. This ideal seemed to disappear in many cases at the next stage of life, when only 18 percent of the parents age 55 to 59 were living with a married son, and 41 percent were living apart from their married sons. The tendency of elderly parents to live in empty nests changes only when they become very old, normally beyond the age of 70. The empty nest families dropped to 28 percent and 22 percent in the last two age cohorts that I surveyed, while the percentage of stem families increased to 68 percent and 72 percent respectively (see Table 7.1). In other words, elderly parents do not have many choices during the last years of their lives, and the best arrangement seems to be to return to a married son's family, regardless of the living conditions there.

Parent Abuse and Intergenerational Conflicts

In 1998 and 1999, I asked about elderly support, including a set of questions about the provision of food, clothing, shelter, and petty cash, ways of communicating with the elderly, and gestures of caring and emotional bonding. Chief among them was whether the elderly parents or parent could enjoy the same quality of food the rest of the family did. When adequate supplies of food, clothing, and shelter are not provided in a given household, I consider it a case of parent abuse. Using this simple standard, I was able to identify eleven cases in which the elderly were treated improperly.[3] The older the parents the more likely they were to be subject to abusive behavior from their married sons and, most often, from their daughters-in-law.

Six of the eleven instances of parent abuse involved senior villagers over the age of 70 in 1998. One elderly couple, ages 71 and 73, had been literally thrown out by their third son after living in his house for more than three years. According to other villagers, the elderly couple had had some personal savings and lived with their youngest son, as was customary among villagers. The third son, however, managed to convince his parents to move to his house, because it was rumored that they had a lot of savings. Things went sour when the third son and his wife realized the old couple really did not have much savings (or, as some villagers noted, after they had pocketed all of their parents' money). The young couple often scolded their parents about trivial things and, more than once, the daughter-in-law physically pushed them and cursed them loudly. During a heated conflict in 1997, she grabbed her father-in-law from behind and pounded his head against the wooden furniture several times. With bruises and wounds all over his head and body, the old man finally took his son to court. The local court quickly found the third son and his wife guilty of parent abuse and also blamed the other three sons for neglect. All four sons were required to share equal support for their parents, who, after their traumatic experience, insisted on living separately.

As predicted by many villagers, the elderly couple did not benefit from their ostensible victory in court, because, after all, it was still up to the four sons to carry out the court order in everyday life. After paying a handsome amount of gift money to the judge and some other local officials, the third son and his wife avoided any further legal punishment for their cruel treatment of the parents, and they publicly announced that they were severing the parent-child relationship. The other three sons argued over who had responsibility for parent support, and they gradually in succession stopped paying their shares. By the time I investigated this case, the parents were living in a small, run-down house, relying on their four daughters for both money and other kinds of support. Each of them was most worried about what would happen to the other after one had died.

This elderly couple was by no means the only one with abusive children. At least two men, ages 73 and 75, and two women, ages 70 and 61, had either been thrown out by their married son or been forced to flee the household of an abusive son and ended up living alone during the last stage of their lives. The 73-year-old man had five sons and the 75-year-old man had two sons, but they shared the same fate: because no son wanted to take them in, they had to learn how to cook, wash their clothes, and do other household tasks in their old age in order to survive on their own. These two old men were lucky, however, commented many informants, because both had daughters who could look after them and comfort them during frequent visits.

To escape from the miserable life of dependence on an unfilial son, one 64-year-old widow decided to remarry, despite all the prejudices and stigma against remarriage among the elderly in rural China. The strongest opponents to her remarriage were her only son and his wife, who believed they would lose face in village society. But neither of them wanted to take her into their house, to say nothing of treating her well. In the end, the old lady did remarry, but not without paying a price. Because of persistent demands from her daughter-in-law and strong pressure from her late husband's kinsmen and some other relatives mobilized by her son, she was forced to go through a humiliating ritual. She left her house for her new home in the dark of night, without any celebration or greetings from relatives; even worse, she was not allowed to leave by the front door of her house, but was forced to climb out the back window as if she were a thief on the run. Her daughter-in-law argued that unless she performed this ritual her remarriage would bring great bad luck to the household. I could not interview the elderly woman, who had already moved to her second husband's village, but I heard that she had accused her daughter-in-law, among others, of being inhuman and feudalistic, because such rules against widow remarriage were supposed to exist only in the old society, that is, before the 1949 revolution.

It was unusual for the daughter-in-law, who is in her early forties, to be such a devout believer in the old taboos. Her real motivation may well have been, as some villagers commented, the simple wish to punish her mother-in-law for remarrying. Ironically, in pre-1949 China, it was the mother-in-law who abused her daughter-in-law; if the latter became a widow and wanted to remarry, the mother-in-law punished her with these humiliating rules. It is also noteworthy that, again, neither the village office nor the local government tried to stop the daughter-in-law's aggressive and abusive behavior. Instead, the local officials all turned a deaf ear, even when other villagers complained.

The elderly who live with a married son generally do not need to worry about basic provisions such as food and shelter, and, in many cases, they are treated reasonably well, at least materially. A minority of elderly parents even enjoyed very high status and still held power in the stem family, but, without exception, they were themselves powerful or rich (or both) individuals in the village. The majority literally needed to earn their own keep in the stem family. Many old men did most of the farming, enabling the married son to seek temporary work in an urban area; and the old women were responsible for household chores such as cooking, babysitting, and tending the pigs and chickens. According to my informants, a simple measurement of the power balance between mother-in-law and daughter-in-law was who did the cooking. My informants told me a popular joke: When a daughter-in-law marries into a family, do you know what happens to the mother's cooking routine? The mother either cooks for one person more or for one person less, because if the daughter-in-law stays in the parents' house she will not cook; if the daughter-in-law cooks, it means she must have already left the house with her husband (thus the mother no longer cooks for her son).

Serious parent abuse was uncommon in Xiajia village in the late 1990s, and in families where it existed there was always a history of family disputes. Emotional quarrels, conflicts, and sometimes fights between the senior and junior generation were much more common than outright abuse. The most common complaint from elderly parents was the lack of respect and concern from their adult children and daughters-in-law, and they unanimously blamed the daughters-in-law for being *buxiaoshun* (unfilial or without filial piety). For most parents, the lack of filial piety was a far more serious problem than parent abuse in material life. While my 1998 survey shows that 13 percent of the elderly age 60 or older had been treated improperly in material life by adult children and thus constituted cases of parent abuse, sixty-two of the parents I interviewed (more than 80 percent) regarded their married sons and daughters-in-law as unfilial.

The married children, however, felt unfairly accused. They insisted that they had tried to support their elderly parents and thus should be praised as filial. The real problem, they argued, was the feudal thoughts commonly held by the older generation. For instance, many old parents could not stand to see a married son display affection or intimacy toward his wife outside the bedroom, and when the young couple disregarded their parents' wishes, family quarrels were inevitable. It is interesting that while the young couples criticized their parents for being closed-minded and feudalistic, the latter accused the former (often the daughter-in-law) of being inconsiderate and lacking respect. Obviously, the two generations held different views of proper elderly support and filial piety, views that had been contested for the previous five decades.

Intergenerational Reciprocity

In an excellent case study of rural northern China, Guo Yuhua, a Chinese anthropologist, examines the emerging crisis of support for the elderly from a social exchange perspective (Guo 2001). Regarding support for elderly parents as a reciprocal obligation by adult children, Guo argues that the logic of this intergenerational exchange has been altered over the past several decades. The breakdown of the traditional mechanism of elderly support has led to the current crisis. Ethnographic evidence from Xiajia village echoes Guo's findings in many respects. In light of Guo's study, I further explore the competing discourse and practices regarding old-age security and filial piety across generational lines.

Local Notions of Appropriate Support for the Elderly

Support for the elderly was not a research topic that I chose; rather, I was forced to look at it after being showered by villagers' comments on the issue during my fieldwork. I thus gradually came to comprehend its urgency and importance. In reading through my eleven years of field notes I realized that some of the complaints about the crisis of elderly support could be traced back to the 1980s, and that some new complaints emerged during the 1990s. The discourse on elderly support itself, therefore, represents a dynamic process of change and transformation in intergenerational relations.

When talking about the prospects for old age, villagers used two terms interchangeably. One, *yanglao*, is descriptive, very close to "support for the elderly" in English; the other, *xiaojing* (or *xiaoshun*), is a more traditional term and carries more meanings. According to older villagers, the first term, yanglao, contains two layers of meanings. At the basic level, it involves the provision of food, clothing, medicine, and shelter by the younger generation, mainly the married sons. The character *yang* is also the same as that for raising children; it therefore indicates a delayed reciprocity by the children. However, yanglao also refers to caring and emotional bonding, such as physical assistance with everyday activities, attending to the sick bed, and moral support of and emotional attachment to one's elders. In the villagers' own accounts, yanglao includes *duancha songshui* (offering a cup of tea or serving hot water), *wenleng wenre* (asking about [a parent's feeling of] cold and hot), and *jiantang weiyao* (preparing the herb medicine and feeding it to a sick parent). Such assistance and caring are critically important for elderly parents, especially when they become unable to take care of themselves. Villagers said that this second part of yanglao was just as important as the first part.[4]

While retaining all the connotations of yanglao, the more traditional term xiaojing (which is used interchangeably with xiaoshun) stresses the superior status of parents and its permanence over time. The term is composed of two Chinese characters: filial piety and respect. Etymologically, therefore, the term calls for the subordination of children to their parents and, by extension, all senior kinsmen within the domestic hierarchy. According to older villagers, the essence of xiaojing lies in the children's unconditional obedience and respect for their parents. Filial children never talk back to their parents, said these villagers, and they should always be polite and obedient. "Parents always have good reasons and they are always right," said a 71-year-old woman; "even if they are wrong sometimes, you must also listen to them and pretend they are right." She then recalled that she always swallowed incorrect accusations from her parents-in-law when she was young and remained an obedient daughter-in-law. Another man over 70 pointed out that the notion of xiaojing also applies to sibling relations if there is a big age gap between two siblings. In the late 1940s he once fought with his elder brother who was fourteen years his senior, and this became a serious family concern. He was ordered by his parents and other senior kinsmen to formally apologize to his elder brother during a family gathering, and fortunately, he recalled, his parents were kind enough to allow him to stand, instead of to kneel, when he made the apology.

To be xiaojing, children must also always provide the best foods and other material items to their parents and always remember to burn incense and send paper money to their ancestors. Filial sons should perform solemn funerals when their parents die because a funeral is considered the most important reward and status symbol at the end of one's life. In local system, the term *yanglao* (elderly support) is always followed by the term *songzhong* (end-of-life farewell), which means providing the right ritual service and a respectable funeral.[5]

These more traditional notions of elderly support, however, have been constantly challenged by younger generations, and consequently there are intergenerational differences among villagers over the principle of intergenerational reciprocity and the actual arrangement of old-age security. Let us start with the views from the parents' generation, loosely defined here as those age 45 or older.

Views of the Parents' Generation

In general, parents claim that elderly support is the ultimate responsibility of every individual and the moral trait that distinguishes human beings from animals. Such an understanding is deeply rooted in the *renqing* ethics of Chinese culture. As I argue elsewhere (1996), according to renqing ethics, an individual is indebted to a number of people and/or institutions for favors and help received throughout one's life called renqing, a complex notion that contains both moral obligation and emotional attachment, as well as material concerns. Among the kinds of renqing, *enqing* represents the most significant favors and help that one receives that influence the long-term course of one's life. Because enqing is the greatest favor, the recipient is indebted to the grantor for a lifetime. Ordinary favors generally can be exchanged, but the highest kinds of favors—enqing—cannot. The most common and highest kind of enqing is that from one's parents, who give life to their children

and raise them, which is called *yangyu zhien*. The notions of yanglao and xiaojing, therefore, are based on the primary assumption that parents grant
the highest kind of favor to their children, and the children should, according to renqing ethics and the principle of reciprocity, repay their parents
during their old age. And, because the enqing from one's parents is the highest kind of enqing, its repayment is endless and limitless, including both
moral and emotional as well as material components. In other words, it is
impossible for anyone to fully reciprocate the enqing received from one's
parents; by implication, in addition to yanglao (elderly support), one must
also practice unconditional and consistent xiaojing (filial piety).

It is against such a moral and emotional background that older parents expect reciprocity from their children. From the parents' perspective, the very
fact that they gave life to their children already constitutes the foundation of
enqing, and their efforts in raising their children only strengthen the vastness
of enqing. Therefore, when parents do not receive the expected return from
their children, they are not only upset and disappointed, but also dishonored.
Older villagers express disappointment with local phrases such as *bai yang le*,
meaning that it is fruitless to raise their children, or *bu zhi de* (it is not worth
it [to raise the children]). The local expression of dishonor is *diuren xianyan*,
which can be roughly translated as "shameful and disgraceful."

Because enqing can never be fully repaid in money or material goods (although in practice the repayment of enqing frequently takes material forms),
in the Chinese renqing system some older parents express a strong sense of
entitlement to respect and obedience from their married sons. A village friend
of mine, for instance, did not allow his sons to raise their voices when they
talked with their parents in the family, even if the parents were wrong. He
argues that this practice prevented his sons from becoming spoiled. But only
a few elders in Xiajia village could maintain their patriarchal power like this
old friend. Most elders had accepted that they were dependents and no longer
fit into the fast-changing society; they thus had better keep their mouths shut
and try their best to make themselves useful. According to my informants, it
was common for a married son to reproach his parents in public or to neglect
them during a conversation. I also noticed that during my investigation of
old-age security issues, the elders rarely spoke up when the younger members of a family were also present. The chances that an elder would actively

participate in my household survey were so slim that I eventually had to conduct follow-up interviews specifically targeted at older informants.[6]

Deliberate neglect is another frequent complaint from the elderly. Those
who live separately from their married sons complain that they can only see
their sons when they have something useful to offer, such as taking care of
their grandchildren or tending to household chores. An old lady told me in
the summer of 1997 that she had not seen her daughter-in-law since the
Spring Festival, even though they lived fewer than ten houses apart. Another
elderly woman's situation was even worse. Although she lived with her married son in a household of six, she was not allowed to eat at the dining table
because one of her granddaughters said she smelled bad, and rarely did anyone come into her little dark room to talk with her. Gradually, she became
ashamed of herself and avoided contact with anyone in the household. "During mealtime I would wait in my room until all the others had begun to eat at
the dining table in the big room," she told me. "Then I would quickly sneak
into the kitchen and snatch a full bowl of rice, putting whatever dish that was
left in the cooking pot on top of my rice, and then escape back to my room as
quickly as possible." When asked why she did this furtively, she replied that if
she met anyone in the kitchen they would not speak to her, and such neglect
made her feel humiliated and hurt.

Views of Married Children

Married children viewed the same issues quite differently. (My informants in
this group included mainly married sons and their wives, and only a few married daughters.) No one questioned the moral legitimacy of supporting the
elderly. All of the married children said they wanted to support their parents
in their old age, and all agreed that it is morally wrong to mistreat elderly parents. Even two married sons who had previously been brought to the local
court or the village office by their parents for abandonment and neglect
firmly denied that they did not want to fulfill their obligation of elderly support. One insisted that he wanted to have his 68-year-old father live with his
family (his mother had died early), but the old man wanted to live alone because he enjoyed the freedom and quiet. Yet other villagers reported that he
had thrown his father out of the house, only allowing him to take his personal

belongings and daily necessities. The other married son argued that he had done the best he could, because he did not want to be accused of showing off by his four siblings. "There are five of us, and we have to make sure things are done fairly," he explained.

In addition to formally endorsing the notion of elderly support and making up excuses for avoiding the obligations in practice, the married sons I talked to in the 1990s also made some points that reflect the changing perspective of the younger generation. Many of them rejected the traditional idea that giving life to a child is the parents' enqing to the child and that the child cannot repay this highest debt. They argued that giving birth to a child is just a natural event that transforms a couple into parents, not a great favor to the child, because the child has no choice about birth. Once a child is born, it is the parents' duty to raise the child, they said (see also Guo 2001); everyone will do the same, and even animals give the greatest love and care to their children. For this generation of villagers, the moral and ideological components of biological parenthood that once gave it such elevated status have been reduced. They emphasized instead the social aspects of parenthood.

Some criticized their parents for not adequately helping them start their own households after marriage. By the end of the 1990s, this meant building a house, offering a handsome bridewealth of 45,000 yuan or more, and for daughters, offering a dowry of between 3,000 and 15,000 yuan. The new house and marital gifts constitute almost all of a newly married couple's conjugal funds, so young couples try to acquire as much as possible at the time of their marriage.

Married sons often said that parents should treat all of their children equally at home, although their individual notions of fairness differed. For some, parental fairness was closely tied to the distribution of family property. In other words, parents should provide the same amount of money and material goods to each son; likewise, they said that the responsibility for elderly support should also be equally distributed among the married sons. Yet others also mentioned parental caring and loving, recalling how much they were hurt by a perception that their parents liked their siblings better when they were young. Villagers describe such fairness as *yiwanshui yao duanping*, meaning "to balance a bowl of water evenly"; any imbalance will spill the water, indicating a breakdown of the normal operation of intergenerational reciprocity.

Younger villagers frequently mentioned the case of parent abuse in 1997 in which the father was beaten up by the wife of his third son and was forced to take his four sons to court. Some younger villagers argued that the father was also guilty because he had long treated his third son better than the others, spoiling him when he was young. Before the elderly parents were lured into the third son's house, they were well treated by their youngest son. Because the father liked the third son best and wanted to leave his personal savings to him, the parents moved in with him, only to be abused by him a few years later, after having appropriated all of his father's savings. Angered by their father's unequal treatment, the three other sons refused to take in their parents after they were thrown out by the third son. Hence the drama at the local court. Had the father not been so unfair and stupid, commented the young villagers, the elderly couple would have lived a happy life in their old age. Of the eleven cases of parent abuse that I documented, nine involved complaints of parental unfairness from the younger generation.

It is clear that villagers in the two generations did not share the same notion of elderly support. The parents believed in the sacredness of parental authority and the superiority of parents at least in a moral sense, though they accepted the need for compromise and had already retreated in the face of the rising power of the younger generation. They also believed in the power of enqing, namely, that the greatest favor that parents grant their children is giving them life. Parental love in most societies is considered the most altruistic form of love, and the exchange between parents and children is what anthropologists call "generalized reciprocity," involving no immediate expectation of return or even an equal return. However, because China has no socialized support system for the rural elderly, intergenerational reciprocity remains the only tangible resource that aging parents can draw upon. So, from both a moral and a pragmatic perspective, parents feel a strong entitlement to support from their children.

Although accepting the obligation and duty of supporting their elders, the younger generation sees the issue from a different perspective. For them, giving birth and raising children are parental duties, which they are also performing (many of them are in their thirties and early forties). The idea that human reproduction is sacred is no longer accepted by younger villagers. Consequently, unconditional filial piety, which was based on the sacredness of parenthood, no longer exists. For younger villagers, intergenerational reciprocity, like other types of reciprocity, has to be balanced and maintained through consistent exchange. If the parents do not treat their children well or are otherwise not good parents, then the children have reason to reduce the scope and amount of generosity to their parents. The major reason for the current crisis in elderly support, therefore, is the introduction of a new logic in intergenerational exchange (see also Guo 2001).[7]

Parental Investments for Old Age

Many parents are aware of the changing ideology and practice of elderly support and have responded by investing for their old age and working to secure their children's support. This is particularly true among middle-aged or "aging" parents, namely, those between the ages of 45 and 59, many of whom have just become grandparents but may still be living with their youngest unmarried child. According to an informant in this age cohort, the most important principle is to not hurt the good feelings of either generation (*buyao huxiang shang ganqing*); as a parent, one must do one's best to win the hearts of one's children and at the same time build up one's own retirement funds. Several important strategies are commonly used and deserve a closer look here.

In order to build stronger emotional bonds, many parents actively help their married son(s) establish an independent conjugal household. Recognizing the younger generation's increasingly common desire for an early family division, some parents prepare for it even before their sons marry; many more parents facilitate the division once a young couple makes a proposal. This is a win-win situation for both generations, particularly for parents in their forties and early fifties who can continue working for ten years or more and build up their own retirement funds. Early division may also motivate the younger couple to work harder, which in turn reduces the possibility that they will take advantage of the accumulated family wealth.

A 45-year-old man told me in 1997 that he had initiated the family division with his only son because he wanted to break the "big common pot" (a popular political idiom) and to encourage his son to work harder. He and his wife thus cut the family wealth into two halves, giving one half, including, for example, two of the four diary cows and half of the family tractor, to their son, who still lived in the family compound with his wife. Because the son was too young to receive a share of contracted land during the 1983 decollectivization, the father also gave him half of his contracted land. But this family division did not separate the parents from their son in the conventional way. From 1997 to 1999, the young couple did not cook a single meal; instead, they ate with the parents without making any contribution. When asked why he did this, the father responded that the family division was a working strategy toward cultivating a deep and solid bond with his married son and daughter-in-law. He told me: "Eventually, everything we own will belong to my son, whether I like it or not. Therefore, it does not make any sense for me to be too selfish now, or to intimidate my son and his wife, because my wife and I will only suffer from their bad treatment in our later years. Now, the younger ones may take advantage of us, but in the future we will depend on them. This is all preparation for the day when we are too old to do anything on our own."

According to a man in his early forties, parents must be open-minded enough to follow contemporary social trends in dealing with their adult children, and they must also be sincere and caring with their married children to win the children's hearts. He recalled that he acquired his first poker cards at the age of 12, but his father soon destroyed the cards in order to force him to concentrate on school. "I was deeply hurt," he said; "I never did that kind of thing to my two sons. I always tried to talk with them and understand their needs." He said that all those parents who failed to care for their children wholeheartedly ended up living miserably in their old age, such as the two who ultimately committed suicide. When asked his plans for old age, this middle-aged man did not give me any specific answer, except to name the things he and his wife had already done and were prepared to do for their two sons, including building a house, buying an employment opportunity in a state-owned enterprise, and letting their married sons live in the new houses and thus skip over the period of patrilocal coresidence. But they did have a long-term goal—to live with one of the two sons when they became too old to live on their own.

Many parents work to improve intergenerational communication in order to maintain a strong emotional bond with their married children. In the 1980s and 1990s fathers and sons often chatted for hours while drinking and smoking. At least four fathers and three mothers told me that family meetings to resolve difficult issues in intergenerational relations were effective

and mutually beneficial to the two generations. From the younger generation, although I heard some positive comments about their parents' efforts
to open channels of communication, more often I heard complaints about
how difficult their parents were to talk to. The younger generation, particularly the young daughters-in-law, seemed to have higher expectations of
their parents than the reverse.

Maintaining a good relationship with married daughters has become an
increasingly important investment strategy for old age. Many parents began
to allow young daughters to keep whatever income they earned from working outside the family in order to provide a bigger dowry when the daughters married or as a friendly gesture to the sons-in-law. As a result, married
daughters visited their natal families much more often than they did earlier.
These good relationships with their daughters were especially important to
parents who did not get along well with their married sons and daughters-
in-law (an almost universal circumstance at the end of the 1990s).

The close relationship between a married daughter and her natal family
was long overlooked by the villagers themselves, as well as by students of
the Chinese rural family.[8] The traditional stereotype of a married daughter as
spilled water has changed. In the aforementioned several cases of parent abuse,
for instance, the daughters were the elderly parents' last resort for help when
the married sons refused to fulfill their obligations. A more common pattern, however, is for daughters to visit their parents frequently, providing the
care and emotional support that neither a married son nor a daughter-in-law
can offer. During my 1999 visit several informants mentioned that when an
elderly father had had a serious stroke his three daughters and their husbands took turns taking care of the old man, including feeding and bathing
him daily, while his only son and his wife only occasionally paid him short
visits.

The key to the increasing importance of a married daughter for elderly
support, ironically, is the rising power of the daughter-in-law in family life: a
married daughter cannot really take good care of her own parents if she remains a submissive and bullied daughter-in-law. As one daughter told me,
"There is a natural bond between me and my parents because they gave me
my life and raised me. But what did my parents-in-law do for me? Nothing!
Thanks to the new society [the recent social changes], I don't have to pretend
I care for them [the parents-in-law]. Why should I?" In other words, why

should a woman care for her parents-in-law more than she cares for her own parents? A married woman transferred her loyalty from her natal family to her husband's family only because she was pressured by the institutional arrangement of Chinese kinship, by the cultural constraints of traditional ethics, and by her husband. These traditions have been greatly weakened over the past five decades, and more and more married daughters have begun to look after their own parents more frequently and regularly, while neglecting their previously ascribed duties as a daughter-in-law. Although elderly parents complained about the unfilial behavior of their married sons and daughters-in-law, they told me that they were lucky to have good daughters. It is clear that by the end of the 1990s married daughters had become a major source of caregiving and emotional support, which in turn has had a significant impact on local fertility culture (see Chapter 8). Xiajia villagers recognized this interesting development and, accordingly, had started to invest in their daughters for old-age security.

Parental investment in old age has gone beyond the boundary of personal strategy and gained social significance. Many parents complained that they could not keep up with other parents in meeting their children's needs. Some said that because village cadres had more political advantages and larger networks, they also had more capital to help their children negotiate better marriage deals for their sons and find jobs. In turn, those same cadres complained that urban parents were setting a bad example by meeting so many of their children's demands and that they too could not keep up. One cadre told me that when he bought a motorcycle for his son, he expected to be "rewarded" by some appreciation or a smile. But the son merely told the father that he would have had a motorcycle five years earlier if he had been born to a better-off family in a city. Obviously, parental investment in old age has become a publicized and competitive phenomenon whereby parents have to outdo at least some of the neighbors in order to convince their children that they have done their best.

Finally, there is also a psychological factor in the cycle of intergenerational reciprocity. A number of parents pointed out to me that their moral obligation and love were the strongest motivations for parents to work on behalf of their children. They called it simply the "heart of parents" (*fumuxin*), which means the parents' limitless benevolence and love of their children. Many commented that no matter how much their children disappointed them or even abused their caring and love, they were still concerned with their children's well-being and worried that, without their support, the children would make bad farming plans, indulge in bad consumption habits, or worse. They told me that there are only heartless children in the world, no heartless parents, because the hearts of children need to be cultivated, while the hearts of parents are part of human nature. The nature of parental love, they argued, makes parents want to win their children's hearts, which in turn makes them more vulnerable to opportunistic children.[9]

Filial Piety under a Pincer Attack

When asked to describe the current problems related to elderly support, older villagers all claimed that their own parents had enjoyed a higher status and were treated well during the collective era. They maintained that decollectivization was a temporal divide marking the collapse of filial piety and the beginning of a crisis in old-age security. Many have fond memories of the collectives, which not only offered food and shelter to the childless but also provided a secure and warm social environment in which older members of the collectives could live a comfortable life. Their statements contradict existing knowledge about the radical periods of socialism, when filial piety, patriarchy, and familism were under serious attack, and they also challenge scholarly assumptions that market-oriented reforms and the restoration of family farming are likely to lead to a return of patriarchal power. Thus one wonders whether the major cause of the crisis of filial piety and elderly support was the state-sponsored social transformation during the first three decades of socialism (1949–78) or the impact of the market-oriented reforms in the following two decades. This is one of the fundamental questions I address in the concluding chapter about all changes in the sphere of private life. Here I look at it only in relation to the collapse of the notion of filial piety.

The Powerless Law and Self-Conflicting Ideology

Throughout the history of China, the state and the cultural elite regarded filial piety as a fundamental ethical and social norm; accordingly, imperial law was designed to protect the powers and privileges of the senior generation, particularly the senior members in the family. Parents could ask local government to prosecute an unfilial son, and the authorities would demand no further evidence because "no parents in the world are wrong" was held as truth as well as the guiding principle of the legal system. But a son who dared to scold a parent or a grandparent faced a sentence as severe as death by strangulation. "And if a parent or grandparent should commit suicide in a fit of anger at a son's behavior, the latter would be decapitated for causing the death" (Baker 1979: 115).

After the 1949 revolution, the party-state launched ideological attacks on the notion of filial piety through various political campaigns, such as the Great Leap Forward, the Cultural Revolution, and the "Criticize Lin Biao, Criticize Confucius" campaign in the early 1970s. But the party-state has never tried to attack the traditional practice of elderly support in rural areas. Instead, in the 1950 Marriage Law and its later versions, elderly support is a legal duty of Chinese citizens and is thus backed up by state sanctions. The same law, nevertheless, also emphasizes and promotes equality among family members both across generations and across gender lines.

In its ideological propaganda, the state rarely challenges the traditional practice of "raising a son for old age" and other related cultural ideals. When male preference in reproduction became an obstacle in family planning, the state did try to promote the idea that raising a daughter is also good for old age. But traditions remain intact in rural China, where daughters do not make property claims (except for dowries), and sons take the responsibility for supporting elderly parents (in urban areas the situation is different; see, for example, Davis-Friedmann 1991; Ikels 1996). It is fair to say, therefore, that a fundamental change in the elderly support system was never the intention of the state, but the state indeed made the notion of filial piety less important in order to promote loyalty to the party-state.

Because of the gap between law and practice, and because of the conflicts between the party-state's promotion of equality in the family and attack on patriarchal power on the one hand and its reliance on traditional methods of elderly support on the other, the new marriage laws proved to be quite useless for elderly parents when support was in question. A married son was rarely punished by the legal system for parent abuse or abandonment. According to a former official in the civil affairs department of the local government, there was not a single arrest on charges of parent abuse during his tenure over the previous fifteen years. The local court sought consultation and mediation, and the final settlement of irreconcilable conflicts between parents and their married sons was to force the sons to pay for their parents' living expenses. There was no way for the local government or the court to deal with other aspects of elderly support, such as respect and communication, daily assistance and caring, and emotional comfort. Most important, legal intervention, while forcing married sons to provide material support to the elders, also reduced the moral and emotional components in the parent-child relationship. Once a family conflict is brought to court, the family members are no longer bound by renqing ethics and kinship obligations (going to court violates renqing ethics), and the end result is often a complete breakdown of the parent-child relationship. Unlike in the past when severe punishment of unfilial sons could have a deterrent effect on the public, contemporary legal intervention does not have any power beyond economic sanctions, and ultimately it cannot alter the imbalances of power between elderly parents and married sons.

The Silence of Public Opinion

State-sponsored attacks on related "feudalistic ideas," such as patriarchy, lineage powers, and arranged marriages, have greatly shaken the image of parenthood and the sacredness of filial piety. In village society, public opinion is far more important than the legal system in regulating people's behavior in general and elderly support in particular. Until the early the 1950s public opinion was overwhelmingly in favor of older parents, whether the parents were right or wrong. But in the following decades of the collective period, young people became much more active in public life and exerted a greater influence on public opinion.

Public opinion has been further silenced since decollectivization. My informants singled out three reasons for this radical change. First, more and more villagers consider it improper to intervene in other people's personal and family affairs. As the villagers put it, nowadays even the seventh house on a street does not know what happens in the eighth house (*qi jia bu zhi ba jia shi*). This may reflect the villagers' increased sense of privacy, as well as their decreased interest in community affairs.

Second, changes in judgment about a person's social standing also affect public opinion on elderly support issues. Unlike in the recent past, when filial piety was regarded as a high virtue and when a *laoshi* (obedient and honest) person was the ideal mate for young women in the village, under the influence of the market economy and an urban culture, an individual's ability to make money is now considered most important. Those who have been able to advance their economic and social standing quickly are called *nengren* (capable persons). Their moral failure to provide elderly support can easily escape the critique of public opinion because few individuals are willing to risk offending them. Once public opinion cedes itself to the power of some individuals, its moral authority and power decrease accordingly.

Third, measurements of elderly support are also changing as a result of the interactions between older parents and their married sons. The most obvious change is the graduate disappearance of xiaojing (filial piety) as a basic component of elderly support. Fewer and fewer parents can expect formal obedience and ritual respect from their married children, and almost no one in the younger generation considers unconditional obedience to one's parents to be a moral norm. Arguments with parents, on the other hand, are no longer regarded as bad behavior by adult children, as long as the arguments do not develop into impolite or offensive quarrels. Moreover, as the demands for intergenerational communication and emotional bonding emerge, and as parents began to invest in old age emotionally, older villagers became reluctant to make critical comments about the behavior of village youths.

Collapse of the Symbolic World

In a similar pattern, the state-sponsored attack on beliefs and rituals in popular religion severally undermined the status of parents in the family, while the market-oriented reforms accelerated the waning of parental authority and power in the symbolic world.

Ancestors were traditionally worshipped in solemn rituals twice a year in this region, namely, during the Qingming (grave sweeping) Festival and the Spring Festival (the lunar New Year). Before the revolution, male members of larger agnatic groups gathered on each occasion to visit the ancestral tombs or to perform an incense-burning ritual in front of an ancestral scroll hung in the main room at the home of the most senior man in a lineage group. Both rituals involve the performance of a kowtow rite to the ancestors, after which the lineage members also hold a banquet.[10] Villagers who belonged to smaller agnatic groups did not have such a highly organized ritual, but they performed ancestor worship rituals at individual homes.

Recalling the ritual details and the moral messages of the rituals were the older villagers' favorite part of our conversations whenever I interviewed them on related subjects. One articulate villager related his childhood experience of ancestor worship:

> The spectacle of kowtowing and incense-burning was grand and very impressive. Just imagine that! I was on my knees among my cousins, and I looked around and saw my father and uncles also kneeling in a row in front of me, and several grandfathers in the far front row. I looked up and I saw two huge white candles and a lot of burning incense; amidst the smoke I also saw the blurred image of the ancestors on the painted scroll and the names of the deceased. I was really scared and did not dare to breathe. Afterward I had bad dreams for several nights and always thought about the blurred image of the ancestors and the white candles. I was overwhelmed!

He went on to comment that such rituals served to educate both young children and adults about one's moral duty to respect and obey one's parents and grandparents. Although not as analytical, the testimony of other older villagers confirmed this man's view that the ritual itself could help parents maintain their higher status at home.

Large-scale rituals of ancestor worship ended after the 1949 revolution, in part because lineage funds for such activities were eliminated and in part because of radical socialist campaigns against feudalistic customs during the late 1950s. Domestic worship continued until the Cultural Revolution and then was resumed during the early 1980s. But the rituals were largely held by households for immediate ancestors, and organized activities among agnates were not resumed. After the deaths of some elderly villagers who were keen to resume ancestor worship in their families, even the domestic cult began to disappear in the 1990s. During my visit to Xiajia in 1999, I could find only two families who actually performed an ancestor worship ritual during the 1999 Spring Festival; the majority had ancestor scrolls hanging on the wall or placed in the storage room but did not bother to perform the ritual, a clear sign that the custom is once again (and probably forever this time) dying out. A major reason, according to several older villagers, is that elderly parents have lost their influence and cannot persuade their married children to continue this old custom.

In addition to the rituals, some beliefs that helped to maintain the superiority of parents in the traditional Chinese family have also disappeared. One schoolteacher pointed out that, before the revolution, the villagers all believed in the power of an omnipotent Heaven that could punish or reward the living in accordance with their moral behavior. Most people also believed in the existence of an afterlife, and, in general, people were afraid of the final judgment day when the king of Hell would decide one's fate in the afterlife. During thunderstorms, the schoolteacher recalled fondly, parents told their children that the god of Heaven was sending the Thunder god and Light goddess to catch unfilial children and, if a child committed serious offenses of unfilial piety, the gods would strike the child with light and thunder. Or, the king of Hell would send the unfilial son to the depths of Hell, forcing him to undergo terrible torture and suffering. Similar messages were conveyed through the performing arts and religious texts as well as through oral literature. All of these beliefs are now condemned as superstitious and are criticized in school textbooks, newspapers, and public performances. As a consequence, the younger generations do not believe in the supernatural world and therefore have nothing to be afraid of.

The attack on traditional symbols and popular religion continued in the 1990s. One example is the funeral reform that took place in 1993–94 in Xiajia village and the surrounding area. The local government had long enforced funeral reforms, which had featured mandatory cremation and deep burials since the 1970s. In accord with government policies, villagers cremated their dead but still buried the ashes in a traditional way, by building a tomb in a public cemetery. By the early 1990s some villagers secretly buried the dead without cremation because, as many villagers noted, older people still regarded cremation a horrible way to begin one's final journey to the other world. When the local government decided to launch another campaign for funeral reform, villagers were forced to dig up the tombs, cremate the remains, and rebury the ashes. For an entire week, people in Xiajia village were deeply disturbed when nine families had to dig up the buried members of their families. When the human remains were dug up and pushed around, some villagers began to doubt the meaning of life in old age. A 69-year-old man said: "When *gongjia* [the local government/the state] does not respect the deceased, and when we move the remains of our parents back and forth as material things, how can we expect our children to respect us?"[11]

The collapse of parental superiority in religious and kinship domains leads to what I call the "demystification of parenthood." Without the backup of a traditional kinship system and religious beliefs and rituals, the notion that parents grant their children the highest enqing (moral, emotional, and material favors), *fumu zhien*, began to weaken, and the basis for intergenerational relations became more rational and self-interested. As a result, intergenerational reciprocity is no longer a presumed gift of life from parents, but an exchange of material and nonmaterial items in everyday life. This is precisely the argument insisted upon by the younger villagers, although they do not use the scholarly language of social exchange theory.

Economic Deprivation and the Ruthless Logic of the Market Economy

Once parenthood lost its moral ground to economic concerns, the position of elderly parents became disadvantaged, even morally. When land reform and the collectivization campaign deprived villagers of all economic standing of private ownership of farmland and other means of production, the traditional way of accumulating family wealth through inheritance ended. The prolonged state policies that gave industry priority over agriculture led to a generalized poverty in rural China for more than two decades. And by the eve of decollectivization, older villagers had little accumulated family property. Most family property was accumulated in the reform era, during which the younger generation has proven to be more adaptable to the emerging market economy and their contribution to family wealth quickly exceeded that of their parents. When older parents had almost nothing to give to their married sons during family division, one result was the serial form of family division. In other words, older villagers were deprived economically to such an extent that they could no longer fulfill their traditional parental duties to pass property on to their married sons, simply because there was no property to pass on.

Having little to exchange with their married sons in the game of intergenerational reciprocity, parents found themselves in a vulnerable position once the mystified image of parental superiority collapsed and the younger generation rejected the principle of filial piety. A number of older parents sensed their embarrassing position and felt both helpless and hopeless. As an older woman put it: "Honestly speaking, we did very little for our children—

did not feed them well or clothe them well—because we were so much poorer before; we did not provide them with the best wedding for the same reason. When my three sons left the old house one after another, we had nothing to offer them except to buy them some basic kitchen utensils. No wonder my daughters-in-law are angry with me—I did not have the money to buy a gold ring for them." In a separate interview, an old man told me that in the early 1950s his parents still lived with his grandparents and three uncles who were all married and had children: "My grandparents were extremely powerful, because they could tell a son to leave the house if they thought he was unfilial. Without family property, it was extremely difficult for a son to survive, especially if he was kicked out of the house because of his lack of filial piety. Nowadays, parents have nothing to give [to their married son], and of course they have lost all their power."

To conclude, the most significant change with respect to elderly support, in my opinion, is the disintegration and ultimate collapse of the notion of filial piety, the backbone of old-age security in Chinese culture. In traditional China, the primacy of filial piety was sustained institutionally by imperial law, public opinion, patrilineal kinship organizations, the religious system, and family ownership of property. All these institutional bases were undermined under radical socialism from the 1950s to the 1970s as part of a process that I call the demystification of parenthood and filial piety. The introduction of new values associated with the market economy was the fatal blow to the notion of filial piety; contemporary rural youth now perceive elderly support from a new perspective of individual achievement. Without the traditional forms of support, the notion of filial piety lost cultural legitimacy and social power. Under a new set of ethics prevailing in the market economy, intergenerational reciprocity is evaluated more often by a rationally calculated principle of balanced exchange, a principle that elderly parents cannot possibly adhere to because of their economic deprivation under radical socialism. Contrary to villagers' nostalgic memory of the collective period, filial piety and the traditional provision of old-age security began to decline in the 1950s, and the trend continued to the 1990s after being caught in a pincer attack.

CHAPTER EIGHT

Birth Control and the Making of a New Fertility Culture

Of all the state-sponsored programs of social engineering since 1949, birth planning (*jihua shengyu*) is perhaps the most dramatic and far-reaching, fundamentally altering the family structure and redefining the private lives of the Chinese people—urban and rural alike. In Xiajia village, residents were caught by surprise by the official birth control policy and thereafter experienced a painful process of resistance, coping, and adjustment during the 1980s and 1990s.

Although the propaganda and education program for birth control started in the mid-1970s, Xiajia villagers did not pay much attention to it until a team of birth planning workers arrived in late summer 1977, a year before I left the village to begin my college education. I recall seeing the villagers assembled at educational meetings in the headquarters of production teams to learn the three-point program "*wan, xi, shao*," meaning "late births, larger spacing, and fewer births." At that time, most villagers could not accept the argument that having fewer children would benefit their own families and the country.

During one of the meetings, Mr. Zhao, an outspoken man and father of three daughters, openly challenged the state policies and confronted the birth control workers from the township government. He became an instant hero when he shouted in the face of a woman doctor: "I want to see who can control how many times I knock up my own wife!"

Mr. Zhao learned a hard lesson in subsequent years. First he was fined for having two more daughters; then he had to abandon his hopes for a son when his wife was sterilized during the harsh birth control campaign in 1983. When I met the man again in 1989, he still had not fully recovered from a feeling of despair. He had become an alcoholic, often tearfully complaining about his bleak future as a man without a son.

The third time I met Mr. Zhao was during a wedding banquet in 1998; he appeared to be happy, healthy, and affluent. Fellow villagers told me that Zhao had actually benefited from his five daughters, all of whom were hard workers in factories outside the village. More important, he had not spent much for their marriages and had been enjoying care and help from his daughters and sons-in-law. When I congratulated him on a good life, Zhao accepted it matter-of-factly and said: "I knew all along my daughters would be good to me. They are better than boys. As Chairman Mao said, times are different; men and women are the same."

Another anecdote concerns a well-built young man nicknamed "Iron Pole," who was born in 1966 and married in 1986. In January 1987, about four months after his wedding, Iron Pole's wife gave birth to a baby girl. The couple named the child Jing, meaning "glitter" or "shining," a vivid reflection of their happiness. In November 1988 the couple had a second baby girl and was fined 1,400 yuan for violating the birth control regulations. They could have waited two more years and applied for a permit for a second try because their first child was a girl; but Iron Pole had been so eager to have a son that he could not wait. Disappointed by the sex of their second child, Iron Pole named her Pan, meaning "to long for," which showed his determination to have a son. The second girl's name attracted the attention of Ms. Wang, the veteran leader of the Women's Association in Xiajia, who had worked as a birth control cadre since 1978. Ms. Wang made extra efforts to see that Iron Pole's wife used contraceptives and tried to persuade Iron Pole not to violate the policy again. Ignoring many people's advice and his wife's poor health and reluctance to become pregnant again, Iron Pole impregnated her again and they had a third child in 1992—this time a boy. He happily agreed to pay the heavy fine of 6,000 yuan and named his son Delong, meaning "receiving a dragon." The dragon is a positive and powerful symbol in Chinese mythology, representing the *yang* element, lightness, good luck, masculinity, and more important, the emperor in imperial China.[1] The boy's name reflected Iron Pole's happiness as well as his high expectations for his precious son.

During my interview with Iron Pole in 1993, he was delighted to recall how he had cleverly cheated the birth control cadre, Ms. Wang, convinced his wife, and finally had good luck. However, when we met again in 1997, Iron Pole was no longer excited by his reproductive triumph because he and his wife had been experiencing economic hard times in raising their three children. At our last meeting in 1999, Iron Pole openly admitted the mistake of ignoring the birth control regulations in 1988 and said: "If I had waited for a few more years I could have received permission for a second child and I probably would have a son." Then he told me that his youngest brother and sister-in-law had had a daughter the previous year and had decided not to have a second child; this too, in his opinion, was a mistake: "They are too young to consider things seriously, just as I was ten years ago. But I don't know who is more stupid—my brother or me."

Iron Pole's brother is not alone. By 1999 more than a dozen young couples in Xiajia village whose only child was a girl had decided not to have a second child. A closer look at the demographic changes in Xiajia shows that in their response to the birth control program many villagers had transcended their fertility ideals and behavior while others had made adjustments. As a result, a new fertility culture is in the making, and by the end of the century the state-sponsored birth control program had begun to shift toward to a more individual-oriented family planning program.

In the following pages I review the birth planning program in the village during the 1980s and 1990s and examine how the villagers coped with the state policies. I analyze the social and cultural factors that have contributed to the emergence of a new fertility culture and conclude by discussing the significant implications.

Two Decades of Birth Planning

The birth planning program in Xiajia that began in late 1977 started modestly, relying mainly on propaganda and educational meetings. Although many villagers openly rejected the idea of birth control, some found it a helpful solution. According to Ms. Wang, nine Xiajia women voluntarily underwent sterilization between 1978 and 1979 because they did not wish to have more children.

State policies became much stricter in 1980, and in order to rapidly reduce the population growth, the single-child policy was implemented, first in cities and then in the countryside. In Xiajia village, a fine of 700 yuan was imposed on any couple who had a second child (or more) after April 1, 1980. Married women of fertility age were required to use contraceptives, and newlywed couples had to apply for permission to have their first child. These policies encountered strong resistance from many villagers whose lifetime goal was to have as many children as possible, especially sons (see Li Yinhe 1993; Wasserstrom 1984). To reduce the massive discontent and anger, the Xiajia Production Brigade provided a subsidy of 420 yuan so that people could pay the 700 yuan fine for having more children.

It was not until 1983 that Xiajia villagers truly experienced the impact of the powerful birth planning program. Unlike in the previous years when the focus was on propaganda and education, the emphasis in 1983 was on the insertion of intrauterine devices (IUDs) and female sterilization (tubal ligation). All women of fertility age who had had a son by 1983 were required to be sterilized, except those with serious health problems. Women whose first child was a girl were required to get an IUD. Individual will was ignored. Six middle-aged women who had voluntarily used contraceptives long before the campaign began asked to be spared the sterilization because they did not want to have more children in any case. Their requests were rejected, and they had to undergo the operation. In addition to the government-imposed fines, the collectives punished birth control violators by withholding grain rations and other benefits for newborns. Most informants agreed that they were terrified by the very strict campaign, and few dared to resist.[2]

By the end of the 1983 campaign, 102 women in Xiajia village had been sterilized. Virtually every family had either an immediate member or a close relative who had had the operation. As informants recalled in the 1990s, anxiety, discontent, grief, and strong feelings of helplessness had been typical emotional responses in 1983. Men who did not have male offspring reacted the most strongly and, for a short period of time, despairing husbands were commonly seen drunk on the streets. Two men cried out loud in the hospital while their wives were undergoing the operation.

Women suffered even more, enduring both physical and psychological pain (see Greenhalgh 1994a). According to my female informants, four women were taken to the operation table literally by force when at the last minute they had refused to have the surgery. At that time, the local hospital was poorly equipped for such a large number of operations in both human and material terms; it did not have enough beds or painkillers to treat all the women. One woman told me that she had been rushed to the county hospital in the middle of the operation because of massive bleeding. "I felt I was dying right there on the table. But I kept thinking of my three children and that helped a lot," she recalled. After the operations, the women were transported back to Xiajia village in small groups by a tractor-drawn wagon. As the wagon bumped roughly along the unpaved country roads, many women could no longer control themselves and cried out loud.

Villagers believe that when a woman is sterilized her *qi*, that is, the essence of her body, flows out. She simultaneously loses both her reproductive abilities and her physical strength. In fact, many women who underwent the operation complained that for a time afterward they felt weak and easily became ill. In addition, both men and women regarded female sterilization as akin to male castration. They used the word *qiao* to refer to female sterilization, which usually is only used to refer to gelding and spaying animals, especially pigs. Although the medical term for both male and female sterilization is *jue yu*, ordinary villagers did not refer to it in this way.[3] The fact that villagers insisted on using the term *qiao* indicates that female sterilization produced a great deal of anxiety and unhappiness.

To compensate for losing part of their bodily essence (qi) and to ease the anxiety and despair of both the women and the men in the community, the women created a gift-giving ritual. As on other ritualized gift-giving occasions (see Yan 1996: 52–67), relatives and friends visited the woman who had been sterilized, bringing eggs, brown sugar, canned fruits, preserved meat, and other kinds of food considered by the villagers to be nutritious. According to my informants, large-scale gift-giving began when one woman fell seriously ill after being sterilized; thereafter all women who were sterilized began to receive gifts and the new ritual of gift exchange was created.

As in other rural areas, the local government and cadres in Xiajia village relied on the imposition of fines to force the villagers to comply with the birth control regulations; the size of these fines was constantly increased. The heavy fines did have a deterrent effect on some villagers. When asked why they did not continue trying to have a son, some who had had multiple births, going against the official plan, gave me the same simple answer: *"fa pa le,"* meaning they were afraid of the repeated fines. Table 8.1 summarizes the fines imposed during the 1980s and 1990s.

The fines frequently increased, their imposition more and more arbitrary by the late 1990s, and a wide range of fines was created for each category of births that defied the official plan. Xiajia villagers complained to me that in practice the local government always imposed the heaviest fines possible because the government benefited economically from them. When a family accumulated too many unpaid fines, the village office had the power to confiscate the family's contracted land as further punishment. The fines were shared

TABLE 8.1.

Fines for Unplanned Births, 1980–1999 (yuan)

Period	Fines for first birth	Fines for second birth	Fine for third or higher-order birth
April 1980–January 1983		700	Same as for second birth
February 1983–December 1987		1,200	Same as for second birth
January 1988–September 1989		1,400	Same as for second birth
October 1989–January 1990	2,200	4,200	6,200
February 1990–June 1994	3,000	6,000	9,000
July 1994–present	1,000–5,000	5,000–30,000	10,000–60,000

NOTE: Since October 1989 couples have been required to apply for a certificate of a planned birth after their marriage. A first birth without a permit is regarded as an unplanned birth and thus is subject to fines.

between the village office and the local township government. The village office kept 40 to 60 percent of the fines to use as rewards for one-child households. The rest of the collected fines went to the birth planning committee in the local government to be used as part of its operating budget. For obvious reasons, therefore, both the local government and the village office were keen to impose and collect the fines.

A large-scale campaign of female sterilization was relaunched every two or three years after 1983, but it never was as coercive or massive as the first. The last campaign took place in 1994 when twelve Xiajia women underwent sterilization. Since then state birth control policies have been relaxed. Women with a son no longer have to be sterilized; instead they are allowed to use an IUD or to take birth control pills. In addition, beginning in 1987, couples whose first child was a girl were also allowed to have a second child if the wife was 28 or older and the interval between her first and second birth was four years or more. These policy changes eased the worries of villagers who wished to have at least one male heir. More important, new fertility ideals were created among the younger generation in the 1990s.[4] Table 8.2 summarizes the demographic changes during the 1980s and 1990s.

The obvious and most important change is the dramatic drop in higher-order births. As shown in Table 8.2, there were a total of 383 live births from 1979 to 1998: 221 were first births, 102 were second births, 37 were third births, and 23 were fourth or more births.[5] A clear line can be drawn in 1992, when the last third and the last fourth births occurred. Actually, fourth (or more) births were rare as early as 1984, with only two during the subsequent fifteen years. Similarly, the number of third births also declined to one or two per year after 1984.

As a result of the reduction and eventual elimination of higher-order births, the total number of births per year dropped from 34 in 1979 to 11 in 1998, and the percentage of first births among all births increased from 32 percent in 1979 to 91 percent in 1998. By the end of the 1990s not only had the fertility rate decreased significantly, but birth parity had shifted to a predominantly first-birth pattern. It should also be noted that in the 1990s there was only one illegal second birth; all other second births conformed to the revised policy that allowed couples whose first child was a girl to have a second child. Consequently, the percentage of second births also dropped dramatically from 29 percent in 1979 to 9 percent in 1998.[6]

TABLE 8.2.
Distribution of Births by Parity, *1979–1998*

	First birth		Second birth		Third birth		Fourth or higher birth		Total number of births	Total number by sex (male:female)
	Number	Percent	Number	Percent	Number	Percent	Number	Percent		
1979	11	32	10	29	8	24	5	15	34	16:18
1980	11	35	12	39	6	19	2	6	31	15:16
1981	9	32	7	25	4	14	8	29	28	16:12
1982	10	34	11	38	5	17	3	10	29	14:15
1983	11	48	7	30	3	13	2	9	23	12:11
1984	12	67	4	22	1	5.5	1	5.5	18	8:10
1985	14	74	5	26					19	8:11
1986	7	41	9	53	1	6			17	8:9
1987	10	45	9	41	2	9	1	5	22	9:13
1988	12	60	6	30	2	10			20	9:11
1989	13	72	3	17	2	11			18	8:10
1990	7	50	6	43	1	7			14	9:5
1991	10	77	2	15	1	8			13	7:6
1992	13	76	2	12	1	6	1	6	17	10:7
1993	11	79	3	21					14	8:6
1994	14	82	3	18					17	10:7
1995	13	93	1	7					14	6:8
1996	12	100							12	6:6
1997	11	92	1	8					12	7:5
1998	10	91	1	9					11	6:5
All year total	221		102		37		23		383	192:191

198 BIRTH CONTROL AND THE NEW FERTILITY CULTURE

The ratio of male to female births is another interesting figure shown in Table 8.2. Although the sex ratio of newborns fluctuated in 1980s and 1990s, overall there were 192 boys and 191 girls born during this twenty-year period. But this surprising ratio of 100.5 boys to 100 girls is largely the result of the first decade of birth control, during which there were 115 newborn boys and 126 newborn girls, a ratio of 91:100. The higher birth rate of girls in subsequent years is a direct result of parents' efforts to have male offspring. This trend took a remarkable turn in 1990 when the number of newborn boys was almost twice the number of newborn girls, and this continued in most years during the decade. The ratio increased to an alarming 118:100 during the second ten-year period, echoing the national pattern of strong preference for males among Chinese parents in both the cities and the countryside.[7] Paralleling the rise in male births, the number of illegal births declined significantly. This suggests that some villagers might have taken a more direct strategy to secure a male offspring, a rather common nationwide phenomenon in the 1990s.[8]

Xiajia villagers are aware of the demographic changes, and they attribute the radical drop in the number of births to the new mentality of the younger generation as well as to the state birth control campaigns. Ms. Wang, the birth control cadre in Xiajia, told me that her job had become much easier in the 1990s because many young couples preferred to have fewer children and their parents had also given up the old ideal of *duozi duofu* (more sons, more happiness). Consequently, Xiajia village maintained an excellent record of birth planning for six successive years after 1993, with only one birth outside the plan. According to the official birth quotas issued in late 1998, Xiajia village was allowed to have eleven first births and two second births in 1999. These quotas, Ms. Wang told me, were more than enough for Xiajia; based on past records and her own information, she predicted that the village would not even reach its quota. Simple evidence of this new trend, Ms. Wang said, were her difficulties in issuing second-birth permits to the qualified couples. In the late 1980s, applying for such a permit cost only twenty yuan. A number of young couples applied for the permit, but not all of them had a second child. In 1992 the local government decided to add a registration fee of 500 yuan, the sole purpose of which was, according to the villagers, to increase the revenue of the local government, particularly that of the birth planning committee. This proved to be a bad strategy, at least in the Xiajia case. Ms. Wang told me that only ten couples applied for the permit from 1992 to 1997 (nine had a second child). "Unless a couple has made a definite decision, they don't want to spend the 520 yuan for a piece of paper. Who knows when the state policies will change again," she explained, as she showed me several blank permits for a second birth. Not long ago, these permits had been regarded as scarce resources.[9]

Ironically, by the end of the 1990s, cadres in local birth planning agencies had begun to worry about the radical changes that they had contributed to bringing about. Because fewer and fewer villagers were violating the state policies, fines and the sale of second-birth permits declined, and the cadres faced a serious shortage of revenue. As a schoolteacher humorously noted, Xiajia village's perfect score in birth planning was bad news for many cadres in the local government.

Individual Choice and Reproductive Strategies

After carefully examining the interactions among the central state, the local state (represented by the village cadres), and the ordinary villagers, Susan Greenhalgh suggests that the family planning program in rural Shaanxi has been "peasantized" in the sense that both the state and the villagers have retreated from their original positions. The state was forced by strong peasant resistance to change its original radical policies, and it gradually relaxed the single-child policy, allowing some villagers to have a second child if their first child was a girl. Although this change reinforces the traditional preference for male children, villagers have begun to change their opinion about the ideal number of children, with many concluding that the ideal is one son and one daughter—the "optimal two" (see Greenhalgh 1993).

What I find most intriguing about Greenhalgh's study is the idea that nothing was immutable in the two decades of birth planning in rural China, and the results were derived from the dynamic contestations and negotiations among the parties involved. In light of Greenhalgh's findings, I went further in my own research and tried to understand who, at the individual level, made what choices and why, taking into consideration the interactive relationships among the state, the local cadres, and ordinary villagers. Some clues about individual strategies can be gleaned from Table 8.3.

The data presented in Table 8.3 differ from those in Table 8.2 in several respects. First, the numbers represent the couples, instead of actual births, whose status in childbearing is defined by their most recent birth. A couple with three children is still counted as one couple in the category of "third or more births outside the plan." Second, as mentioned, enforcement of the birth control policies in Xiajia began on April 1, 1980. Before that, villagers did not have to make any choices about childbearing. So, couples who had children before 1980 are not included here, but the five couples who had their first child in early 1999 are. Third, in grouping the individual cases, I draw a line after 1986 because after the implementation of policy changes in 1987 some couples qualified for a second child. Another divide is in 1992, when the birth planning program in Xiajia took another turn, as shown by the near-disappearance of illegal births thereafter.

Facing increased pressure from the birth control policies, villagers had to choose between complying with or defying the policies. Customarily, local birth planning cadres classify villagers into two large categories: *jishenghu* (planned-birth households) and *chaoshenghu* (households in which one or more births do not conform to the birth rules). One hundred and sixty-two couples observed the birth control regulations and had either an only son, an only daughter, or two children with a planned second birth after 1987. Another eighty-nine couples defied the state policies by having more children, including both second births and higher-order births.

Planned-Birth Households

The fifty-nine couples who were the parents of an only daughter were eligible to have a second child, but by the summer of 1999 they had not done so. Their unconventional choice challenges the widely accepted assumption that Chinese peasants universally prefer male offspring (see, e.g., Li Yinhe 1993).

A focused survey of this group revealed, however, that thirty-two of those couples had had their first child in or after 1993 and were therefore qualified for a second child for only a short period of time or were too young to be qualified. In either case, it is hard to know whether or not they intended to have a second child. In addition, of the twenty-seven couples whose only

TABLE 8.3.

Villagers' Childbearing Status Defined by Last Birth, April 1980–July 1999

Period of childbirth	Planned birth[a]			Unplanned birth[b]			
				Second birth		Third or higher birth	
	Only-daughter	Only-son	Second birth	Did not have a son before this birth	Had a son before this birth	Did not have a son before this birth	Had a son before this birth
1980–1986	6	10		21	17	16	6
1987–1992	21	32	12	10	7	10	1
1993–1999[c]	32	38	9	1			
All years	59	82	21	56		33	

[a] A planned birth is a birth that conforms to the official birth control regulations.

[b] An unplanned birth is a birth that does not conform to the offical birth control regulations.

[c] Because my last field research was conducted in July–August 1999, birth data for 1999 are incomplete. Four first births and one planned second birth were expected when I left the village.

daughter was born before 1993, eight were unable to have a second child because of health-related problems or the death of spouse. This narrowed my investigation down to the remaining nineteen couples.

The official birth control records show that among the wives of the nineteen families, seventeen had IUDs and the other two had been taking contraceptive pills since giving birth to their first child. Some of the women had had their first child in the late 1980s, and their only daughters were already in primary school. Had they decided to have a second child, the interval between children would have been nearly ten years. According to Ms. Wang, these couples were content with an only daughter, and all except one had expressed the intention of not having a second child. They were officially recognized as *dunuhu* (only-daughter households); the other twenty-one similarly qualified couples who had given birth to a second child during this period were still referred to as "planned-birth households" (see Table 8.3).[10]

Through interviews and household visits I found that these parents of only daughters shared several things in common. They were born either in the late 1960s or the early 1970s (with one exception), and all had established their conjugal households shortly after their weddings. Economically, they formed a rather homogeneous group slightly above the village average—having a new house, major electric appliances, and some savings. However, in their consumption of food, clothing, and leisure goods, such as music tapes and videos, these couples lived much better material lives than the average, even comparable to the rich in some respects.

Moreover, many husbands in this group were landless laborers, because they were too young to be given a share of contract land during decollectivization in 1983. Only two men had a full share of contract land, seven had received a half-share (because they were 16 or 17 years old in 1983), and the remaining ten had not received any contract land. Seeking temporary work in cities, therefore, was the main channel of income for these young men, and, with one exception, they regularly spent six months or so per year working in urban areas. Their experiences working and living in cities no doubt affected their mentality and behavior, and many were among the most open-minded individuals in Xiajia.

When asked about the unconventional idea of having an only daughter, the most common answer from these parents of only daughters was *yatou xiaozi buzhongyao, guanjian shi xiaoshu*, meaning "it is unimportant whether the child is a son or daughter, the key is to have a filial child." The wives seemed to be even more open-minded and vocal during my interviews, and several provided detailed stories about sons who had failed to support their elderly parents. Among the six husbands, four admitted that they would probably have wanted to have a son had their wives agreed to having a second child; but it was also fine with them to have an only daughter because many daughters were indeed better caretakers of their elderly parents. Five men and eight women in this group also identified quality of life as their primary concern in deciding not to have a second child, and their excuses were either *yangbuqi* (cannot afford) or *zhaogu bu guolai* (cannot take care of [so many children]).

When I discussed my findings with Ms. Wang, the birth control cadre in the village, she told me that these new ideas regarding childbearing had emerged in the 1980s and that the first couple to have an only son had decided to do so in 1981. But in the 1980s most villagers were just playing with words, and it was only in the late 1990s that more and more young couples became serious about having only one child. Ms. Wang then called my attention to another group—the eighty-two couples with an only son (see Table 8.3), and said: "I am not sure the parents of an only daughter won't change their minds because they still have the time to do so. But I can assure you these only-son families will stay the same, unless the government policies change again." Her confidence was due to the almost perfect record of the birth control program in Xiajia village, which also reflected Ms. Wang's hard work.

I found Ms. Wang's statement convincing because most parents of an only son were in their early thirties or late twenties and shared the same social background and economic status as the nineteen parents of an only daughter. Given the fact that some open-minded young couples had found an only girl household acceptable, it was likely that most of these eighty couples would continue to comply with state policies—although some might do so by default.

Households with Births in Defiance of the Plan

By 1999, fifty-six couples had two children and thirty-three couples had three or more children. Did they all want to have a son so ended up with more children than they were allowed to have? Some did, but others did not.

Of the fifty-six couples who were fined for having a second child, thirty-two did not have a son before the second attempt, and twenty-four did. This means that only some of these couples decided to violate the state policies in order to have a son; others may have been hoping to have a daughter, or simply a second child. Male preference, therefore, was not the sole motivation for villagers to have a second child.

How many couples achieved their sex preference goal when they risked having a second child? Table 8.3 shows that of the thirty-two couples whose first child was a daughter, fifteen had a second girl, and seventeen had a boy. Similarly, of the twenty-four couples who already had a son but decided to have a second child, thirteen had daughters and eleven had sons. If the gender was their priority in having a second child, their chances of success were about fifty-fifty.

But some couples cared less about the sex of their second child than about having two children. Several villagers explained to me that they felt it was unfair for the first child to grow up alone. "Everybody needs to have siblings and relatives," claimed one middle-aged mother. This sentiment was particularly strong among couples whose first child was a son. In other words, contrary to widely accepted scholarly wisdom, gender may not be the only reason for a second birth in defiance of the birth control plan.

Male preference, nevertheless, seems to be the major motivation among those who had three or more children. The majority of the couples who chose to have a third or fourth child (twenty-six out of thirty-three) did not yet have a son. By 1992, the last year of a higher-order birth, only fourteen of the twenty-six couples had had a son, and the other twelve couples ended up having three, four, or even five girls. Again, when couples tried a second or third time to have a son, the success rate was about 50 percent. This may also explain why in the 1980s the sex ratio of newborns was unusually low, because many of the higher-order newborns were girls. These couples had a much stronger male preference in the first place, so an unsuccessful second attempt led them to third and fourth attempts. Of these thirty-three couples, eighteen had three children, nine had four children, four had five children, and two had six children. So, by 1992, these thirty-three couples had produced 122 children, which translates into a fertility rate of 3.69 per woman in this small group, much higher than the average of 1.8 births per woman among the cohort of reproductive age from 1980 to 1999 in Xiajia village.

Seven couples had already had a son by the time they had their third child, but six had the higher-order birth in either 1980 or 1981 when the birth control polices were not strict. For these six couples, the direct cost of having a third child was tolerable because the collectives subsidized a major part of the 700-yuan fine. After the 1983 birth control campaign, however, only villagers with a strong desire for a son defied the state policies to have a third or fourth child.

The only exception was the couple who had their fourth child in 1989. It may not be coincidental that the husband in this couple was known for being an extremely conservative and patriarchal tyrant at home, and economically the household was way below average in the late 1980s. They could not afford to pay the rising fines for higher order births—they were fined 6,000 yuan for their third child and 9,000 yuan for the fourth—and went even deeper into debt.

A lower economic status is perhaps the most salient feature of this group. Twenty-four of the thirty-three couples in the multiple-birth group were poor, and the other nine had barely average incomes. Even worse, twenty-eight couples owed fines to the village office and many were also in debt to relatives. Although most husbands in this group were old enough to have received contracted land in 1983, their land had long ago been confiscated by the village office to pay their accumulated unpaid fines. The everyday struggle of raising several children dragged these couples further down. Their impoverished multiple-birth situation was vividly described by fellow villagers as *yue qiong yue sheng, yue sheng yue qiong*, which means "the more poor, the more children; the more children, the more poor"—a vicious circle. Consequently, many couples in this group were looked down upon by other villagers and thus also suffered from a lack of self-esteem and social prejudice against them. A few couples in this group regretted their choices or were interested in rethinking their reproductive strategies, but the majority still insisted on the ideal of "more sons, more happiness." Their insistence on traditional notions may also be explained by their age; they were generally in their early forties or older in 1999 and thus had spent their youth during the collective period.

Understanding the New Fertility Culture

The above analysis demonstrates that villagers did not respond homogeneously to the birth planning program imposed by the powerful state; instead they employed different strategies to cope with it. No single explanation, such as repression, resistance, or adaptation, reflects the richness and individual variations of their lived experiences in this aspect of their private lives. And the fact that a large number of young couples were content with having an only child—an only daughter in some cases—indicates that a new fertility culture had emerged by the end of the 1990s, which can be examined in economic, demographic, gender, and communal terms.

The Cost and Utility of Children: The Economic Factor

Economic considerations emerged as a major factor contributing to changes in fertility behavior among the young villagers.[11] Recall that a number of young parents of an only daughter said that not being able to afford or to take good care of another child were the major reasons not to have a second child. Many parents of an only son held the same view, though they did not use it to justify their reproductive choice. The interesting point is that, as shown in the above analyses, parents of an only child tended to enjoy a better economic status than those who violated the birth control policies to have more children; yet it was the former rather than the latter who seriously considered the cost of raising children when making fertility decisions. Having said this, I must stress that, by the late 1990s, all informants—regardless of age, sex, and or fertility situation—agreed that they could hardly keep pace with the increasing costs of raising children.[12]

When reviewing the cost of raising children, villagers seemed to be most concerned with *linghuaqian* (incidental expenses); this newly emerged category that had little to do with life's necessities has been rising rapidly. Toys are incidental expenses; but the most incidental expenditures were for food items, including candy, soft drinks, ice-cream bars, cookies, fruits, fried instant noodles (which are consumed as snacks by children), and sausages. By the end of the 1990s, these incidental expenditures were a must for families with small children, poor and rich alike. The average daily expenditure per child was 1 yuan in summer 1998, or 360 yuan per year, nearly one-tenth of the average annual household income (4,000 yuan). Influenced by the urban culture, young parents competed with one another to buy fancy toys and plentiful snacks to show affection toward their children (in many cases, an only child), a practice that, interestingly, attracted little criticism from the older generation.

By the late 1990s children had become accustomed to such daily luxuries and had developed a strong sense of entitlement. In the summer of 1999, when two children (ages 6 and 10) learned that their mother, a schoolteacher, had received a salary increase, they demanded that she also increase her monthly incidental expenditures on them from 70 yuan to 100 yuan. The mother told me that her parents had never spent extra money on her when she was young, buying only necessary food and clothing. "It is amazing that these little people dare to ask for a raise," the mother complained while holding both children in her arms and smiling.

Although incidental expenses attracted a lot of attention, the more important expenses are for basic daily needs. According to several villagers' accounts, to raise a child from birth to age 20 a couple needs at least 200 yuan per year for clothing, 160 yuan per year for medicine and emergencies, and 800 to 1,000 yuan per year for food. Since the late 1980s, education has become increasingly costly, and many parents complained that they could no longer afford to send their children to school. The normal cost of education was estimated at 240 yuan per year (an average of the costs of primary and middle school).

The most expensive item, however, is a marriage.[13] The custom of providing a generous bridewealth and dowry has flourished since the 1980s, and the average cost of marriage (for a son) increased more than tenfold over the five decades after 1949, reaching 30,000 yuan in 1999. With young people demanding conjugal independence and individual property rights, a new house is now also a precondition for marriage. This means that a son's marriage normally costs his parents 40,000 to 50,000 yuan (it is much less costly to marry off a daughter because the parents need only provide an acceptable dowry). In total, my informants estimated that parents had to spend 70,000 yuan or more for a son and 40,000 yuan for a daughter over a period of twenty years.

Although these figures are derived from individual accounts rather than a systematic survey, they still provide a rough estimate of the rising costs of raising children and their impact on the current generation of young parents. In fact, the estimations of the Xiajia villagers approximate those from survey results. A 1995 survey in rural Shaaxi found that the total cost of raising a child from birth to the age of 16 was 30,120 yuan, but this figure did not include the largest expenditure—the cost of marriage (see Zhu and Zhang 1996).[14]

While the costs of raising children are on the rise, their perceived utility has been decreasing at an equally rapid pace. As is widely recognized in both scholarly work and among the public, children are valuable as potential laborers for the family economy, future providers of aged parents, carriers of the family/descent line, and a source of parents' happiness and psychological fulfillment. The existence and importance of these roles vary from one society to another according to the specific conditions of social and economic development. In contemporary American society, it is the latter that matters the most, while in rural China, scholars have long considered the first three to be the most important reasons villagers want more children.

The Xiajia case reveals some astonishing changes in this respect. First, the shortage of land and other employment opportunities has led to a serious surplus of laborers since the early 1980s. It is at least unwise, if not suicidal, to invest in children as laborers. This is obvious to the villagers because children born after 1983—the year of decollectivization and land redistribution—did not receive a share of rationed land, not to mention per-male-laborer-based

contract land. Second, the new custom of early family division further reduced the potential of adult children contributing economically to their parents' home; they all left to establish their own conjugal household shortly after marriage. Third, the traditional notion of filial piety is collapsing, and
elderly support has become increasingly problematic. Although adult children (mainly married sons) still fulfilled their responsibilities to feed their
parents, a number of elderly parents were forced to live alone to avoid heart-
breaking conflicts with unfilial sons. Both ideologically and as a practical
matter, the first two values of children—as family laborers and providers of
elderly support—are quickly declining.

This is particularly true regarding the marginal utility of high-birth-order
children. When it comes down to the matter of elderly support, married sons
tend to shift the responsibility from one to another, but an only son has no
such ability. As a result, everything else being equal, elderly parents of multiple sons found themselves worse off than their counterparts with only sons.
In this connection, it is noteworthy that a 1996 survey of 660 households in
three different rural areas showed that 60 percent of elderly parents lived
alone, with a pattern whereby the more sons aged parents had, the higher the
chance they would live alone (see Peng and Dai 1996: 57–58). Improvements
in the medical system and the drop in child mortality have further undermined the marginal utility of multiple sons. By the end of the 1990s, villagers
all agreed that the number of sons did not count for much in terms of old-age
security; it was best to have one filial son. Similar reflections have been reported from many other areas of rural China as well (see, e.g., Li Yinhe 1993;
Peng and Dai 1996; and Ye 1998).

A New Generation of Parents: Demographic Factors

Some Chinese scholars have disputed the applicability of the cost-utility
model to rural China because the demands for children are deeply rooted in
a cultural tradition that is characterized by familism and the worship of fertility. The perpetuation of the family line through reproduction is what
makes life meaningful to Chinese villagers, and it is for this reason that children (particularly male offspring) evoke a kind of religious feeling of fulfillment that cannot be measured by economic gains or losses. In this view, the
cost-utility model cannot explain why so many villagers had multiple chil-

dren regardless of the price they had to pay and why in some developed rural areas of southern China the fertility rate remained high even after the cost of children increased and a better social system of elderly support was put into place (see Li Yinhe 1993; Chen and Mu 1996: 127).

In my opinion, such a cultural perspective is important in understanding the persistence of the traditional fertility culture and peasant resistance to birth control policies. However, scholars of this view tend to regard the conservative characteristics of peasant culture as timeless and immutable and also to assume that Chinese villagers homogeneously refuse to accept new fertility ideals. The Xiajia case proves otherwise in two ways.

First, traditional notions of fertility have changed to a great extent. By the end of the 1990s, few Xiajia villagers still upheld the old ideal of "more sons, more happiness" (*duozi duofu*); instead the view had changed to "more sons, more worries" (*duozi duochou*). Villagers also began to question the notion of *yang er fanglao* (raising sons for old age) and tried to increase old-age security by establishing personal savings and cultivating close relationships with married daughters. Although most villagers still perceive the continuation of the family line only through sons, the pressures to produce a son for the family have begun to wane: third births among parents of two daughters are rare, and only-daughter households are no longer exceptional. Similar changes in the fertility culture are reported from other parts of rural China as well (see, e.g., Peng and Dai 1996).

Second, it is not accidental that births that defied the official policy dropped sharply in the early 1990s and then ended entirely in the late 1990s in Xiajia village—the secret lies in the demographic transition of parents of fertility age. Young parents in the 1990s were born in the early 1970s and grew up in a social environment where birth control was emphasized as a fundamental strategy for national development. This constitutes a sharp contrast to the social environment of their parents, who grew up during the Great Leap Forward and Cultural Revolution when the traditional notion of "more sons, more happiness" was translated into the Maoist slogan of "more people, more power." These young parents, therefore, have been less affected by the legacy of the old fertility culture and are also more ready to accept the reality that their fertility desires must comply with the state birth control policies. Actually, few still consider the birth of a child to be a purely private and family matter. On several occasions, young villagers asked me what it was like to live in a country where one can have as many children as one wants. They simply could not imagine this from their own lived experiences. In other words, the notion of planned birth has become part of the mind-set of the young generation, and this alone may help us to understand the relative ease with which young villagers comply with birth control policies.

But the generational differences go beyond the impact of state ideology and policy implementation. Many young parents view the meaning of life differently from their older siblings and parents. Based on data collected from 1989 to 1994, I elsewhere document the rise of a youth subculture in three villages in northern China and argue that village youth of the 1990s had a much stronger desire than their elders to pursue happiness in their personal lives. Their notion of happiness was more individualistic than that of their parents or elder siblings and, more often than not, was defined by material comforts such as fashionable clothing, good housing, and better jobs (Yan 1999: 80–81). The same group of village youth that I previously studied was married and had become young parents by the end of 1999. Following their footsteps in life, I could see clearly the continuing influence of the youth culture in their family lives, including fertility planning. Their pursuit of material comforts made them particularly aware of the rising costs of children; their awareness of individual rights led them to cast doubt on traditional fertility notions; and the national trend of consumerism further raised their life aspirations (see Yan 2000). During my interviews, young parents frequently cited the difficult lives of their own parents as unsatisfactory and even unworthy of living, saying that they could not understand why their elder siblings were willing to pay heavy fines to have several children and end up living in poverty.

When a Wife Is in Charge: The Gender Factor

Generational differences matter, and so does the gender relationship. Household surveys and interviews revealed a link between the choice of an only child on the one hand and a wife's status at home and the quality of the husband-wife relationship on the other hand. For instance, among the nineteen couples whose only child was a daughter, twelve wives (63 percent) were in charge of family affairs at home; in contrast, only three husbands were in a similar position of power. In the remaining four couples, husbands and wives enjoyed an equal relationship in decision-making and household chores. Moreover, eleven of the nineteen couples were also known for "having good feelings" (*ganqinghao*) toward each other in local terms, which means that their conjugal relationship was close and affectionate.

A similar pattern existed among the forty-seven couples whose only son was born before 1993. Again using the power relationship as a measurement, twenty-seven only-son families were wife-led (57 percent), nine were husband-led (19 percent), and in the remaining eleven the husbands and wives enjoyed an equal relationship at home (23 percent). This suggests that when a wife is in charge of family affairs the couple is likely to comply with birth control policies and, in some cases, young couples manage to overcome the traditional preference for a male child.

Additional supporting evidence can be found among the opposite group—the couples who defied the control policies. Among the twenty-four couples who had had a son before having their second child, there were ten husband-dominant families, five wife-led families, and nine couples with an equal relationship. Given the current trend among the younger generation for more wives to be in charge of family affairs, the percentage of husband-led families in this particular group is obviously higher than the average. It is conceivable that if more wives had played a leading role in this group there would have been fewer illegal second births.

Either way, the Xiajia cases reveal that the status of women, particularly that of young wives, may be one of the key elements in determining a couple's reproductive strategy. Couples in wife-led families tended to easily accept the new ideal of childbearing and most chose to have only one child. In households where the husbands were in charge, the couples tended to follow the traditional ideals and violate the birth control regulations in order to have more children or to fulfill their desire to have a son. One can infer that in those families it was the husband and/or the relatives of the husband who opposed the new policies. Since children are now less useful as a source of labor and less reliable for elderly support, the continuity of the descent line has become a major motivation for having more children; this concern was, understandably, more prevalent among the husbands and their relatives than among the wives. Moreover, when the conjugal relationship is based on affection, respect, and companionship, resulting in a more equal gender relationship, it is likely that the couple will pay more attention to the quality of family life and will rationally calculate the pros and cons of births that defy the regulations.

In this connection Hill Gates's finding from Taiwan and the city of Chengdu, Sichuan province, is particularly noteworthy. In both places women who own small businesses tend to have fewer children, and their choice is a strategy of both work and life (including kinship practices):

> Chinese women do not choose to limit this burden only because childcare and childbearing are sometimes uncomfortable, painful, and exhausting, and at worst fatal. They do so as well because they have access to a secondary model of kinship relations that is submerged within a more visible kinship ideology. This model, especially clear among petty capitalists, rationalizes childbearing as a measurable contribution made to meet a specific obligation, and also rationalizes its limitation. (Gates 1993: 255)

Cunfeng: The Community Factor

Finally, the community also plays a role in influencing villagers' fertility desires and demand for children. When discussing birth planning with me, Ms. Wang, the local birth control cadre, repeatedly pointed out that Xiajia village benefited from a good *cunfeng*, which literally means "village wind" but may better be translated as the "village trend" or "village mood." What Wang meant were the established community practices that provide the social norms for the villagers to follow.

Initially, birth planning work in Xiajia proceeded more smoothly than in surrounding villages, primarily because of Xiajia's strong and relatively clean leadership and its successful collective economy in the late 1970s and early 1980s, which gave the cadres enough resources to use both sticks and carrots as incentives.[15] The absence of serious kinship-based fights within the village also contributed to the emergence of a new fertility culture, and the established new fertility norms in turn regulated the people's behavior.

In addition to its economic function, a family's manpower—the physical power of men—is socially important in rural communities where disputes and other conflicts are often resolved by kinship intervention rather than legal procedures. The number of sons in a family often serves as a direct gauge of a family's influence and status, and this is particularly true if there are frequent kinship-based violent conflicts.[16] In Xiajia village, the kinship structure emphasizes marriage-based alliances rather than lineage-based power. The fact that more than 80 percent of the villagers in Xiajia were related significantly reduced the perceived needs to develop family manpower to deal with kinship-based conflicts. There have been violent conflicts between families in the recent past, but the new patterns of alliance-making depend more on friendship and affinal ties, and actual practice is even more fluid and individual-centered (see Yan 2001). The need for manpower in violent conflicts alone, therefore, can no longer motivate Xiajia villagers to demand more children.

Established practices in a community have more regulating power on its members, and this is the underlying meaning of what Ms. Wang calls cun-feng, the village trend or mood. During my interviews I frequently heard informants cite *sui daliu* (following the big trend) as their rationale for making a particular fertility choice. A middle-aged couple with two sons and three daughters told me that in their time (the late 1970s and early 1980s) many neighbors had several sons, "so we figured we must not have only one son." After paying fines for their fourth and fifth children, the couple luckily achieved their goal; but many others were not so lucky. Similarly, a number of young parents with an only son admitted that they did not want to have a second child because no one else did.

As a result of interactions and readjustments, community norms have emerged and evolved over the years, and villagers consciously use the new norms to guide their actions and judge those of others, labeling them as either *heli* (reasonable) or *buheli* (unreasonable). For instance, having a third child in order to have a son was regarded as reasonable until the early 1990s, but it was considered unreasonable in the late 1990s. At the end of the 1990s, although the ideal number of children in a family was two, not a single couple with an only son had tried to have a second child after 1993 because it was regarded as not only unreasonable but also immoral to compete for the limited birth quota with those couples whose first child was a girl. Yet the nineteen couples with an only daughter were also regarded as a bit strange by the majority of villagers because they did not follow the big trend (sui daliu) and went beyond the community norms.[17]

From Birth Control to Family Planning

In short, the long-term interactions among the state, its local agents, and ordinary villagers made birth planning a much easier task in Xiajia, and a new
fertility culture had emerged by the end of the 1990s. By examining the villagers' individual choices and reproductive strategies, I reveal how ordinary
villagers made their childbearing choices when they were facing an unprecedented intrusion into their private lives by a powerful state. Passive resistance,
the most popular form of peasant response, was certainly a part of their strategy, but they have also established a new fertility culture. It is time, therefore,
to pay closer attention to the villagers' capability to transcend older values
and norms (and to a certain extent even themselves) in human reproduction.

The new fertility culture, however, is still evolving; most changes thus far
involve only the number—ideal or actual—of children. There have not yet
been obvious changes in the other two, equally important, aspects of rural fertility culture: the sex of children and the time of birth. The fact that nineteen
couples intended to remain the parents of only daughters certainly marks a
significant development in the battle against the age-old preference for male
children, yet the alarmingly high ratio of male to female births (118:100) in
the 1990s prevents one from being too optimistic in this respect. State birth
control policies only reinforced the traditional ideal of early birth; fertility
itself is now regarded as both a privilege and a scarce resource. A common
strategy, therefore, is to marry earlier and to give birth earlier, pushing the
average age of first births among Xiajia women down to 21 (many village
youth even lied about their age in order to marry earlier).[18]

The emerging fertility culture involves another significant change—the
shift from state-imposed birth control to a family planning program that is
based more on individual choice and family strategy, as revealed by the two
anecdotes at the beginning of this chapter. Back in the 1970s, villagers regarded childbearing as a natural matter determined by the supernatural, including the goddess of fertility and one's own fate. That is why Mr. Zhao did
not believe that anyone (probably not even he) could control the frequency
of his wife's pregnancies. Such a cultural construction of fertility as a natural/
supernatural process ended after April 1980. Once the believed mystery of
fertility was destroyed by abortion, sterilization, and contraceptive devices,

individual choice and strategies became the new foundation for fertility desires and childbearing. Many parents of an only child are officially recognized as vanguards in family planning because their choices and strategies are sanctioned by state policies. Yet those who resisted the birth control program and managed to have additional children also actively engaged in family planning in their own way, such as Iron Pole, who not only planned the last two births but also manipulated many people in order to have a son. In this sense, the shift toward a more liberal form of family planning has begun, albeit initially due to the intervention of a powerful state.

Based on her fieldwork in the late 1980s, Susan Greenhalgh correctly points out that the Chinese concept of birth planning differs from the Western liberal notion of family planning in that the role of the state is paramount and individual choice is either dismissed or suppressed (1994: 6). In the late 1990s, some Chinese demographers also reflected on the previously narrowly defined notion of birth planning (see Gu 1996). In this connection, the Xiajia case may shed new light on both scholarly inquiry and the continuing implementation of birth control policies in China. Now a key question is: when will the matter of family planning in Xiajia village be based entirely on individual choice and family strategy, balancing the number, sex, and time of birth? The hope may lie in the continuing development of the new fertility culture and with the new generation of young parents, as signaled by the fertility choice of Iron Pole's youngest brother.[19]

Conclusion

The Socialist State, the Private Family, and the Uncivil Individual

In this concluding chapter, I summarize the major family changes in Xiajia village from 1949 to 1999 and then address two issues with importance for this study: the rise of the individual and the role of the socialist state in transforming family life. My attention to the rise of the individual sets this case study apart from most earlier studies of the Chinese family. First, I take a closer look at youth autonomy and agency, particularly among young women, as well as emotionality and desire in contemporary family life. Second, I argue that the socialist state has been a major force in initiating or causing family change over the five decades from 1949 to 1999. This has resulted in a paradoxical transformation of private life that is characterized by a surge of egotism and the rise of the uncivil individual, who emphasizes the right to pursue personal interests yet ignores his or her moral obligations to the public and other individuals.

The Rise of the Private Family

The most obvious change in the felt flow of moral experiences among Xiajia villagers is the transformation of the domestic power structure, namely, the decline of parental power, authority, and prestige, which was accompanied by a rise of youth autonomy and independence. This ongoing process began with land reform in the late 1940s. Over the subsequent five decades, the shift of power and authority from the older to the younger generation has continued in virtually every aspect of family life, from spouse selection, postmarital residence, management of family property, and intrafamily relations to support for the elderly. By the end of the 1990s patriarchy as an institutionalized power no longer existed in Xiajia families, although androcentric power still prevailed in many aspects of both the public and private spheres. What remains unclear is how the sometimes tense negotiations and adjustments between the two generations will play out. More than half a century ago, Francis Hsu stated that the traditional Chinese person, family, kinship, and culture were all "under the ancestors' shadow" ([1948] 1967: 240–60). This statement is no longer true. Coming out of the ancestors' shadow is the principal change in the private lives of villagers in Xiajia village.

The waning of the patriarchal order has opened up new horizons for the individual-centered development of romantic love, intimacy, conjugality, and the pursuit of personal space and privacy. Women, particularly young women, have gained more control over their own lives and have played a decisive role in transforming the domestic sphere. As a result, the previous logic of intergenerational reciprocity needs to be redefined and new norms of elderly support are under negotiation, which in turn are facilitating the growth of a new fertility culture centered on the happiness of the conjugal family rather than the continuation of the family line. In these newly developed areas of family life, emotionality, desires, and personal freedom have become not only legitimate aspirations but also part of everyday practice. Unlike in the traditional family, where an individual was nothing more than the personification of the family line, the contemporary individual is concerned with the well-being of the private family and personal happiness in the present; these new concerns are reflected in the decline of ancestor worship, the crisis of filial piety, the rise of conjugality, and the new status of children.

What occurred over five decades represents the transformation of private life in a dual sense: the rise of the private family and of the lives of the individuals within the family. This private family, which had emerged by the end of the 1990s, is characterized by the relatively weak influence of public forces, the greater control of the individuals over the observability of their behavior by others, the centrality of companionate marriage and conjugal relationships, and an emphasis on personal well-being and affective ties. The essence of this transformation, I stress, lies in the rise of the individual, rather than in household size or family structure, though the latter have changed significantly as well.

Admittedly, the general trend in the transformation of private life in Xiajia village is hardly new; the changes described in the preceding chapters have been similarly reported (though not necessarily in their entirety) in some urban areas (see, e.g., Gates 1993; Jankowiak 1993; and Whyte 1993). From a broader perspective, we can see that the transformation of private life began to occur in western Europe in the seventeenth century and in North America at the turn of the nineteenth century (see, e.g., Coontz 1988, 2000; Goode 1963; Mitterauer and Sieder 1982; and Prost 1991). What makes the Xiajia case theoretically noteworthy are the local expressions of the historical trend and the specific ways things changed, rather than the outcome. More important, the Xiajia case demonstrates the increasingly important role played by the individual in the transformation of private life, which has by and large been overlooked in previous studies that relied on the corporate model of the Chinese family.

As far as the timing of this transformation is concerned, there was no one-time rupture or direct link between family change and political-economic change; it is thus pointless to draw a boundary, say, between the collective and the postcollective periods. Almost all of the contemporary aspects of the transformation are deeply rooted in the early stages of socialist practice, either directly or indirectly. Even the emergence of a new fertility culture in the 1990s is related to the youth culture and new patterns of intergenerational reciprocity, both of which originated during the early decades of radical socialism. More broadly, the Xiajia case represents the latest rural development of a national trend in family revolution. C. K. Yang (1965) points out that the origin of the family revolution among the educated upper class can be traced back to as early as the late nineteenth century.[1] According to Deng Weizhi, the slogan of a "family revolution" first appeared during the 1911 revolution and was further popularized among educated youth during the subsequent New Culture Movement in the 1920s. From the 1930s to the 1940s, attempts to reform the family moved beyond ideology to social practice, along with the promulgation of the Law of Kinship Relations in 1930 by the Nationalist government. However, most of these reform efforts were limited to educated urbanities and were rarely supported by political and economic reforms in larger social settings. It was only after the Chinese Communist Party (CCP) took national power that a much wider and deeper campaign of family reform was carried out at the grassroots level and coordinated with other aspects of the socialist transformation sponsored by the socialist party-state (see Deng 1994).[2]

More often than not, the unintended consequences of state-sponsored family reforms and national policies turned out to be critical for the transformation of private life. The social problem of elderly support, for instance, is clearly an unintended consequence of undermining parental power. The most important unintended consequence deserving our close attention, however, is the rise of the individual.

Autonomy, Emotionality, Desire, and the Uncivil Individual

The rise of the individual, or the development of individuality, is best reflected in the greater autonomy and independence, the intensification of emotional attachment and intimacy, and the expansion of personal desires among several generations of villagers. Because village youth are most sensitive and receptive to social change and more individualistic than their parents, the following discussion focuses on the young people in each generation.

Youth Autonomy and "Girl Power"

Youth autonomy constitutes a critical issue in intergenerational conflicts and defines the rising individuality in many aspects of family life, from spouse selection, postmarital residence, and conjugal power to fertility choices. Over the past five decades young villagers have acquired the power to make decisions and act on them (see Gold 1991; Yan 1999), and their autonomy and independence have carried over to awareness of individual rights and a need for self-expression.

Awareness of individual rights is clearly reflected in intergenerational negotiations over marital gifts (pre-mortem inheritance) and the distribution of family property, but it can also be seen in other areas of family life, such as spatial relations. The fundamental difference between the current practice of family division and its counterpart in the past, I argue, is that the younger generation—married sons and their wives—have a strong sense of entitlement to their share of the family property and indeed have taken determined action to claim it. As a young woman put it bluntly: "What I am trying to get is mine in the first place," referring to a lavish dowry that was partially based on what she had earned by working as a domestic worker over the previous three years. Such a strong sense of entitlement is based on individual autonomy and thus differs from a person's wishful thinking or fantasies.

Another feature of the rising individuality is a willingness and ability to express personal opinions. In the debate over the logic of intergenerational reciprocity, contemporary village youth challenge age-old notions of filial piety and mystified parenthood and insist on a new principle of exchange. Similarly, a number of young husbands defend the new patterns of gender dynamics and conjugal intimacy by accusing their parents of being feudalistic or of interfering in other people's private business. Such debates across generational lines were not uncommon during the 1950s when one's right to choose a spouse was still questionable, but the focus of discussion among engaged couples in the 1980s changed to the appropriateness of premarital sex. The villagers' capacity to develop and express individual opinions became much stronger in the postcollective era, a result of both the richness of their own life experiences and the loosening of political control. My interviews with the villagers of Xiajia during the 1990s revealed a diversity of opinions on almost every issue, a sharp contrast with my experience of living in the same village during the early 1970s, when a dominant voice (more or less official) was always obvious. The demand for autonomy and independence also led to the making of a rural youth culture characterized by antiauthoritarianism and an awareness of individual rights in public life (see Yan 1999).

The generation-based youth experiences are important for understanding both generational gaps and links among Xiajia residents. There are at least four generations of youths in Xiajia whose experiences were dramatically different from those of their parents: (1) the illiterate and newly awakened young revolutionaries in the 1950s; (2) the idealistic youth in the 1960s; (3) the post–Cultural Revolution youth of the 1970s; and (4) the more individualistic and materialistic youth in the post-Mao era (see Yan 1999; see Gold 1991 for an insightful analysis of the youth cohorts). By the 1990s, the youth who sang love songs during the Great Leap had become grandparents (see Blake 1979), and the young activists who had been fond of volunteer work and political campaigns during the 1960s had become grandparents or parents with marriage-age children (see Chan, Madsen, and Unger 1992; Parish and Whyte 1978). The youthful experiences of these grandparents and parents affected their later attitudes toward contemporary youth. Each generation underwent its own particular kind of "breakthrough" in rural youth culture and in challenging generational superiority; each subsequent generation of youth also enjoyed more autonomy and independence. And when these youths became elder siblings and parents they demonstrated more tolerance toward the autonomy of the next generation. The long-term effects of the youth experience have contributed significantly to the transformation of private life.

Although village youth of both sexes were instrumental in changing the private life sphere, the agency of young women deserves closer attention.[3] As discussed in the previous chapters, many young women took the initiative in courtship and postengagement "dating," continuing to expand the previously forbidden area of premarital intimacy. Young women have been particularly active in negotiating marital gifts, especially since the introduction of the new custom of "converted bridewealth" that allows them to take possession of most of the bridewealth. And, to a great extent, the daughter-in-law now determines the duration of postmarital residence with her husband's parents and the power balance across generational lines in a stem family. Nevertheless, young women could not have accomplished all these changes alone and usually had a supportive fiancé or husband. In this sense, "girl power" is merely a manifestation of youth power. But their previous marginality has made young women particularly receptive to new family ideals based on egalitarianism and more active in pursuing autonomy and independence in the domestic sphere than young men.[4]

Emotionality, Desire, and Consumption Demand

The increasing importance of emotionality and sentimentality in family life is one of the themes that I stress throughout this book. The rise of the private family can also be regarded as the transformation of the family from a disciplined corporate group to an emotional, and often sentimental, refuge for individuals. At the micro level, this transformation occurred because the subjective world of villagers has been enriched over the past five decades, so much so that young people consider the ability to express one's inner feelings and affections to be an important quality of an ideal spouse. Romantic love, intimacy, and conjugality have become irreplaceable in the villagers' moral experiences; yet the discussions of intergenerational tensions, contestations, and conflicts are equally related to emotions, albeit less joyful ones, such as anger, jealousy, grief, and despair. Many villagers are as emotional as they are rational in dealing with family issues, and emotional attachments have become much more important mechanisms within the family, as reflected by changes in attitudes toward conjugality and elderly support (see also M. Wolf 1972 for mother-son bonds). As Myron Cohen notes, filial piety should be regarded as a cultural construction of emotional relations on the one hand and as a concept related to the corporate family on the other.[5] Indeed, what most upsets and disappoints older villagers in Xiajia is precisely the waning of the emotional and moral aspects of the notion of filial piety, because in most cases the basic life provisions in old age have not been threatened.

Although emotional responses and ties of affection have become increasingly important in rural family life since the 1950s, few scholars have addressed them. This is because most existing studies of Chinese family life are influenced by the corporate model, which regards the Chinese family primarily as an economic group and a social institution organized according to rational corporate principles. As powerful an approach as it is, the corporate model nevertheless is confined to the fixed norms, rules, and structural formation of the family. Looking through the lens of the corporate model, we see that "it was not the family which existed in order to support the individual, but rather the individual who existed in order to continue the family" (Baker 1979: 26). The family thus becomes a corporate mini-lineage whereby "family attachments have been stripped of 'ordinary emotions' by the demands of a family's practical activities" (Fei [1947] 1992: 84–85). As a result, Chinese villagers are often portrayed as rational and ascetic pragmatists, which this study of Xiajia demonstrates is at least incomplete and perhaps distorted.[6]

Publicly expressed personal desires constitute another sign of the development of individual subjectivity. It is true that youthful self-indulgence and the desire for a good life and easy work are not new; but in the traditional family ideology most personal desires were either controlled or stigmatized as improper. For instance, village youth now prefer to stay in bed late in the morning, but their parents consider that practice to be a serious flaw in peasant virtue. The key issue is not extra sleep per se, but the extent to which one should indulge one's basic desires. While the older villagers consider self-indulgence to be morally unjustifiable for a peasant, the younger generation insists that everyone deserves better treatment in life. In another example, a young man resented seeing urban women walking in and out of office buildings that he had helped to build, because he thought his beautiful wife also deserved a more comfortable and modern lifestyle. During interviews, he (and more than a dozen others, both young and old) repeatedly questioned the lower status of peasants and asserted that villagers deserve the same life advantages as urbanites. This mentality that said "I (or we) deserve . . . " is a new, bold, and individualistic claim based on a clear consciousness of one's rights. This contrasts sharply with peasant mentality during the collective period, when villagers admired the better fate of urbanites and complained about theirs, but rarely felt they deserved the same life chances as urban dwellers. Once this mentality emerges, the object of the statement "I deserve . . . " can be anything, from a consumer durable to an ideal family.

Admittedly, most desires are materialistic and ultimately lead to the desire for consumption, which is more and more possible as China rapidly becomes a consumer society (see Yan 2000). During fieldwork young villagers expressed a strong desire to take control of family property largely because of their somewhat different perception of the meaning of property, particularly with regard to consumption matters. From a conjugal and individual perspective, a well-to-do extended family is characterized by a larger amount of accumulated family property and a stronger labor force; but it does not necessarily mean a higher quality of life because individuals have little access to family property and even less power over consumption. To the younger generation of villagers, money was meant to be spent and goods to be consumed. In Xiajia village young people in nuclear households spent more money on food and clothing than their parents and older siblings; they were also more likely than older villagers to follow consumer trends, such as replacing black-and-white TVs with color sets or purchasing motorcycles.

Consumption was probably not an important issue when most rural families were struggling at a subsistence level and when most individual desires had to be held in check. In those conditions, thrift and endurance of hardship were regarded as the highest virtues among the older generation of villagers. From 1978 to 1984, however, peasant net income grew at an enviable annual rate of 17.6 percent, and living standards in rural areas improved considerably. Although the growth of peasant net income slowed in the late 1980s, overall living standards have improved continuously since the late 1970s (Statistics Bureau 1988; Chai 1992; Ma and Sun 1993: 259–52). As a result, consumption has gained new meaning in rural family life, and more and more village youths have begun to define themselves and their quality of life in terms of consumption satisfaction.

The first national wave of mass consumption in China was triggered by the sudden increase in peasant demand for consumer goods in the 1980s (see Chao and Myers 1998; Qiu and Wan 1990). Consumption and lifestyle are particularly significant for the younger villagers who grew up in the 1990s when the party-state worked hand in hand with global capitalism to promote consumerism as the new cultural ideology (Yan 2000). To date most studies have focused on how the rural family as a production unit enabled its members to develop a household economy; few ethnographers, however, have considered how the family as a unit of consumption may affect its constituent members' everyday lives. This is, in my opinion, another blind spot due to the predominance of the corporate model of the Chinese family in contemporary scholarship.

Egotism and the Uncivil Individual

The new legitimacy of personal desires by the 1990s reveals an important feature of the development of individual subjectivity in the private sphere—that is, the felt entitlement to defend one's rights against other individual members of the family and to claim one's share of the family estate. The emphasis on these individual rights is best reflected by requests for lavish bridewealth and dowries and the demand for early family division. The establishment of the separate conjugal unit is key to these requests. Recall the story of one young man who in 1989 encouraged his prospective bride to ask for a large amount of bridewealth from his parents and then used it to establish his conjugal home shortly after their wedding. That young couple was bold and determined in claiming their rights to the family estate, yet they can hardly be seen as autonomous and independent individuals; their ability to establish an independent household was contingent on receiving sufficient financial support from the young man's parents.

Unfortunately, this case represents a common trend in the 1980s and 1990s. When dealing with their parents or parents-in-law in other aspects of family life, such as the use of domestic space and elderly support, young villagers tended to show little respect for the latter's interest while fiercely pursuing their own. The emphases on romantic love and conjugal intimacy both serve the interests of the individual, not that of the family. The development of these self-centered emotions, together with the legitimacy of personal desires, is in conflict with the traditional emphasis on emotional bonding with parents and self-sacrifice for the good of the extended family. Such a tendency to emphasize one's rights while downplaying one's obligations calls into question the extent to which the individual is truly autonomous and independent.

The short answer is that the development of individuality among village youth is incomplete and unbalanced. It is incomplete because most changes are confined to the sphere of private life; it is unbalanced because the emphasis on individual rights is not complemented by equal respect for other individuals and a commitment to civic duty. What has been rapidly developing since the 1980s, in my opinion, is an extreme form of egotism that justifies individual incivility. To understand such an unexpected consequence of the transformation of private life, we must take a closer look at the socialist state, which is, to a great extent, the creator of the freak of the uncivil individual.

The Socialist State and the Paradoxical Transformation of Private Life

Despite vast disagreements regarding the timetable and sequence of family change in the West, most scholars relate the rise of the private family to the formation of a modern society characterized by industrialization, urbanization, internal migration (or a high mobility rate), and a market economy. The classic explanation of this grand narrative of the birth of the modern family and its globalization is provided by William Goode in *World Revolution and Family Patterns* (1963). More recently, in an inspiring study of the link between the making of modern subjectivity and family change in a Spanish village from the 1960s to the 1980s, Jane Collier identifies the shift from an agricultural economy to a market economy, particularly the villagers' participation in a national labor market, as the major cause of change: "When a family's income and lifestyle appeared to depend on the occupational preferences and achievements of its members, a young couple's actions testified to their intentions and emotions" (Collier 1997: 69).

In contrast, Xiajia village, like many other communities in rural northern China, was not, and still is not, directly influenced by either industrialization or urbanization. Instead, many of the family changes resulted from state-sponsored social engineering programs and national policies that aimed at fixing the villagers to their farmland and securing Xiajia as a basic unit of agricultural production in the national economy. This contrasts with the situation in the West where state regulation of family life is usually a consequence of industrialization and urbanization (see, e.g., Goode 1963). As Davis and Harrell correctly note, in China, "state power and policies have been the creators, not the creations, of a transformed society" (1993: 5). It thus is impossible to understand post-1949 China without taking into account the role played by the state.

Debating the Role of the State

Scholarly assessments of the relationship between the Chinese state and the family have developed in several directions. Impressed by the radical social changes in the 1950s, early studies tend to emphasize the active role played by the state in family reform. C. K. Yang commented: "The present urge toward state collectivism calls upon the individual to sacrifice for a group far different from the family; and whatever its ultimate fate under the Communist regime, individualism has already performed the function of alienating the individual from family loyalty" (C. K. Yang 1965: 173).

That assessment was replaced by new findings from empirical research. Parish and Whyte, for instance, were among the first to argue that, except for during the Great Leap Forward (1958–60), the CCP seems to have favored a more traditional family structure, while trying to change the balance of power between senior and junior generations (Parish and Whyte 1978: 131–32). Along the same lines, many scholars in the 1990s generally agree that despite the state's constant threats and attacks, family loyalties and obligations have survived (see essays in Davis and Harrell 1993).

Regarding gender equality, Kay Johnson and Judith Stacey find that the state has been passive in delivering on its promise of family reform. They argue that the "family mode of production" in China prevented the CCP from making good on its promises, and the new marriage law and policies ended up strengthening the traditional values and creating new forms of the patriarchal family (Johnson 1983; Stacey 1983). Although believing in the original sincerity of the Communist revolutionaries to promote gender equality and family change, Margery Wolf similarly emphasizes the failure of both family reform and the feminist revolution (M. Wolf 1985; see also Judd 1994).

The positive role of the state in facilitating family change is reemphasized by Neil Diamant in a counterargument. Criticizing the earlier feminist works for overlooking women's agency and failing to see the complexity of the state at different political and geographic levels, Diamant claims that the 1950 Marriage Law indeed had a profound impact on family dynamics and women's status both initially and throughout the 1950s and 1960s. He argues that those who took full advantage of the liberal components of the state-sponsored family reform were not modern, well-educated urbanites but rather illiterate rural women who had never heard of gender equality (see Diamant 2000).

Taking a more balanced view, Davis and Harrell give more credit to the state for pushing family changes from the 1950s to the 1970s, but they anticipate the reversal of this trend in the postcollective era. They argue that simply because the state was so powerful in the past, "the retreat of the state during the 1980s may have permitted a revival of cultural preferences and economic forces that the Maoist state held in check but did not eliminate" (1993: 6). What Davis and Harrell fail to consider, however, is that the social space opened up by the retreating state has not been filled by the surviving values of traditional culture alone; instead, there are also contesting forces of the market economy, consumerism, and the legacy of radical socialism. The outcome will depend on how ordinary people cope with these forces in the context of the new political economy and public life.

What can the Xiajia case tell us about the role of the socialist state in family change?

There is no doubt that the socialist state played a key role in directly initiating the transformation of private life during the collective period and in indirectly facilitating the continuation of that transformation in the postcollective era. In most cases the state changed the family by changing the local moral world where individual villagers live their lives; a more thorough assessment of the state's role cannot be made unless one understands what the state has done to the local moral world over the past five decades (see Chapter 1 for a detailed account). However, the state is also directly responsible for promoting family change in several ways, especially during the first three decades of radical socialism.

First, state intervention deprived the family of many of its public functions. In prerevolution Xiajia village, as in other parts of rural China, most social activities were organized within the family and kinship networks where power and authority were based on the superiority of the senior generation over the junior generation, the older over the younger, and men over women (see Fei [1947] 1992; Levy 1949; Thornton and Lin 1994; C. K. Yang 1965). The traditional family organized a whole range of social activities, such as socialization, education, and migration, in addition to production and consumption; it is thus incorrect to categorize its multifunctional role in terms of the "family mode of production." To avoid economic determinism, it is better viewed as a "familial mode of social organization" (to follow Thornton and Fricke 1987).

The familial mode of social organization was challenged during land reform when the local CCP branch and its associated organizations replaced kinship-based communal power, and the authority of elder kinsmen was undermined by that of the revolutionary youth. It was then seriously contested when the collectivization campaigns ended family ownership of land and other means of production in the mid-1950s. During the subsequent two and a half decades, agricultural production was organized by the collectives, and individual villagers were assigned tasks by their team leaders instead of by their parents or lineage leaders. Parental authority was further challenged in public life when a gap appeared between the experience and knowledge of older and younger villagers in their encounters with ideological education, political campaigns, and new agricultural machinery, chemical fertilizer, pesticides, and other innovations.

This trend has continued to develop in the postcollective period because household farming did not entirely restore the familial mode of social organization. In agricultural production, although specific farming work is organized within the family, the household economy as a whole is directed by state policy and market demands. Moreover, owing to the diversification of the rural economy and increasing opportunities for outside employment, a large number of villagers engage in nonfarm work in industrial and semi-industrial organizations. The organization of work constitutes only one aspect of the mode of social organization (albeit an important one), and there are many other areas where individual villagers' activities are organized by nonfamilial modes of organization, such as formal education and leisure.

The marriage law and state policies of family reform constitute the second direct cause of the transformation of private life. The 1950 Marriage Law and its 1980 revision legally empowered the young and women in spouse selection and marriage life (see Diamant 2000; Whyte 1992, 1995). It is interesting to note that villagers tended to stress the potential threat of divorce rather than freedom of mate choice to both patriarchal and androcentric powers. In discussions of the impact of the marriage law, many older villagers cited a local saying from the 1950s: "With their status rising, women began to wear new-fashioned pants; they start with romance and end up with divorce" (*funu tigao, chuanku daibao; xiantan lianai, houda badao* [*badao* is the local term for divorce]). Yet the divorce rate remained very low in Xiajia: there were no more than ten divorces in the five decades before 1999. This is because, among other reasons, the threat of divorce itself is often effective in helping women win their rights in family life. Village men were afraid of divorce because of their mobility disadvantage in the local marriage market and the high cost of remarriage. In contrast, because the household registration system gives them greater mobility, divorced women generally do not have difficulty remarrying.

In addition to political campaigns, the state sponsored ideological attacks on patriarchy, male dominance, and familism and implemented strict birth control policies, all of which had a direct impact on the family institution. The traditional system of family values also underwent a secularization process as many community rituals, calendar festivals, folk beliefs, and family ceremonies (including but not limited to ancestor worship) were stripped of their sacredness and meaning by the ideological attacks on superstition and the official attempts to reform local customs (see Jing 1996; and Siu 1989). One recent example in this connection was cremation and burial reform in the early 1990s, which caused serious anxiety and cynicism among villagers (see Anagnost 1997 for discussions on the construction of socialist subjects).

Third, the state privatized the family by first detaching it from the communal structure and then bringing it directly into a modern social system. The state replaced the previous informal power structure based on kinship and community elite with a formal administrative system and the bureaucracy of cadres (see Jing 1996 for an account of this topic). This traditional informal power structure was the "third realm" (P. Huang 1993: 223–26) between the official and the folk, or between the imperial government and peasant families. The third realm was also filled with symbols and meanings, forming a local "cultural influx of power" (Duara 1988) in which family life was deeply embedded. The corporate family dominated the lives of individuals but was subject to the scrutiny and interference of the informal communal power. After the 1949 revolution, the state was able to remove the traditional communal power structure and, through the collectives and local government, reach every peasant household in both public and private life. This led to a twofold result. On the one hand, never before had the family and individuals been exposed to state power and the formal administration system so closely; on the other hand, to a great extent individual villagers were liberated from the control of the corporate family, kinship organization, and other informal communal powers. In other words, the state privatized the family by destroying traditional communal power and created a new social space for individual development by politicizing the family. Here again the Xiajia case constitutes an interesting contrast to cases in the West where the family was privatized mainly through the separation of work from home brought about by industrialization and urbanization.[7]

The State and the Rise of the Individual

It may seem ironic to identify the socialist state as a major contributor to the enrichment of the subjective world of villagers and the rise of the uncivil individual; but the causal relationship becomes clear once we take a closer look at the unintended consequences, rather than at what the state originally intended. Through collectivization and the Great Leap Forward, the state tried to promote collectivism and to shift the loyalty of villagers from the family to the collectives and ultimately to the state. In order to accomplish this goal, it was necessary to destroy the old social and family hierarchy and transform villagers from loyal family members into individual citizens.[8] By promoting loyalty to socialist collectives as opposed to one's family, and by replacing familism with collectivism, the CCP and the state opened up a new social space and created the social conditions necessary for the development of individuality, as in the case of romantic love and spouse selection. The availability and accessibility of social space outside the family and kinship constitute the vital condition for the enrichment of the subjective world and the development of individual identity. This is what Parish and Whyte found in their early study of mate choice in rural southern China (1978: 180). My study shows that this insight applies to other aspects of the rise of the individual as well, which, again, have been largely ignored in most early studies because of the limitations of the corporate family model.

It is doubtful that the CCP leaders wanted to make the villagers into independent individuals in the first place; participation in public life was always strictly controlled by the party-state. The power of rural youth derived by and large from the top-down impact of collectivization, the marriage law, state policies, and political campaigns, rather than from a bottom-up, spontaneous movement in which individuals fought and sacrificed in order to gain their rights. Even when young women were mobilized by the state to participate in production and politics during the heyday of radical socialism, they rarely pursued their own goals and thus did not demonstrate a clear gender perspective in their worldview. As a result, young villagers' pursuit of individual rights in the domestic sphere was not always accompanied by an equal effort to gain autonomy and independence in the public sphere.

Since the early 1980s the socialist state has gradually loosened its control over ordinary people's private lives and has focused on the most critical areas of the economy and politics (see Walder 1995). Consequently, values of the market economy, the mode of commodity production, and globalizing consumerism have become new dominating forces of family change in particular and of social change in general, which makes the Chinese case more like its counterparts in the West. Nevertheless, the state remains powerful in some aspects of villagers' private lives, such as birth control and marriage.[9] The birth control policy has been reshaping both the family ideal and various practices throughout the postcollective era, ranging from childbearing, property management, and the conjugal relationship to elderly support. It is therefore premature to ignore the continuing influence of the state on people's private lives in the contemporary context of market-oriented reforms.

Moreover, precisely because of the state's intrusive influence in everyday life during the collective period, its retreat in the postcollective era has produced an equally strong yet perhaps more negative impact on the private lives of individual villagers—that is, the development of the ultra-utilitarian individualism in a unique context where the survival of traditional culture, the legacy of radical socialism, and global capitalism are competing with each other.

Although generations of youth were encouraged by the state to fight against patriarchal power and traditional values in private life during the collective period, they did not have much true autonomy and independence in public life, where individualism and self-organization by the masses were not allowed. Instead, under collectivization and the household registration system, villagers fell into "organized dependence" (Walder 1986; see also Oi 1989), in which they had to depend on the collectives and the cadres to meet their everyday needs. During the collective period, all public activities were sponsored and organized by the collectives, and the new sociality invariably bore the imprint of the official ideology of the socialist state, emphasizing the submission of individuals to an officially endorsed collectivity. Accordingly, a socialist morality was promoted through various political campaigns, which started as a powerful critique of the traditional paradigm for moral discourse and soon established itself as a radical Maoist paradigm of ethics (see Madsen 1984, esp. chaps. 3 and 4).

The socialist morality quickly collapsed after the collectives were dismantled and the state withdrew from many aspects of social life. With neither traditional values nor socialist morality, villagers faced a moral and ideological vacuum in the postcollective era. It is in that special historical context that the villagers, along with their involvement in commodity production and the market, quickly embraced the values of late capitalism characterized by a globalizing consumerism, which emphasizes the "I deserve . . . " perspective and the legitimacy of personal desires (for its impact on the popular culture in China, see Gold 1993). The demand for individual rights and personal desires thus prevails and even threatens the fragments of the traditional culture that survived radical socialism, such as *renqing* ethics (see Chapter 1 for the instrumentalization of *guanxi* and *renqing*).

The increasing flow of information and people since the 1980s causes another unexpected consequence. Villagers, particularly young men and women, have been exposed to the proliferation of modern life images projected by television and other mass media, and many have worked in cities. The rapid expansion of their imaginary world raises their life aspirations and sometimes creates a sense of helplessness because the modern lifestyles from Hong Kong or Shanghai are so desirable yet unattainable. This also explains why so many young villagers ruthlessly extract money from their parents for the "modernization" of their own private lives.

There has not been any countermechanism to balance this ego-centered consumerism. If there were autonomous societal organizations and if villagers were able to participate in public life, a more balanced individualism might have developed, in which the individual obligations to the public and to other people could be emphasized as well. But just the opposite has happened. Beginning in the 1980s, public life declined, social order deteriorated, and the village community disintegrated. Local government and village cadres became increasingly predatory and exploitive in order to extract more and more resources from the villagers to support the ever-expanding bureaucratic system and meet their own personal desires. To make the situation even worse, the state remained hostile to any organized societal forces even after it withdrew its political and economic support of public life at the local level. Having been excluded from political participation and public life, villagers were forced to retreat to their private homes and have grown increasingly cynical about any moral discourse. As a result, their sense of duty and obligation to the community and to other people as equal individuals continue to shrink in both the public and private spheres.

The rise of the individual that I describe throughout this book is a combined result of the socialist engineering of the local moral world during the collective period and the powerful impact of commodity production and consumerism on the community in the postcollective era. During both periods the party-state played a critical role in initiating or causing the changes, albeit in different ways and for different purposes. The transformation of private life in Xiajia village has manifested itself as a paradoxical process with three features: (1) the socialist state is the ultimate creator of a series of family changes and of the growth of individuality; (2) as the state became less intrusive in the postcollective era, the blossoming of private life paralleled the decline of public life caused by the destruction of local societal forces; and (3) the development of individual identity and subjectivity has been confined mostly to the private sphere and has evolved into a kind of egotism. Consequently, the individual feels fewer obligations and duties toward the community and other individuals and thus has lost much of his or her civility.

Given that the socialist state remains hostile to independent societal forces and autonomous actions in the public sphere, the disjunction between the public and the private is likely to continue, as is the imbalance between civil duties and self-interest in the growth of the individual. The transformation of private life under socialism, therefore, appears to be a mixed blessing for the villagers in Xiajia. And if one views the Xiajia case as a Chinese alternative to the Western pattern of individual development and the modernization of the family, one can clearly see that there are still many more critical issues and significant implications waiting to be explored.

Character List

ai	爱
airen	爱人
bai yang le	白养了
banpei	般配
beikang	北炕
buheli	不合理
buhui shuohua	不会说话
bu yao huxiang shang ganqing	不要互相伤感情
bu zhi de	不值得
caili	彩礼
chaoshenghu	超生户
chengbao tian	承包田
chuanmenzi	串门子
cunfeng	村风
dadao de laopo, roudao de mian	打倒的老婆，揉倒的面
dajian	大件
dayuantao	大院套
danguo	单过
dangjia	当家
delong	得龙
dongwu	东屋
duancha songshui	端茶送水
dui piqi	对脾气
duixian	对象
duozi duofu	多子多福

duozi duochou	多子多愁
enqing	恩情
erpihua	二屁话
erxifu yi jin men, fuquan jiu bei dadao	儿媳妇一进门，父权就被打倒
falungong	法轮功
fa pa le	罚怕了
fangbian	方便
fenjia	分家
fengjian	封建
fengliu	风流
fengliu hua	风流话
fumu baoban	父母包办
fumuxin	父母心
fumu zhi en	父母之恩
fumu zhi ming, meishuo zhi yan	父母之命，媒妁之言
funu tigao, chuangku daibao, xiangtan lianai, houda badao	妇女提高，穿裤带包，先谈恋爱，后打八刀
fushi	服侍
ganqing	感情
ganqing hao	感情好
ganzhe	干折
geming duixiang	革命对象
gen	跟
gen erzi guo	跟儿子过
gongtong yuyan	共同语言
guanxi	关系
guiju	规矩
heli	合理
huishuohua	会说话
huokang	火炕
jihua shengyu	计划生育
jishenghu	计生户
jia	家
jiaji suiji, jiagou suigou, jiagei biandan tiao zhe zou	嫁鸡随鸡，嫁狗随狗，嫁给扁担挑着走

jia nai zhousi fuyu zhi hexie zhengti;	家乃宙斯赋予之和谐整体;
yun tianlun zhile, nai xinfu zhi	蕴天伦之乐，乃幸福之源泉，
yuanquan, wennuan zhi xiangzheng	温暖之象征
jiawushi	家务事
jiantang weiyao	煎汤喂药
jiaoyou	教友
jieshao duixiang	介绍对象
jin	金
jing	晶
jingshen chuhu	净身出户
jueyu	绝育
kaidan	开单
kang	炕
kangtou	炕头
keting	客厅
koulian tian	口粮田
ku	库
laoshi	老实
laoshiren	老实人
liang ge ziyou	两个自由
liangtoutiao	两头挑
linghuaqian	零花钱
majiazi	马架子
mai dongxi qian	买东西钱
man	满
meiyou fengdu	没有风度
mianzi	面子
mu	亩
nankang	南炕
nannu pingdeng	男女平等
neiren	内人
nengren	能人
nengzheng huihua	能挣会花
pan	盼
pojia	婆家

qi	气
qidao dian	祈祷点
qiguanyan	妻管严 (气管炎)
qijia buzhi bajia shi	七家不知八家事
qiao	劁
qingming	清明
rizi zong shi ziji guozhe shunxin	日子总是自己过着顺心
renqing	人情
shenqin	神亲
shengmi zhu cheng shufan	生米煮成熟饭
shunxin	顺心
shuo le suan	说了算
shuo xifu	说媳妇
sifangqian	私房钱
siheyuan	四合院
sishi	私事
songzhong	送终
sui daliu	随大流
ting	厅
tongxinglian	同性恋
tunqin	屯亲
waiwu	外屋
wan, xi, shao	晚稀少
wenleng wenre	问冷问热
wo ai ta	我爱他
wuyuexian	五月鲜
xifu	媳妇
xiwu	西屋
xiaguan bieren de sishi	瞎管别人的私事
xiaxiang	下乡
xianyou houjia	先有后嫁
xiang gansha jiu gansha	想干啥就干啥
xiaobailian	小白脸
xiaojing	孝敬
xiaoshun	孝顺

yatou xiaozi bu zhongyao,	丫头小子不重要,
guanjian shi xiaoshun	关键是孝顺
yang	阳
yang	养
yangbuqi	养不起
yang er fang lao	养儿防老
yanglao	养老
yangyu zhien	养育之恩
yao	窑
yaokang	腰炕
yiwanshui yao duangping	一碗水要端平
yin	银
yinsi	隐私
you fengdu	有风度
you huashuo	有话说
youli youwai	有里有外
yuqin kuzong	欲擒故纵
yuzhou	宇宙
yuanzi	园子
yueqiong yuesheng,	越穷越生,
yuesheng yueqiong	越生越穷
zeou	择偶
zijiaren bu neng suan tai qing	自家人不能算太清
ziliudi	自留地
ziyou	自由
ziyou duixiang	自由对象
zhao duixiang	找对象
zhao dinghun xiang	照订婚像
zhaogu	照顾
zhaogu bu guolai	照顾不过来
zhao pojia	找婆家
zhuang yan qian	装烟钱

Notes

1. In Chinese it reads: "*Jia nai zhousi fuyu zhi hexie zhengti; yun tianlun zhile, nai xinfu zhi yuanquan, wennuan zhi xiangzheng.*" In his usual understated way, Mr. Hu once told me that he had learned these expressions from other sources; but it was his idea to use them to describe the family. Because the word *zhousi* is the Chinese translation of the god Zeus in ancient Greek mythology, I asked Mr. Hu how he came up with the idea that the family was created by a Greek deity. He was surprised to learn the meaning of the word *zhousi* and told me that he misunderstood it to be the same as *yuzhou*, which means the "universe." Hence I translated the second half of the first sentence as "created by the universe."

2. The family is complex in both structure and economic management. The main breadwinners were Mr. Hu's wife, who had taught at the village school since the early 1960s, and his eldest son, who co-owned the village shop. The eldest son and his wife were responsible for taking care of the family's land as well as the shop. The daughter studied at an occupational school about six hundred kilometers away from home and depended on parental support. Mr. Hu's second son was a low-ranking army officer stationed in another province who could barely support himself. The wife of the second son spent almost equal amounts of time living (and working) in three places: with her natal family, at her husband's military station, and in Mr. Hu's house; but she regarded the latter as her family home, where she had a permanent room and was registered as an official household member. The only person who did not have a steady income or major responsibility for household chores was Mr. Hu, the household head, who nevertheless was respected by his adult children and was in charge of the household finances. Here we see an interesting case of a dispersed family economy and organization based on a common estate (see Cohen 1976). However, Mr. Hu's joint family dissolved into a stem family in the middle of the 1990s after his daughter married out and his second son returned from the army and obtained a factory job in the town seat, moving his own conjugal unit out of the old house.

3. See, e.g., Baker 1979; Freedman 1966; Gallin 1966; Harrell 1982; Pasternak 1972; R. Watson 1985a; Wolf and Huang 1980. C. K. Yang (1959) offers perhaps the most comprehensive account of the impact of the Communist revolution on rural families in the early 1950s.

4. The other side of the coin is that the Chinese family itself has been changing (see Parish and Whyte 1978; Whyte 1995; Yan 1997), and with this change, the private lives of individual members within the family have undergone a process of transformation.

5. There is a close link between the corporate model of the Chinese family and the structural-functional theory of family change in Western social science, developed mainly by Talcott Parsons and William Goode (see Cheal 1991: 4–7). This theory assumes that any major social institution must ensure the well-being not only of individuals, but also of the society upon which those individuals depend. Families are believed to perform essential functions for family members and for society as a whole. The fit between family and society, therefore, remains the central issue in discussions of family change and social development. The most noteworthy example of this is Goode's hypothesis that industrialization and urbanization lead to a shift from an extended family system to a conjugal family system (1963, 1982). Perhaps the most systematic study of the human family and its variations across cultural and ethnic boundaries is Harrell 1997.

6. Studies of urban families tend to be more individual-oriented than those of rural families; see, e.g., Davis-Friedmann 1991; Ikels 1996; Jankowiak 1993.

7. For detailed documentation and discussions of this transformation of the family, see especially the chapters in volume 3 of *A History of Private Life: Passions of the Renaissance*, edited by Roger Chartier (Ariès and Duby 1989).

8. As Martin Whyte points out, many of the changes in rural family life did not begin with the economic reforms, so we should not regard the collective and post-collective periods as representing a sharp contrast in family life (1992: 320). This is why the present study aims to address both continuity and change in the family institution and private life across the two periods.

9. Here, one may compare Kleinman's dichotomy of ethical discourse and moral experience with P. Bourdieu's distinction between official kinship and practical kinship. According to Bourdieu, the former refers to the abstraction of norms, rules, and regulations of kin groups and the latter refers to the transformation of such an abstraction into strategies of practice by active agents in everyday life. While the function of official kinship is to order the social world and to legitimate that order, practical kinship is used by individual agents to achieve social goals in everyday life (1977: 33–38; 1990: 166–87).

10. It is easy to understand that informants are reluctant to reveal confidential information regarding, say, income or savings, or "face-losing" matters such as family conflicts. But sometimes villagers and scholars see things differently (which is frequently when the most rewarding data are revealed). The issue of gender equality (locally called *nannu pingdeng*, literally the equality between men and women) serves

as a good example in this connection. Almost without exception, village women agreed that men should take on more responsibilities in dealing with public affairs, although in actuality many women were actively involved in public life. Moreover, few women wanted to admit that they exercised more power in the family than their husbands, despite the fact that many actually did. All these examples relate to concern about the man's face, which, arguably, is a residual of the traditional family ideology. So, during the initial interview with a couple, for instance, it was common for the wife to claim that she was a submissive woman, always listening to her husband, while her husband sitting at her side would not make any comment. But if a crosscheck with her neighbors and relatives revealed the opposite, I brought the issue up again when interviewing the woman the second or third time. In our discussions of specific family anecdotes and events, such as a spousal quarrel or a recent family ceremony, she would begin to tell me what decisions she made and why she wanted things to be done her way. I encountered this pattern many times during multiple fieldwork visits. Experience has taught me that a really submissive wife does not feel at ease talking about gender issues with an interviewer in the first place. The same holds true for men. Usually only those men who were regarded as powerful and decisive at home felt free to declare that their wives were in charge at home. In initial interviews I thus took their claims with a grain of salt and then double-checked their validity through an indirect channel. Then I revisited these informants after days, months, or even years, and more often than not, we discussed the same topics from a new perspective.

11. According to Russell Bernard, that informants sometimes lie about certain things is just part of the practice of fieldwork (Bernard 1994: 168–69). The interesting question is, when and why do informants lie?

12. A related issue here is how to look at change. Strictly speaking, change and continuity are not separable; there is no social institution that can change from A to B without any remaining link between the two. In other words, at any moment in the process of change, there are always elements that remain unchanged. In many cases what is emphasized depends on the observer's perspective. In my case study, I tend to focus on new developments. I also acknowledge the remnants of the traditional family, such as the structural form of the stem family, the male-only inheritance pattern, and the absence of romantic love in many cases of spouse selection. But overall, I pay more attention to what has changed and what is changing, because they represent the current dynamics and possible directions of future developments.

CHAPTER 1

1. As an administrative unit, Xiajia also officially incorporates a neighboring community of approximately 400 people. My research, however, is confined to the core community of Xiajia.

2. During land reform, nine landlords and six rich peasants were identified in Xiajia. Such land concentration was a social phenomenon commonly found in northeastern China. After the 1911 revolution, the formally Manchu and imperial land was sold at low prices to powerful local elites and officials.

3. C. K. Yang's *A Chinese Village in Early Communist Transition* (C. K. Yang 1965) is perhaps the best ethnographic account of land reform in a village setting. See also relevant chapters in Friedman, Pickowicz, and Selden 1991; Hinton 1966; Potter and Potter 1990; and Siu 1989. For a detailed explanation of the system of class labels, see Kraus 1977 and Unger 1984. These class labels were officially abolished in 1979 when the economic reforms were launched nationwide.

4. The term "thought work" can refer to many means of controlling people, from personal persuasion, informal interrogations, and study workshops to public, often violent, struggle.

5. Madsen classifies rural cadres into four types in accordance with their moral character: the Communist gentry, the Communist rebel, the moralistic revolutionary, and the pragmatic technocrat (1984: 243–57).

6. The transformation of local government and village leadership in the postcollective era appears to be path-dependent; that is, it depends on conditions that favor economic development, such as the legacy of collective enterprises, the availability of overseas investments, transportation links, and entrepreneurial traditions. In localities where one or more favorable conditions exist, local government tends to be corporatist and developmental, actively involved in the local economy, and cadres either hold strong positions in local enterprises or form a symbiotic relationship with private entrepreneurs (see Blecher 1991; Chan, Madsen, and Unger 1992; Oi 1998; Pieke 1998; Ruf 1998; Wank 1995).

7. For a systematic review of changes in state capacities both centrally and locally, see Baum and Shevchenko 1999: 351–60.

8. The reach of the state remains an unresolved topic among China scholars, deriving from an earlier debate between Vivienne Shue (1988) and Jonathan Unger (1989).

9. Xiajia is by no means unique with respect to the practice of village endogamy. My surveys in Shandong and Hebei provinces show that in many multi-surname communities marriage within the village was considered an advantage for the bride and her natal family. As in Xiajia, the number of intravillage marriages increased during the collective era. These findings echo earlier observations in Guangdong province, where not only village endogamy but also intralineage marriages began to emerge after 1949. According to Parish and Whyte, "Marriage to people of the same village and lineage clearly increased through the mid-1960s, although there may have been a slight reversal of this trend recently" (1978: 171). In their view, these changes were due to the reduced importance of lineage organizations and the rise in personal selection of one's spouse (1978: 170–72). Potter and Potter (1990) report on the breakdown of the taboo against same-surname marriages in single-lineage villages in Guangdong province during the collective era. A similar "marriage revolution" is discussed by Chan, Madsen,

and Unger (1992) in their village study. They find that "within just a few years, as it became evident that having a daughter close at hand promised an extra measure of security for old age, marriage within Chen Village became the *preferred* match, involving some 70–80 percent of the total" (p. 191).

10. According to my 1991 survey, 126 men in Xiajia had chosen wives from within the village (accounting for 35 percent of the household total of 365), of which 102 were married after the 1949 Revolution. These 126 men were connected, by direct affinal ties, to 102 other male household heads, who were either their fathers-in-law or brothers-in-law. Thus the total number of households connected by affinal ties was 228, or 62 percent of the total households in Xiajia.

11. Elsewhere I explore the fluid and flexible nature of kinship as reflected in the lived experiences of individual villagers and examine some features of current kinship practice in Xiajia village, including the elasticity of kinship distance, the uncertainty of kinship alliance, the active role played by women in network building, and the shift in emphasis from cross-generation links to same-generation connections (see Yan 2001).

12. In a given guanxi network, the immediate family and closest agnates and affines constitute a "core zone" of social connections; good friends and less close relatives who can always be counted on for help form a larger "reliable zone"; and finally, an "effective zone" that embraces a large number of distant relatives and friends in a broader sense (see Yan 1996: 98–102; see also Kipnis 1997).

13. My inquiry into guanxi networks began with a collection of villagers' gift lists. In Xiajia village, as in most rural communities in China and some other East Asian societies as well, for each major family ceremony they host, villagers compile a gift list—a document that records the names of the gift-givers as well as a description of all gifts received. Families carefully keep these gift lists and use them for future reference when reciprocal gifts need to be offered. From a researcher's point of view, a gift list may serve as a repository of data on the changing nature of interpersonal relations and as a social map that vividly displays guanxi networks. In my 1991 fieldwork I collected forty-three gift lists based on a stratified selection of households and added to them a computer database containing a total of 5,286 individual gift transactions (for more details about gift lists, see Yan 1996: 49–52).

14. Relatives constituted 37 percent of the donors in villagers' gift-giving networks; by contrast, nonkin, who include fellow villagers, friends, and colleagues, constituted 62 percent of the donors. Within the system of kinship ties, affines constituted 21 percent and agnates only 9 percent (Yan 1996: 112–14).

CHAPTER 2

1. The first step, however, was to alter their birth dates in the official household register, a practice that involves offering expensive gifts or money to the local official in charge.

2. See the works by Beach and Tesser, Chu, and Hsu cited in Jankowiak 1995b: 166.

3. The urban situation is somewhat different. Extramarital affairs have gained more publicity and tolerance in recent years, and some trendy young people date and live together for several years without a clear goal of marriage. See, e.g., Li Yinhe 1998: 47–69, 251–77; Xu 1997: 217–63.

4. The term can be used to refer to an "object," when combined with a modifier, such as in *geming duixiang* (the object of revolution). But it always refers to the beloved other when it stands alone.

5. I used documentary data to track the marriages and then gathered ethnographic data on them through personal and group interviews. Documents included the 1982 and 1990 census, village household registers, and records of population control in 1999. It is impossible to gather complete information about marriages of Xiajia women, because there is no written record of female marriages; and when a young woman marries out of the village her household register is transferred to her husband's village.

6. As suggested by my informants, I skipped the years 1959 through 1961 in my survey because it was the period of famine, when the top priority for all villagers was the search for food, not for romance or a spouse.

7. In an excellent analysis of romantic love and cross-cousin marriage, De Munck argues that the dichotomy between romantic love and arranged marriage prevented scholars from understanding the richness and complexity of the emotional world of villagers. By showing that more than 70 percent of the cross-cousin marriages arranged by parents actually involved romantic love beforehand, De Munck maintains that "contrary to conventional wisdom, romantic love does play a significant role in a community where parents officially select an offspring's mate" (1996: 711).

CHAPTER 3

1. In his provocative study of divorce and family change in China, Neil Diamant finds that rural women are more active and efficient than their urban counterparts in taking advantage of the new marriage law to seek divorce and freedom of mate choice. A major reason, argues Diamant, is "a culture of openness about sexuality and sex-related problems that allowed peasants to divulge domestic problems to state authorities in a frank and feisty fashion (2000: 12). He also notes that the contrast between an open peasant sexual culture and a conservative elite sexual culture exists not only in China, but also in France, Russia, Turkey, and Japan (Diamant 2000: 79–80, 172–76, 197–98).

2. To illustrate the point, let me cite one anecdote from my personal experience. I worked as a shepherd in a village in Shandong province from 1968 to 1971, and during this period I was very close to Uncle Liu, an elderly shepherd from the neigh-

boring production team who taught me a great deal about local culture and life. We always mixed our herds together in the fields and chatted while watching the sheep grazing. One day (in 1969 or 1970) Uncle Liu asked me: "Do you know what Chairman Mao did last night?" I had no idea and asked him back: "What did he do?" "Oh, he was riding on top of Jiang Qing [Mao's wife] and fucking her really hard. All of a sudden, Chairman Mao stopped pounding and talked to himself: 'I wonder how our troops are doing in Vietnam; hope they beat the Americans again.'" Uncle Liu then burst into loud laughter, enjoying his joke and my confused reaction immensely (as a 15-year-old, I could not fully understand the joke and asked Uncle Liu why Chairman Mao had to stop). Years later, the more I learned about Maoist radicalism during that period, the more I appreciated Uncle Liu's courage and common-sense insights; he was able to see Mao Zedong as a man with human desires at a time when he was worshipped as a deity by most (if not all) elite and educated people in China. But Uncle Liu obviously did not (and could not) know that by the late 1960s Mao had long stopped having sexual relations with his wife and was probably busy with several other women (see Li Zhisui 1994).

3. Although I learned of some interesting extramarital affairs, I decided not to write about them in order to protect the privacy of the villagers. Another important yet highly sensitive topic is homosexuality. The only case in Xiajia that I am aware of involved two women, whose relationship some villagers identified as a living example of *tongxinglian* (homosexual love).

Born in 1949 and 1950 respectively, these two women grew up together as best friends and worked in the same production team for many years. They rejected all their marriage proposals and swore loyalty to each other. For nearly ten years they shared a room in the younger woman's (or, as they prefer, the younger sister's) brother's house. Because both of them had worked in the collective before, and after decollectivization had engaged in small family sidelines, they could financially support themselves. In 1996 the younger gay woman went to visit a relative in southern China; after seven months' separation, the older gay woman died of a cerebral hemorrhage. Many villagers believe, however, that the woman died simply because she missed her "younger sister" too much.

The folk explanation might have some basis in truth because, as the deceased woman's own sister told me, after the younger woman had been gone more than three months, the elder sister began to lose weight and did not sleep for several days before her sudden death. In response to my question whether she thought the relationship between these two women was special, the deceased woman's younger sister answered: "Sure, they are *toxinglian* [homosexual]." I was stunned by her candid answer. She then described in detail the everyday life of the two women, such as how they openly and frequently hugged and kissed each other. She also showed me photos of her elder sister's funeral and the beautiful tomb that she had built for her sister. She told me that she planned to bury the two women together when the younger woman died, which was her late sister's last wish.

4. According to a large-scale survey in 1989–90, 75 percent of the sampled college students viewed premarital sex positively, but 79 percent of the married urban and rural couples in the same sample pool disapproved of premarital sex (Liu Dalin 1995: 305). In another study in the late 1980s, Xiao Zhou reports a rapid increase of premarital sex: "In my sample, 87 percent (n = 100) of urban working women and 11 percent (n = 100) of rural women had had premarital sexual intercourse" (Zhou 1989: 283). This trend, as might be expected, continued in the 1990s, as my study of the Xiajia villagers shows.

5. This development of sexuality within the framework of engagement is quite similar to what David Schak found in Taiwan during the late 1960s and early 1970s (see Schak 1974).

6. There is a humorous side to this tale of the muskmelon. A melon picked up in a cornfield during an autumn harvest has only one possible origin—it has grown out from human excrement, a byproduct of melon consumption during the summertime. Although melon seeds growing out of human excrement is not uncommon, the chances that they will survive and eventually produce edible fruit are very small. This is why my informants found this story so interesting and funny.

7. The formerly negative connotation of the word, however, is still used in everyday life. For instance, a person involved in an extramarital affair is also regarded as being fengliu.

8. Studies of urban China are more positive in this respect, because scholars at least recognize the existence of romantic love among urban youth; see, e.g., William Jankowiak's pioneering work in a northern city (1993, 1995). But as yet there has been no systematic investigation of the subject.

9. It is doubtful that such a unified American way of expressing love exists, except in Hollywood movies. As Vincent Crapanzano notes: "We know for example that American middle class wives like their husbands to tell them that they love them and that American husbands find it difficult, impossible even, to say, 'I love you'" (1989: 78). In an influential study on love and gender in American society, Francesca Cancian points out that, along with the transformation of an agrarian to capitalist economy, a gender-based split developed whereby women were supposed to specialize in love and caring and men in work and self-development. She calls the process "the feminization of love" (see Cancian 1987: 15–65).

10. Kevin Birth and Morris Freilich describe a transformation of a sexual exchange system into a romantic love exchange system in east Trinidad over a period of thirty years. They attribute the cause of change to both the increased gender equality fostered by economic development and the influence of American media presentations of romance (Birth and Freilich 1995: 270–74).

11. In this connection, a passage from the Kleinmans is particularly illuminating: "There is also a panhuman constraint on the continuities and transformations that represent our lives and our networks which derives from the limited number of social ways of being human. Because of the political economy of experience, that pan-

human constraint is itself twisted and turned by the local contexts of pressure that encourage or oppress our aspirations, that defeat us, that defend us, that are us" (Kleinman and Kleinman 1991: 293).

12. This emergence of what I call "girl power," however, does not suggest that women in general have a stronger sense of agency than men; young women may, as claimed by the villagers themselves, enjoy a better position in the marriage market. I address this in more detail in the concluding chapter.

13. See, in particular, two important collections of essays: Jankowiak 1995; and Lynch 1990; see also Rebhun's 1999 book on love and conjugal relationships in Brazil; and Trawick's 1990 ethnography on love and emotionality in an Indian family.

14. According to Goode, the antithesis of romantic love is conjugal love, "the love between a settled, domestic couple" (1959: 39). Some argue that "the association of trust with love is basic to our distinction between conjugal and romantic love" (Driscoll, Davis, and Lipetz 1972: 3).

CHAPTER 4

1. These figures do not include the population of a small neighboring village that officially has been part of the Xiajia administrative system since the 1950s. Moreover, some of the out-migrating families still maintain their household registration in Xiajia village, and others moved in and out of the village more than once. Exact numbers are therefore difficult to calculate.

2. Household net income alone is not an accurate measure of a rural family's economic position because villagers need capital to invest in agricultural production. In my survey I used both household income and family assets to measure the economic position of a family. The second measurement includes primary tools of production, farm machinery and/or draft animals, and capital for family sidelines such as dairy cows, private enterprises, housing, savings, and consumer durables. For a more detailed account, see Yan 1992: 8–14. My first survey on household economic positions in 1989 has been updated three times, in 1991, 1994, and 1998.

3. I did not distribute questionnaires on these subjects because past experience teaches me that villagers usually do not respond well to formal surveys. As I learned from a survey on gift-giving behavior, many villagers worry about providing "correct" answers because they regard the survey as a sort of test. In addition, many men find it difficult to admit that gender relationships are changing in their own families, and women tend to provide an "ought-to-be" answer when being surveyed. Thus I have found that the results are more accurate and the villagers more objective when asked in person to evaluate their neighbors. A selection of knowledgeable and objective informants is of course one key to the success of this kind of group interview. Finally, if the questions are not too sensitive, villagers tend to be enthusiastic and argue with one another about their differences of opinion. These arguments allow an ethnographer

to extract much additional information and still gather the data he or she wants to collect. Admittedly, information gathered in such a way does not have much statistical significance; it merely provides a rough model from the villagers' perspective.

4. Although Uncle Lu sounds like a diehard patriarchal tyrant, he actually had a very good relationship with his wife. But for the previous two decades the old man had been fighting with his seven sons, all of whom moved out of his house shortly after they married. I was told that this painful defeat in dealing with his married sons made Uncle Lu such an angry old man.

5. Depending on the senior male's age, health, and personality, in the past there were always some stem families headed by a married son instead of the father. But this number was quite small.

6. A similar pattern has been found among families in Taiwan; see Gallin and Gallin 1982: 148–50; Thornton and Lin 1994.

CHAPTER 5

1. According to a well-known story that sounds very much like a Western movie plot, bandits once surrounded the village and tried to make their way into the Wang compound. One of the Wang men who was brave and a good shot became involved in a one-on-one fight with the bandit leader. During the exchange of fire, he fooled the bandit by using a hat to disguise his position in one of the embrasures and then shot the bandit leader to death.

2. This was primarily a male perspective, because village women never had a problem marrying before the 1949 revolution; neither could they have their own house because they married out of the family.

3. Beginning in the 1970s, however, more and more young couples insisted on living in a separate room after their wedding, usually the west room of the house; this arrangement created a need for more heating energy (crop stems, dry grasses, and other materials that could be burned) during the winter and thus for a separate storage shack outside the house.

4. Interestingly, in the cave dwellings (*yao*) in rural Shaanxi, the inner space of a house is divided into two halves, signified by the huge heated bed and the table or tables opposite the bed. The bed is occupied primarily by women, symbolizing femininity and family intimacy, while the table is used by men as a place for public interactions (see X. Liu 2000: 45–47).

5. The family toilet is always outside the house, usually in a remote corner of the courtyard. This too has changed since the 1980s. Earlier, families used a corral for elimination, which was typically located at one end of the house—outside, of course. The entryway was not blocked or covered, and excretions were left for the pigs. When I used this kind of open-air corral-toilet during the 1970s I always carried a stick big enough to scare away the family pig(s), and to make loud noises when I

heard someone approaching. When I returned to Xiajia for my first fieldwork in 1989, I was surprised to find that my landlord had built a pit toilet, which was at the front left corner of the courtyard, fully walled and roofed, with a door that could be locked from the inside. My landlord proudly told me that his toilet was a model for others, as I was to confirm later on. Some older villagers, however, complained that the new-style toilet smelled terrible.

6. There is no space here for me to discuss the notions of personal image and hygiene among the village youth in the 1990s. Suffice it to say that, unlike their parents and older siblings, young villagers of both sexes were conscious of their personal appearance and the importance of hygiene, spending much more time and resources to keep themselves neat and clean. To praise his wife, a husband showed me how clean his shirt collar was; he then told me that his wife would not allow him to wear a shirt for more than three days even if he did not do any physical labor (this is, admittedly, not a high standard from a contemporary American perspective). An old woman said she simply could not understand why her grandson, a young man, spent so much time in front of the mirror, and why he wore good clothing and leather shoes even to herd the cows in the fields.

7. When my family was sent by the Red Guards from Beijing to my father's natal village in Shandong province in 1966, my father was able to reclaim the plot of land on which his parents' house had stood even after being gone for more than twenty years. The house had been demolished much earlier, and a close relative had farmed the plot when no one from my father's family lived in the village. We lived in another relative's empty house and grew vegetables and sunflowers (for the seeds) on our own house plot. In 1979 my father was given back his old job in a factory in Beijing; he sold the house plot to a neighbor before moving the family out of the village again. All this took place during the collective period, and no one challenged the transactions, even though they involved a person with a bad class label. It should also be noted that a major difference between the Shandong village and Xiajia village is the size of the house plot—people in Xiajia enjoyed much larger plots because farmland in Heilongjiang province was so plentiful.

8. Private plot land (ziliudi) was allocated by the collectives to its members, which included a private lot on a per capita basis and "fodder land" based on the number of pigs a family was raising. It was farmed in a household mode of production. In Xiajia each person could receive one-fifth to one-fourth mu of a private plot, and they used the land to grow crops and pig feed for family consumption. But unlike the house plots, the private plot land was frequently reallocated in accordance with the changes in local population, which was also a reminder of the collective owner of the so-called private plot land. During radical periods of socialism, policy was altered several times, and the collectives stopped reallocating private plot land for two years. For more detailed accounts of the policies toward private plot land and actual practice in rural Guangdong, see Parish and Whyte 1978: 118–21; Potter and Potter 1990: 109–12.

9. One family I know very well maintained an additional path through their back garden so that they could reach both the front and back streets from their house. Their neighbors, however, also used this private path; people (including me) entered through the front door of the house, walked through the kitchen while casually greeting whoever was at home, exited through the back door, and went through the back garden to reach the other street.

10. In a Shandong village where the collectives still held a great deal of power in the late 1980s, special effort was made to prevent the relatively well-off families from building larger houses to display their wealth (see Kipnis 1997: 12).

11. Interestingly, when a family has a married son living in the same house, the young couple's bedroom is regarded as more private than that of the parents. During my household survey I was sometimes invited to the parents' bedroom, but never to the bedroom of the married son unless I specifically asked to look at the newlyweds' room.

12. When I lived in the village during the 1970s, on several occasions I heard that parents, usually the mother, reminded the married son and his wife not to exhaust themselves (meaning not to indulge in too much sex) during the night; the evidence that prompted such a reminder was the nightly noise coming from behind the hanging curtain.

13. Until recently adult villagers (men and women) did not wear shorts in public in Xiajia village and the surrounding areas. This local custom, however, began to change in the late 1980s, when village youth began to copy urban fashions.

14. Unlike in rural Heilongjiang, villagers in Hebei and Shandong provinces have long lived in multiroom houses. The separation of the bedrooms from the living room, however, is similarly a recent phenomenon.

15. The seating pattern extended to public life too. During the collective period, mass meetings were held in the headquarters of the production teams, which was built much like the family house except that the heated beds were much bigger. Senior men usually sat on the heated bed near the center, close to the team leaders; the younger members were scattered around the room, and girls typically formed a small group in a corner. When a young man mistakenly took a place reserved for senior people, he was immediately corrected by a fellow villager.

16. Liu Xin notes that in a village in Shaanxi province: "While eating, men are supposed to sit down at the table and not move from their seats; women are supposed to move around the bed, looking after the children and passing the food to the male members of the family" (2000: 46).

17. The issue of privacy has attracted the attention of scholars and the mass media. In scholarly discourse, the protection of privacy is regarded as one of the core elements of private rights (see Liu Zuoxiang 1996). That the mass media focus mostly on legal cases of privacy violation reflects the rising awareness of privacy among urban residents. In the first lawsuits that occurred in 1990, two urban residents sued a novelist for writing a story about their private lives; they won their cases and were awarded 180 yuan and 120 yuan respectively (Li Jun 1999: 8). Interestingly, by the end of the 1990s, while more sensitive about their own privacy, urban residents

seemed to gain a new interest in learning about other people's private lives, which resulted in a hot market for books on the subject of privacy. The following titles were among the bestsellers published in 1997-98: *Juedui yinsi* (Absolute privacy) by An Qi; *Feichang yinsi* (Unusually private) by Zhai Jun and Xue Mei; *Danshen yinsi* (The privacy of singles) by An Qi; *Zhencao yinsi* (The privacy of chastity) by An Jing; and *Zuier de yidianyuan* (The sinful Eden) by Yang Bo. For a special report on the importance of privacy in urban life and its commercialization, see *Xinzhoukan* (New weekly), no. 21, 1998, pp. 13-25.

18. I have to admit that many of my informants thought I was silly, or even worse, when I bothered them with questions like "What does the word 'freedom' mean to you?" Unlike a foreign scholar or even someone from urban China, I grew up in the village and therefore was expected to understand the complex meanings of such a simple word. It always took me some extra effort to explain that I was doing anthropological research, which was different from my living in the village, and thus I needed to hear exactly what they (the villagers), not I, thought about the issues in question.

19. Feminist scholars criticize the depriving function of privacy: by taking public significance out of the private sphere, they say, the unprivileged members—women and children—are put in a helpless situation. For a detailed review of this approach, see Boling 1996: 4-19.

20. The significance of "face" in Chinese society is widely known by now, so much so that the term has entered the English-speaking world. In general, scholars distinguish between two kinds of face: social face based on one's achievement and dignity, and moral face based on a person's feelings of shame. The former works as prestige and is subject to others' evaluation, and the latter functions as a moral self-constraint. Social face is achieved and possessed by people in the upper classes; ordinary people do not care much about their social face (see Hu 1944; King 1988). However, my case study of gift exchange in Xiajia village demonstrates that, by the 1980s, ordinary villagers not only cared about social face but also fought to gain it, an important development similar to their quest for privacy. For a detailed ethnographic account of the "face contest" in Xiajia and a review of scholarly discourse on the concept of face, see Yan 1996: 133-38.

21. Wang Yalin and Zhang Ruli (1995) report a similar pattern of house remodeling in Changwu township, Zhaodong county, which is about 200 kilometers away from Xiajia village. They interpret the change as another positive result of the economic reforms and one more step toward the modernization of the family in rural China.

CHAPTER 6

1. For local patterns of gift giving in ritualized situations, see Yan 1996: 43-73; for a detailed discussion of the childbirth celebration ritual, see page 53.

2. Several such cases of family division occurred earlier in the 1950s and 1960s, but they were isolated incidents resulting from unsolvable family disputes, rather than a common, institutionalized practice accepted by the majority of Xiajia residents.

3. However, when younger sons (those under age 18 in 1983) started to claim the family division in the early 1990s, they were allowed to take only their own subsistence-grain land from the old house—that is, all they were given in 1983. Most fathers are still physically strong enough to farm their own contract land and also need to do so for the unmarried sons still at home. Only those older villagers who were about 50 in 1983 and who reached retirement age in the 1990s may decide to pass their contract land on to their sons (in most cases the youngest sons) in a family division. The situation can be far worse for those who were born after 1983 because they did not even receive subsistence-grain land. To solve this problem yet maintain villagers' confidence in the stability of land policies, the village office made a minor adjustment in 1997–98, allocating each landless youngster or child two *mu* (0.165 acre) of subsistence-grain land. The extra land used for this second distribution was taken from those who passed away or officially moved out of the village during the previous two decades.

4. Interestingly, the current trend of early family division has not weakened the moral-emotional ties and provision of mutual aid among family members and close kin; instead, interactions between postdivision nuclear families have increased. Because of the early timing and the serial form of family division, the newly established nuclear families are more vulnerable and less independent than those derived from a prolonged patrilocal residence. Traditionally, the couple in a newly established household were middle-aged adults with their own children, and they would have inherited an equal share of the family estate (whatever that may have been). In contrast, many of the current new nuclear households consist only of newly married couples, who are in their early twenties and who lack experience in managing a household. Even worse, these young couples do not have a strong economic base since they can only take away their own personal belongings, plus their own share of the farm land, from the husband's parents' house. What they do have, in comparison with the earlier generations, however, is a strong desire for conjugal independence, together with their parents' understanding or tolerance (although the degree of understanding and tolerance may vary) of their early departure. So, on the one hand, the young couples need the support from their parents; on the other hand, parents see it as their moral obligation to help out their married sons. In addition, the emerging crisis of elderly support leads many parents to treat this as an important opportunity to cultivate a good relationship with their married sons, an investment for their old age (I return to this point in Chapter 7). Thus there is a natural demand for a close relationship between the child-family and the parent-family. This is not a unique phenomenon found only in Xiajia village. As early as the mid-1980s, scholars had noted the close relationship and extensive cooperation among postdivision nuclear families. Elisabeth Croll characterizes this as an "aggregate family" and argues that an aggregate family is perhaps the most important family change in the new era. Following Croll's

work, Ellen Judd emphasizes the blurring of household boundaries in everyday life (1994: 181–87). From a modernization perspective, some Chinese scholars regard the embeddedness of rural nuclear families in the web of kinship as a sign of an incomplete trend toward the nuclearization of families (see, e.g., Liu 1990: 38–39; see also Zeng et al. 1993).

5. The local custom of recording marriage transactions allowed me to chart their development over the five decades before 1999. In Xiajia village and the surrounding areas, marriage negotiations usually result in the writing of a formal bridewealth list called *caili dan* (list of betrothal gifts). This gift list is produced, in two copies, during the engagement ritual and it records all monetary and material gifts received at the time of marriage. During my 1991 fieldwork, I collected fifty-one bridewealth lists from several decades and conducted structured interviews with the owners of these lists to gather background information. Every bridewealth list was double-checked with both spouses to obtain data that were as accurate as possible. I then updated the data using the same methods during fieldwork in 1994, 1997, and 1999.

The selected cases are all regarded by my informants as representative because the amount of the monetary gifts and material goods involved in each of these cases was deemed to be average. More important than the actual amount of transferred wealth are the changes in the categories of gifts. It is common practice for individual families to negotiate the amount of the bridewealth and dowry, but the families always follow accepted categories for marital gifts. In this sense, we may say that every betrothal gift list is "representative" in indicating the structure of marriage transfers. During the research, I also found that villagers, especially women, had surprisingly long memories about the details of their marriages. Women could easily recall every betrothal gift, but sometimes they exaggerated the size of their dowry. When this happened, the husbands often corrected them.

6. According to existing theories, bridewealth and indirect dowry (subsidized by bridewealth), by definition, must be properties transferred between the groom's and the bride's families. It should be noted that several scholars who work on China have pointed out that indirect dowry involves an intergenerational transfer of family properties: monetary and material gifts going from the groom's family (in the form of bridewealth) and the bride's family (in the form of the indirect dowry) to the newlywed couple and eventually to the conjugal fund when the couple forms their own household (see Cohen 1976; McCreery 1976; Ebrey 1991; and R. Watson 1991). However, little attention has been paid to the property transferred within the groom's family, which is used to endow the new conjugal room instead of being exchanged between families in the form of bridewealth or indirect dowry.

7. Influential studies on bridewealth and dowry include Comaroff 1980; Goody 1973; Harrell and Dickey 1985; Schlegel and Eloul 1988; and Tambiah 1973.

8. This section is based on a chapter in my 1996 book *The Flow of Gifts*. For a detailed ethnographic description, a discussion of anthropological discourse on marriage transactions, and my analysis of the changes in the local system of bridewealth and dowry, see Yan 1996: 176–209.

9. The monetary amount in the early 1950s was translated into its equivalent purchasing power in the grain market. From the late 1950s to the early 1980s, the Chinese currency, the yuan, was stable. Changes in the betrothal gifts resulted mainly from changes in local economic conditions and living standards, not inflation. However, since 1983–84 inflation has become a problem in China, and fear of inflation reinforces current trends calling for large betrothal gifts.

10. The issue of how long a married woman can hold private property arouses considerable debate in China studies. I do not address this issue in the present study. Cohen suggests that a woman can control her private money only as long as she and her husband remain part of a larger family (1976: 210–11). R. Watson argues that women living in either joint or conjugal families can have their own money, even though the private funds of a woman in a joint family are probably greater than those of a woman in a conjugal family (1984: 6).

11. For example, if A borrows a sack of corn from B and wants to repay B in cash for the sake of convenience, A may ask B whether it is acceptable to convert the value of the borrowed grain into a certain amount of cash. In so doing A may use the word *ganzhe* to indicate the conversion of the value of the goods into cash.

12. This development parallels what Parish and Whyte discovered in southern China: "Items that in many areas used to be part of a dowry (such as furniture and bedding for the bridal room) are now the sole responsibility of the groom's family" (1978: 184).

13. In my 1996 book, which was based on fieldwork in 1991, I noted that housing was not yet regarded as part of the marriage transaction and had not yet entered the bridewealth list in Xiajia village. Only several years later, local practice had changed; housing has become a necessary part of marriage transfers, just as it has in many other areas of rural China (see, e.g., Cohen 1992; Potter and Potter 1990: 209; Kipnis 1997; and Siu 1993: 166).

14. Arguing that the dowry in traditional China should not be seen as a daughter's inheritance right, R. Watson points out that the most valuable part of the dowry is often jewelry, which cannot generate wealth like the property men inherit, such as land or shops (1984: 8). In the 1990s women began demanding income-generating property as part of the converted bridewealth (ganzhe); traditionally such property would have been part of their dowries.

15. Women's "private money" has received substantial attention among China scholars; see Chen 1985; Cohen 1976; Ebrey 1991; McCreery 1976; Ocko 1991; and R. Watson 1984.

16. The local practice of providing a dowry underwent a similar change: in the 1960s it was more like bridewealth, and many parents withheld most of the dowry and the bridewealth they received; in the 1970s an indirect dowry system became more common; and in the late 1980s the offering of lavish dowries prevailed. Daughters played an active role in claiming larger dowries from their parents; for details see Yan 1996: 181–92.

17. Jack Goody notes that in India there is a bilateral transmission by which parental property devolves vertically on both sexes. Dowry—the property that a woman takes with her into marriage to form a conjugal fund—"can be seen as a form of pre-mortem inheritance to the bride" and, as such, part of a woman's property complex (see Goody 1973: 17).

18. Among China anthropologists, there is a disagreement over the mechanisms by which property rights are transmitted across generations through family division. Freedman (1966) and others view family property as a manifestation of jural relations. It is the father who has all the power and legal rights to control family property and, consequently, the father's status is the determinant of family division. Cohen (1976) challenges this widely accepted view by arguing that the married sons actually hold legal rights to family property equal to those of their father and thus can demand family division at any point after their marriage. What keeps the extended family intact is the economic self-interest of the married sons, and family property, consequently, reflects economic relations between the self-interested members of the family. See also Yanagisako's comments on the debate (1979: 170).

19. I remember passing up such an opportunity two or three times precisely because I lived by myself and did not want to overconsume.

CHAPTER 7

1. To date, old-age security in rural China remains an understudied topic. For recent studies of the subject in urban China, see Davis-Friedmann 1991 (expanded edition); and Ikels 1996. Interestingly, Martin Whyte and his research team found that, in Baodin City, Hebei province, family and filial obligations were intact in the 1990s, with little sign of a generation gap between parents and children. Aging parents were still being treated in a filial manner by their grown children, and the adult children were as likely as their parents to express support for traditional family obligations (see Whyte 1997). It seems to me that elderly parents in the countryside tend to face more serious problems of old-age security than their counterparts in cities. Rural parents' lack of a pension and other economic resources is certainly a factor, but the issue is much more complicated and deserves systematic study in its own right.

2. It was reported that by the end of the 1990s the proportion of elderly in China age 60 or older was close to 10 percent of the population, and 7 percent were age 65 or older. Chinese demographers estimated that by the year of 2040, 23 percent of the Chinese population would be age 60 or older (see Tian Xueyuan 1997: 117–43; Wu Cangping, Gui Shixun, and Zhang Zhiliang 1996: 303–21). As White notes, with the rapid fertility decline after 1970, the inadequate system of retirement pensions in urban areas and little coverage at all in the countryside, the country's working-age population will be caught in a double vise: "It will have to provide for child

care and elder care, and do so without benefit of a reliable system of pensions or health care insurance, during a time of great flux in domestic economic institution and policies" (White 2000: 103).

3. In another six households elderly parents were verbally abused by their daughters-in-law but did not live a material life worse than the rest in their respective families.

4. According to Charlotte Ikels, urban residents in Guangzhou use three words to describe aspects of elderly support. The term *yang* means the provision of food, clothing, and shelter; and *fushi* and *zhaogu* mean to look after, to attend to, or to wait on, with the former implying a status difference between the server and the served (see Ikels 1996: 128). For an excellent in-depth discussion of the complex meanings of yang, see Stafford 2000.

5. For an excellent and thorough study of the rich meaning of funerals in Chinese culture, see Watson and Rawski 1988.

6. Usually an anthropologist encounters the opposite situation—being constantly surrounded by elderly informants.

7. According to Deborah Davis-Friedmann, the ground of intergenerational reciprocity shifted much earlier, probably at the time of the 1949 revolution. She argues that there is a marked difference between the attitudes of urban and rural adult children toward elderly support. Urbanities cite the sacrifices and hardships their parents made for them in childhood, and their sense of duty rests more on emotional attachment than anything else. In contrast, rural children tend to be more pragmatic and rational, defining their obligations to elderly parents in terms of the specific financial arrangements between the generations (Davis-Friedmann 1991: 54).

8. A notable exception is Judd 1989. And Davis-Friedmann (1991) documents in detail the strong and close ties between married daughters and their aged parents in urban families; she also notes that, in the countryside, when sons were unavailable daughters became important for the elderly. Emotional attachment, according to Davis-Friedmann, is one of the main reasons that daughters play such an active role in elderly support.

9. Scholarly accounts rarely take into consideration this psychological explanation by the parents. In a modernist critique of the fertility culture in rural China, for instance, the Chinese sociologist Li Yinhe argues that, unlike in the West where the relationship between parents and children is individualistic, in China parents not only invest in children for old-age security but also depend on the latter to continue the family line. Therefore, parents scarify themselves for children because they are driven by the cultural ideal of the longevity of the family, and adult children take parental help for granted because they know it is for the family rather than for them: "This is an egoism that has been expanded to the boundaries of the family, instead of altruism" (Li Yinhi 1993: 113).

10. For an insightful description of the kowtow rite, see Kipnis 1997: 74–83.

11. In order to wipe out the influence of the religious sect of Falungong, the party-state launched another nationwide campaign of "promoting science, against superstition" in late 1999.

CHAPTER 8

1. For a brief explanation of the multifaceted role of the dragon in Chinese culture, see Eberhard 1986: 83–86.

2. The collective economy had been successful in Xiajia village, reaching its peak by the early 1980s. Under the strong leadership at the brigade level, the four production teams had the best headquarters and agricultural machinery and boasted that they were the richest in the commune. Consequently, cadres in Xiajia enjoyed more power and latitude than their counterparts in neighboring villages when enforcing the birth control policies.

3. The sterilization process used was tubal ligation. A tubal ligation does not include oophorectomy (removal of the ovaries); it is merely contraceptive and does not ablate the woman's sexual hormonal secretion. Nevertheless, Xiajia villagers did not make a distinction between tubal ligation and oophorectomy, and they insisted that the sterilized women were castrated. For popular attitudes concerning tubal ligation in Taiwan during the 1960s, see Kleinman 1980.

4. For early trends in demographic transition in China, see Banister 1987; Goldstein and Wang 1996. For a recent overview of changes in family planning policies and demographic structure, see White 2000.

5. These numbers are drawn from the official records of family planning in Xiajia village. However, these numbers do not include data for villagers who moved their household registrations out of the community.

6. A decline in the fertility rate has been a national trend since the 1980s. According to the 1993 statistics, the fertility rate in China was 2.0 per woman, which was even lower than the rate of 2.1 in the United States (Gu 1996: 118). It should also be noted that Heilongjiang province has had one of the lowest total fertility rates—1.71 as shown in a 1990 national sample survey of 1 percent of the population. See Wu, Gui, and Zhang 1996: 216–19; Gu 1996: 115.

7. According to Tyrene White's review, the ratio of boys to girls born in 1995 was 117.4:100, 116:100 in 1992, 113.8:100 in 1989, 111.2:100 in 1985, and 107.2:100 in 1982: "By 1997, the sex ratio reported in China's annual population yearbook for ages four and under was 120 males for every 100 females. This relentless trend left no further doubt about the reality and seriousness of the skew toward males in late twentieth-century China" (White 2000: 10). For views on this issue from a Chinese perspective, see Zeng et al. 1993.

8. There were rumors that several couples had taken advantage of ultrasound technology, which is available at the county hospital, to help them identify the sex of

their child and decide whether to proceed with the pregnancy. Although sex selection by ultrasound is illegal, it is not impossible if one has the right connections and is willing to pay a large amount of money. However, I was not able to collect solid data on this topic.

9. According to Peng and Dai, many people in the villages of southern Jiangsu province prefer to have only one child, thus creating a new pattern of fertility culture: "Actually, in one of our field sites, Yuexi village, there has not been a second birth for many years. The officials from the birth planning committee of Taicang county said that they had to mobilize some qualified villagers to have a second birth, 90 percent of whom voluntarily gave up their quota for a second child" (Peng and Dai 1996: 180).

10. The new phenomenon of an only-daughter household has been reported in some rural areas. In 1991, 2,039 families in Yuyao county, Zhejiang province, voluntarily gave up their quota for a second birth and became only-daughter households (Li Yinhe 1993: 158). In their comparative study of three rural areas, Peng and Dai found that in Taicang county, Jiangsu province, the majority no longer had no longer been influenced by male preference, and the sex ratio there remained at a normal level (Peng and Dai 1996: 150–59).

11. Since the 1970s microeconomic theory has made an important contribution to demography by explaining fertility changes in terms of the changing cost and utility of children in family life, such as Gary Becker's consumer demand theory (1976), Leibenstein's utility maximization theory (1975), and Richard Easterlin's integrated fertility model (1978). Despite the important differences among these scholars themselves, they all view reproduction as an individual or familial behavior based on the rational choice of actors (parents). Parents calculate the costs of raising a child or children as well as the utility (in both material and nonmaterial forms) that children may bring to them. They then decide, based on the principle of maximization, whether to have children, and if yes, how many. These theories were introduced to China in the 1980s and have been quite influential in Chinese demography. According to Chen and Mu, the cost-utility framework has been a leading theory in directing both fertility research and actual policy implementation in China (Chen and Mu 1996).

12. The rising cost of raising children can be attributed to the changing parent-child relationship, the newly emerged child-centered culture, and, of course, the influence of urban life on child development. But these are large subjects and cannot be discussed here owing to the shortage of space.

13. Here we see a fundamental difference between Western scholars and Chinese villagers in calculating the cost of children. The former, regardless of their theoretical differences, normally define the duration of raising a child as eighteen years, from birth to the beginning of adulthood (see Becker 1976; Leibenstein 1975). The Chinese villagers, by contrast, also include the marriage costs for their children because they feel morally and socially obligated to help their children (mainly sons) marry in style. Furthermore, according to Chinese cultural tradition, the child only becomes

an adult after marriage, and in this sense the cost of marriage is indeed part of the cost of raising a child.

14. According to Ye Wenzhen's analysis, the cost of raising a child from birth to age 16 (by 1995–96 standards) was 93,968 yuan in the southern city of Xiamen, 55,437 yuan in Beijing, and 30,120 yuan in rural Shaanxi (Ye 1998: 208). For some recent studies on children's consumption, see Davis and Sensenbrenner 2000; Zhao and Murdock 1996; for essays on children's food see Jing 2000.

15. Remarkably, the cadres in Xiajia continued to comply with the major birth planning regulations throughout the subsequent two decades; there were only a few early marriages and early births (first births without a permit). This, plus Ms. Wang's diligence, certainly helped to ease the tension caused by the birth control program. According to some villagers, however, cadres did not resist because there was too much at stake if they violated the birth control regulations—they could lose their positions, which were worth between 5,000 yuan and 9,000 yuan for a cadre in the 1990s.

16. Interlineage hostility and periodic violent conflicts are more evident in the rural south, where kinship organization is historically stronger (see Baker 1979; Freedman 1966). Along with the revival of kinship power in these regions during the postcollective era, organized and violent fights often broke out between feuding lineages (see He 1998; Xiao 1997). In 1991 in Guandong province, two lineages fought a seven-day war, involving more than 6,000 people armed with both traditional weapons and stolen rifles and handguns (see Yang Ping 1994).

17. My inquiry into the role of the community in birth planning was inspired by both Ms. Wang's repeated emphasis on cunfeng (village wind) and the work of Peng Xizhe and Dai Xingyi. In their 1996 book, Peng and Dai call for close attention to community culture in studies of fertility change in rural China. They argue that differences in local patterns of economic development, elderly support, public security, and interpersonal relations can be used to explain regional variations. A good example is the famous contrast between the so-called Sunan model and the Guangdong model: in southern Jiangsu, regional economic development has led to a decline in the fertility rate, and in similarly prosperous Guangdong province to a rise of fertility desire and illegal births (see Peng and Dai 1996: 184–207).

18. These changes, again, echo the general patterns of demographic change found by large-scale surveys in other parts of rural China. As Gu Baozhang notes, rural China is characterized by the coexistence of a low fertility rate and high population growth because of the trend toward early birth and the concentration of women of childbearing age in the 1990s. Another serious problem is of course the unbalanced sex ratio (see Gu 1996: 88; Tian 1998).

19. Some Chinese scholars argue that an uncompromising birth control program reinforced by the state is the key for any future changes in fertility culture (see, e.g., Li Yinhe 1993).

CONCLUSION

1. Kang Youwei, Liang Qichao, and Tan Sitong, the three major leaders of the 1898 Reform Movement, all proposed radical reforms of the traditional Chinese family. Kang even suggested the abolition of the family as a precondition for social reform (see Deng 1994: 23–27). Among students of the Chinese family, Marion Levy was perhaps the first to document the radical changes of the Chinese family, as encapsulated in the title of his book *The Family Revolution in Modern China*. However, he is mainly interested in the impact of industrialization on family structure and the match between the conjugal family and modernization, a typical reflection of the then dominant structural-functionalist theory of family change (see Levy 1949).

2. In a letter written on August 31, 1944, Mao Zedong elaborates on three aspects of his plan for a family revolution. First, Mao states: "It is necessary to destroy the peasant family; going to the factories and joining the army are part of the big destruction of the family." Second, the key to reforming the peasant family is through mass campaigns: "The transformation of the peasant family from feudalism to democracy cannot be achieved through isolated family members who read some sort of good suggestions from books or newspapers; instead, it can only be done through mass movements." Third, he said, reforming the peasant family will help the development of individuality, because individuals will be organized into new forms of military, political, economic, and cultural organizations (see Deng 1994: 188–91).

3. By "young women" I mean those who are between the ages of 15 and 24, or as defined in social terms, those who are going through the transition from being a teenage daughter to becoming a young daughter-in-law. For a rural woman, this is the most difficult and important period in her life, full of changes and challenges. In a traditional patriarchal family, young women were marginal outsiders who held only a temporary position in the family, because daughters married out and new daughters-in-law were not yet fully incorporated into their new families. Daughters were commonly regarded as a drain on the family wealth, and new daughters-in-law were seen as a potential threat to family order. Thus, in comparison to their male siblings, girls were without status, powerless, and somewhat dangerous; they could only take their proper place in the domestic sphere by becoming mothers. As a result of their longstanding anonymity in family life, young women have attracted little scholarly attention.

4. It should also be noted that "girl power" challenges patriarchal order rather than androcentric order, and therefore it does not necessarily bring about radical changes in gender inequality. In all the areas mentioned above—mate choice, marriage negotiation, and family division, girl power is reflected mainly in the young woman's ability to impose her own will on her prospective (or actual) parents-in-law, such as in demanding marital gifts or early family division. What has been altered is mainly the unfair treatment in the traditional expectations of a virtuous daughter-in-law.

Precisely because girl power is primarily a threat only to the prospective parents-in-law, young women can easily pursue their goals without much resistance from their own parents or their husbands. In other words, young women challenge patriarchal power during the move from their natal families to those of their husbands, when they socially transform themselves from daughters into daughters-in-law (and from girl to wife). In other words, girl power is actually the power of the new daughter-in-law, and it is limited to the cross-family, intergenerational dimension of domestic life. Nevertheless, the traditional Chinese family was designed in such a way that most duties and obligations in everyday life fell on the shoulders of the daughter-in-law, and thus, for practical reasons, her status had to be kept low and her agency could not be awakened. This is why the development of agency and individuality among young women could be such a fatal blow to the patriarchal family. As one witty villager put it: "When the daughter-in-law enters the family door, the father's power is knocked down" (*erxifu yi jin jiamen, fuquan jiu bei dadao*).

5. This is from Cohen's oral comments on several papers delivered in the session "The Practice of Filial Piety in Contemporary China" at the 52nd Annual Meeting of the Association for Asian Studies, San Diego, March 11, 2000.

6. In a provocative review of gender studies in the China field, William Jankowiak concludes: "Most scholars of Chinese gender remain uninterested in exploring the domain of heterosexual intimacy and emotional interdependence. The current emphasis on the interplay between social factors and the production of structural inequality has overlooked the importance of the emotional domain, especially as it pertains to the spheres of pleasure, sentimentality, hope, faith, integrity, decency, obligation, loyalty, compassion, altruism, ardent love, and passionate self-sacrifice" (1999: 36). Interestingly, most responses to Jankowiak's article focus on whether power and inequality have been overemphasized, while the emotional domain is still considered less important. Louise Edwards offers an interesting counterargument by emphasizing that the recent anthropological concern for the emotional is related more to scholarly interest in social phenomena in the West than to interest in China: "Emotional relations between husbands and wives were less important and parent-child relations more significant in Imperial China than in nineteenth century Europe. The state has been far more intrusive into individuals' lives in China than in any European nation or in the United States. This may well justify the concentration of China scholars working on the impact of state policy on gender relations" (Edwards 1999: 45; see also other responses to Jankowiak's article in the same issue).

7. In a similar twist, the privatization of the family in rural China actually promotes the status of women in the domestic sphere. The segregation of family life from social structures that are far more extensive in space and time is perhaps one of the most fundamental features of the modernization project in Western societies. As a result of the privatization of the family, women were assigned strictly domestic roles as caregivers (as opposed to men's roles as breadwinners) and thus were isolated

from public life (Cheal 1991; Sennett 1970; Fischer 1981). Even romantic love was feminized; women were encouraged to devote themselves to love, while men were told to concentrate on work (Cancian 1987). The privatization of the family is therefore regarded by feminist scholars as having a negative impact on women's lives in both public and private (Chalmers and Smith 1987; Cheal 1991; Eichler 1973; Millar and Glendinning 1987). The practice of socialism in China has had a different impact. Women were intentionally mobilized by the state to participate in production and public life (Johnson 1983; Stacey 1983). While the family was privatized in the sense that it was separated from organized kinship power, it was brought closer than ever to the public because of state intervention in people's private lives, especially during the radical political campaigns (Parish and Whyte 1978). For reasons that I argue in this text, this dual process (the privatization and politicization of the family) has enabled the previously unprivileged members of the family—youth and women—to gain more power in relation to the existing patriarchal order.

8. It should also be noted that some state policies and political campaigns were meant to reinforce the traditional patterns of family life or to hinder the trend of change for the sake of social stability. For instance, the household registration system reinforced the old custom of patrilocal postmarital residence, divorce was discouraged at various levels of the local state, and the promise of women's liberation was never fully delivered (Johnson 1983; and Stacey 1983). In the postcollective era, the strict birth control policies strengthened villagers' preference for male children, and the redistribution of land during decollectivization favored men's inheritance rights (see Davis and Harrell 1993; Judd 1994; and Yan 1996, 1997). However, we should also be aware that the same state policy may have had a different impact on family structure and family relations. The state's emphasis on individual obligation to support elderly parents (which is written into the law) tends to reinforce traditional family obligations and encourage the persistence of stem families. But this does not indicate official support for parental power; on the contrary, as shown in the Xiajia case, the majority of stem families are run by the younger generation.

9. I note in Chapter 7 that the local government launched a cremation and burial reform in the early 1990s. In 1998 the county government issued a formal document regulating gift exchange activities among villagers, limiting gift-giving to three family rituals: weddings, funerals, and house construction. In practice, the new rules had never been observed by anyone—cadres or villagers—although some villagers had to pay fines for violating the rules when they were first implemented.

Bibliography

Anagnost, Ann. 1997. *National Past-Times: Narrative, Representation and Power in Modern China*. Durham, N.C.: Duke University Press.

Anonymous. 1997. *"Xiangcun shehui jiegao zai bianhua"* (Rural social structure is changing). *Gaige neican* (Internal reference to reforms), no. 10: 22–24.

Ariès, Philippe. 1962. *Centuries of Childhood: A Social History of Family Life*. New York: Vintage Books.

———. 1989. "Introduction." In Philippe Ariès and Georges Duby, eds., *A History of Private Life*. Vol. 3. Trans. Arthur Goldhammer. Cambridge, Mass.: Harvard University Press.

Ariès, Philippe, and Georges Duby, gen. eds. 1987–1991. *A History of Private Life*. 5 vols. Cambridge, Mass.: Belknap Press of Harvard University Press.

Baker, Hugh. 1968. *Sheung Shui: A Chinese Lineage Village*. Stanford, Calif.: Stanford University Press.

———. 1979. *Chinese Family and Kinship*. New York: Columbia University Press.

Banister, Judith. 1987. *China's Changing Population*. Stanford, Calif.: Stanford University Press.

Baum, Richard, and Alexei Shevchenko. 1999. "The State of the State." In Merle Goldman and Roderick Macfarquhar, eds., *The Paradox of China's Post-Mao Reforms*, pp. 333–62. Cambridge, Mass.: Harvard University Press.

Becker, Gary. 1976. *The Economic Approach to Human Behavior*. Chicago: University of Chicago Press.

Berger, Peter, and Michael Hsiao, eds. 1988. *In Search of an East Asian Development Model*. New Brunswick, N.J.: Transaction Books.

Bernard, Russell. 1994. *Research Methods in Anthropology*. 2d ed. Thousand Oaks, Calif.: Sage.

Birth, Kevin, and Morris Freilich. 1995. "Putting Romance into Systems of Sexuality: Changing Smart Rules in a Trinidadian Village." In William Jankowiak, ed., *Romantic Passion: A Universal Experience?* pp. 262–76. New York: Columbia University Press.

Blake, Fred. 1979. "Love Songs and the Great Leap: The Role of a Youth Culture in the Revolutionary Phase of China's Economic Development." *American Ethnologist* 6, no. 1: 41–54.

Blecher, Marc. 1991. "Development State, Entrepreneurial State: The Political Economy of Socialist Reform in Xinju Municipality and Guanghan County." In Gordon White, ed., *The Chinese State in the Era of Economic Reform: The Road to Crisis*, pp. 265–91. Armonk, N.Y.: M. E. Sharpe.

Boling, Patricia. 1996. *Privacy and the Politics of Intimate Life*. Ithaca, N.Y.: Cornell University Press.

Bourdieu, Pierre. 1977. *Outline of a Theory of Practice*. Trans. Richard Nice. Cambridge, England: Cambridge University Press.

———. 1990. *The Logic of Practice*. Trans. Richard Nice. Stanford, Calif.: Stanford University Press.

Braudel, Fernand. 1967. *Capitalism and Material Life, 1400–1800*. New York: Harper and Row.

Bray, Francesca. 1997. *Technology and Gender: Fabrics of Power in Late Imperial China*. Berkeley: University of California Press.

Cancian, Francesca. 1987. *Love in America: Gender and Self-Development*. Cambridge: Cambridge University Press.

Chai, Joseph C. H. 1992. "Consumption and Living Standards in China." *China Quarterly*, no. 131: 721–49.

Chalmers, L., and P. Smith. 1987. "Wife Battering: Psychological, Social and Physical Isolation and Counteracting Strategies." In K. Storrie, ed., *Women: Isolation and Bonding*. Toronto: Methuen.

Chan, Anita, Richard Madsen, and Jonathan Unger. 1992. Expanded ed. *Chen Village under Mao and Deng*. Berkeley: University of California Press.

Chao, Linda, and Ramon Myers. 1998. "China's Consumer Revolution: The 1990s and Beyond." *Journal of Contemporary China* 7, no. 18: 351–68.

Cheal, David. 1991. *Family and the State of Theory*. Toronto: University of Toronto Press.

Chekki, Dan A. 1988. "Recent Directions in Family Research: India and North America." *Journal of Comparative Family Studies* 19, no. 2: 171–86.

Chen, Chung-min. 1985. "Dowry and Inheritance." In Hsieh Jih-chang and Chuang Ying-chang, eds., *The Chinese Family and Its Ritual Behavior*, pp. 117–27. Taiwan: Institute of Ethnology, Academia Sinica.

Chen Junjie and Mu Guangzong. 1996. "*Nongmin de shengyu xueqiu*" (Fertility demands among the Chinese peasants). *Zhongguo shehui kexue* (*Chinese social sciences*), no. 2: 126–37.

Cohen, Myron L. 1970. "Developmental Process in the Chinese Domestic Group." In Maurice Freedman, ed., *Family and Kinship in Chinese Society*, pp. 21–36. Stanford, Calif.: Stanford University Press.

————. 1976. *House United, House Divided: The Chinese Family in Taiwan*. New York: Columbia University Press.

————. 1992. "Family Management and Family Division in Contemporary Rural China." *China Quarterly*, no. 130: 357–77.

————. 1993. "Cultural and Political Inventions in Modern China: The Case of the Chinese 'Peasant.'" *Daedalus* 122, no. 2: 151–70.

————. 1999. "North China Rural Families: Changes During the Communist Era." *Etudes Chinoises* 27, nos. 1–2: 59–153.

Collier, Jane Fishburne. 1997. *From Duty to Desire: Remaking Families in a Spanish Village*. Princeton, N.J.: Princeton University Press.

Comaroff, J. L. 1980. "Introduction." In J. L. Comaroff, ed., *The Meaning of Marriage Payments*. New York: Academic Press.

Conklin, George H. 1988. "The Influence of Economic Development on Patterns of Conjugal Power and Extended Family Residence in India." *Journal of Comparative Family Studies* 19, 2: 187–205.

Coontz, Stephanie. 1988. *The Social Origin of Private Life: A History of American Families, 1600–1900*. London: Verso.

————. 2000. *The Way We Never Were: American Families and the Nostalgia Trap*. New York: Basic Books.

Crapanzano, Vincent. 1989. "Preliminary Notes on the Glossing of Emotions." *Kroeber Anthropological Society Papers*, no. 69–70: 78–85.

Croll, Elisabeth. 1981. *The Politics of Marriage in Contemporary China*. Cambridge, England: Cambridge University Press.

————. 1987. "New Peasant Family Forms in Rural China." *Journal of Peasant Studies* 14: 469–99.

Dasgupta, Satadal, Christine Weatherbie, and Rajat Subhra Mukhopadhyay. 1993. "Nuclear and Joint Family Households in West Bengal Villages." *Ethnology* 32, no. 4: 339–58.

Davis, Deborah, ed. 2000. *The Consumer Revolution in Urban China*. Berkeley: University of California Press.

Davis, Deborah, and Stevan Harrell, eds. 1993. *Chinese Families in the Post-Mao Era*. Berkeley: University of California Press.

Davis, Deborah, Richard Kraus, Barry Naughton, and Elizabeth Perry, eds. 1995. *Urban Spaces in Contemporary China: The Potential for Autonomy and Community in Post-Mao China*. Cambridge, England: Cambridge University Press.

Davis, Deborah, and Julia Sensenbrenner. 2000. "Commercializing Childhood: Parental Purchases for Shanghai's Only Child." In Deborah Davis, ed., *The Consumer Revolution in Urban China*, pp. 54–79. Berkeley: University of California Press.

Davis-Friedmann, Deborah. 1991. *Long Lives: Chinese Elderly and the Communist Revolution*. 2d ed. Stanford, Calif.: Stanford University Press.

De Munck, Victor. 1996. "Love and Marriage in a Sri Lankan Muslim Community: Toward a Reevaluation of Dravidian Marriage Practices." *American Ethnologist* 23, no. 4: 698–716.

Deng Weizhi. 1994. *Jindai Zhongguo jiating de biange* (Family change in modern China). Shanghai: Shanghai renmin chubanshe.

Diamant, Neil. 2000. *Revolutionizing the Family: Politics, Love, and Divorce in Urban and Rural China, 1949–1968.* Berkeley: University of California Press.

Driscoll, Richard, Keith Davis, and Milton Lipetz. 1972. "Parental Interference and Romantic Love: The Romeo and Juliet Effect." *Journal of Personality and Social Psychology* 24, no. 1: 1–10.

Duara, Prasenjit. 1988. *Culture, Power, and the State.* Stanford, Calif.: Stanford University Press.

Easterlin, R. 1978. "The Economics and Sociology of Fertility: A Synthesis." In Charles Tilly, ed., *Historical Studies of Changing Fertility*, pp. 57–134. Princeton, N.J.: Princeton University Press.

Eberhard, Wolfram. 1986. *A Dictionary of Chinese Symbols.* Trans. G. L. Campbell. London: Routledge.

Ebrey, Patricia B. 1991. "Introduction." In Rubie S. Watson and Patricia B. Ebrey, eds., *Marriage and Inequality in Chinese Society*, pp. 1–24. Berkeley: University of California Press.

Edwards, Louise. 1999. "Historical/Hysterical: China and Western Emotional Needs." *Bulletin of Concerned Asian Scholars* 31, no. 1: 44–46.

Eichler, M. 1973. "Women as Personal Dependents." In M. Stephenson, ed., *Women in Canada.* Toronto: New Press.

Fei Xiaotong. [1947] 1992. *From the Soil: The Foundations of Chinese Society.* Trans. Gary Hamilton and Wang Zheng. Berkeley: University of California Press.

Fischer, C. 1981. "The Public and Private Worlds of City Life." *American Sociological Review* 46(3): 306–316.

Fraser, David. 2000. "Inventing Oasis: Luxury Housing Advertisements and Reconfiguring Domestic Space in Shanghai." In Deborah Davis, ed., *The Consumer Revolution in Urban China*, pp. 25–53. Berkeley: University of California Press.

Freedman, Maurice. [1961] 1979. "The Family in China, Past and Present." In G. William Skinner, ed., *The Study of Chinese Society: Essays by Maurice Freedman*, pp. 273–95. Stanford, Calif.: Stanford University Press.

———. 1966. *Chinese Lineage and Society: Fukien and Kwangtung.* London: Athlone.

Friedman, Edward, Paul Pickowicz, and Mark Selden. 1991. *Chinese Village, Socialist State.* New Haven, Conn.: Yale University Press.

Gallin, Bernard. 1966. *Hsin Hsing, Taiwan: A Chinese Village in Change.* Berkeley: University of California Press.

Gallin, Bernard, and Rita Gallin. 1982. "The Chinese Joint Family in Changing Rural Taiwan." In Sidney Greenblatt, Richard Wilson, and Amy Auerbacher Wilson, eds., *Social Interaction in Chinese Society.* New York: Praeger.

Gao, Mobo. 1999. *Gao Village: A Portrait of Rural Life in Modern China*. London: Hurst.

Gates, Hill. 1993. "Cultural Support for Birth Limitation Among Urban Capital-Owing Women." In Deborah Davis and Stevan Harrell, eds., *Chinese Families in the Post-Mao Era*, pp. 251–74. Berkeley: University of California Press.

Giddens, Anthony. 1992. *The Transformation of Intimacy: Sexuality, Love and Eroticism in Modern Societies*. Stanford, Calif.: Stanford University Press.

Gillette, Maris Boyd. 2000. *Between Mecca and Beijing: Modernization and Consumption among Urban Chinese Muslims*. Stanford, Calif.: Stanford University Press.

Gold, Thomas. 1991. "Youth and the State." *China Quarterly*, no. 132: 594–612.

———. 1993. "Go with Your Feelings: Hong Kong and Taiwan Popular Culture in Greater China." *China Quarterly*, no. 136: 907–25.

Goldstein, Alice, and Wang Feng. 1996. *China: The Many Facets of Demographic Change*. Boulder, Colo.: Westview Press.

Goode, William. 1959. "The Theoretical Importance of Love." *American Sociological Review* 24, no. 1: 38–47.

———. 1963. *World Revolution and Family Patterns*. New York: Free Press.

———. 1982. *The Family*. Englewood Cliffs, N.J.: Prentice-Hall.

Goody, Jack. 1973. "Bridewealth and Dowry in Africa and Eurasia." In Jack Goody and Stanley Tambiah, *Bridewealth and Dowry*, pp. 1–58. Cambridge, England: Cambridge University Press.

———. 1976. *Production and Reproduction: A Comparative Study of the Domestic Domain*. Cambridge, England: Cambridge University Press.

———. 1983. *The Development of the Family and Marriage in Europe*. Cambridge, England: Cambridge University Press.

———. 1990. *The Oriental, the Ancient and the Primitive: Systems of Marriage and the Family in the Pre-Industrial Societies of Eurasia*. Cambridge, England: Cambridge University Press.

Greenhalgh, Susan. 1993. "The Peasantization of the One-Child Policy in Shaanxi." In Deborah Davis and Stevan Harrell, eds., *Chinese Families in the Post-Mao Era*, pp. 219–50. Berkeley: University of California Press.

———. 1994a. "Controlling Births and Bodies in Village China." *American Ethnologist* 21, no. 1: 3–30.

———. 1994b. "De-Orientalizing the Chinese Family Firm." *American Ethnologist* 21, no. 4: 746–75.

Gu Baochang. 1996. *Zonglun Zhongguo renkou taishi* (A synthesis of demographic trends in China). Shanghai: Shanghai shehuikexue chubanshe.

Guo, Yuhua. 2001. "*Daiji guanxi zhong de gongping luoji jiqi bianqian: dui Hebei nongcun yanglao shijian de fenxi*" (The logic of fairness and its change in cross-generational relations: an analysis of cases of elderly support in rural Hebei), *Zhongguo xueshu* (Chinese scholarship), no. 4: pp. 221–54.

Harrell, Stevan. 1982. *Ploughshare Village: Culture and Context in Taiwan*. Seattle: University of Washington Press.

————. 1985. "Why Do the Chinese Work So Hard? Reflections on an Entrepreneurial Ethic." *Modern China* 11, no. 2: 203–26.

————. 1993. "Geography, Demography, and Family Composition in Three Southwestern Villages." In Deborah Davis and Stevan Harrell, eds., *Chinese Families in the Post-Mao Era*, pp. 77–102. Berkeley: University of California Press.

————. 1997. *Human Families*. Boulder, Colo.: Westview Press.

Harrell, Stevan, and Sara Dickey. 1985. "Dowry Systems in Complex Societies." *Ethnology* 24, no. 2: 105–20.

He Qinglian. 1998. *Xiandaihua de xianjing* (The pitfalls of modernization). Beijing: Jinri Zhongguo chubanshe.

Hinton, William. 1966. *Fanshen: A Documentary of Revolution in a Chinese Village*. New York: Vintage Books.

Hirsch, Jennifer. 1999. "'Men Go as Far as Women Let Them: Courtship, Intimacy, and the Mexican Companionate Marriage." Paper presented at the 98th Annual Meeting of American Association of Anthropology, Chicago.

Hollan, Douglas. 1997. "The Relevance of Person-Centered Ethnography to Cross-Cultural Psychiatry." *Transcultural Psychiatry* 34, no. 2: 219–34.

————. 2001. "Developments in Person-Centered Ethnography." In Carmella C. Moore and Holly F. Mathews, eds., *The Psychology of Cultural Experience*, pp. 48–67. Cambridge, England: Cambridge University Press.

Holland, Dorothy. 1992. "How Cultural Systems Become Desire: A Case Study of American Romance." In Roy D'Andrade and Claudia Strauss, eds., *Human Motives and Cultural Models*, pp. 61–89. Cambridge, England: Cambridge University Press.

Hsieh Jih-chang. 1985. "Meal Rotation." In Hsieh Jih-chang and Chuang Ying-chang, eds., *The Chinese Family and Its Ritual Behavior*. Taipei: Academia Sinica.

Hsu, Francis. [1948] 1967. *Under the Ancestors' Shadow: Kinship, Personality, and Social Mobility in Village China*. Garden City, N.Y.: Doubleday.

Hu, Hsien-chin. 1944. "The Chinese Concept of Face." *American Anthropologist* 46: 45–64.

Huang, Philip. 1985. *The Peasant Economy and Social Change in North China*. Stanford, Calif.: Stanford University Press.

————. 1993. "'Public Sphere'/'Civil Society' in China? The Third Realm between State and Society." *Modern China* 19, no. 2: pp. 216–40.

Huang, Shu-min. 1992. "Re-examining the Extended Family in Chinese Peasant Society: Findings from a Fujian Village." *Australian Journal of Chinese Affairs*, no. 27: 25–38.

Hwang, Kwang-kuo. 1987. "Face and Favor: The Chinese Power Game." *American Journal of Sociology* 92, no. 4: 944–74.

Ikels, Charlotte. 1996. *The Return of the God of Wealth: The Transition to a Market Economy in Urban China*. Stanford, Calif.: Stanford University Press.

Jankowiak, William. 1993. *Sex, Death, and Hierarchy in a Chinese City: An Anthropological Account*. New York: Columbia University Press.

———. 1995. "Romantic Passion in the People's Republic of China." In William Jankowiak, ed., *Romantic Passion: A Universal Experience?* pp. 166–83. New York: Columbia University Press.

———. 1999. "Chinese Women, Gender, and Sexuality: A Critical Review of Recent Studies." *Bulletin of Concerned Asian Scholars* 31, no. 1: 31–37.

———, ed. 1995. *Romantic Passion: A Universal Experience?* New York: Columbia University Press.

Jankowiak, William, and Edward Fischer. 1992. "A Cross-Cultural Perspective on Romantic Love." *Ethnology* 31: 149–55.

Jing, Jun. 1996. *The Temple of Memories: History, Power, and Morality in a Chinese Village*. Stanford, Calif.: Stanford University Press.

———, ed. 2000. *Feeding China's Little Emperors: Food, Children, and Social Change*. Stanford, Calif.: Stanford University Press.

Johnson, Graham. 1993. "Family Strategies and Economic Transformation in Rural China: Some Evidence from the Pearl River Delta." in Deborah Davis and Stevan Harrell, eds., *Chinese Families in the Post-Mao Era*, pp. 103–36. Berkeley: University of California Press.

Johnson, Kay Ann. 1983. *Women, the Family and Peasant Revolution in China*. Chicago: Chicago University Press.

Judd, Ellen. 1989. "*Niangjia*: Chinese Women and Their Natal Families." *Journal of Asian Studies* 48, no. 3: 525–44.

———. 1994. *Gender and Power in Rural North China*. Stanford, Calif.: Stanford University Press.

King, Ambrose Yeo-chi (Jin Yao-ji). 1988. "'Mian', 'chi' yu Zhongguoren xingwei zhi fenxi" (Face, shame, and an analysis of Chinese behavior patterns). In Guoshu Yang, ed., *Zhongguoren de xinli* (The psychology of the Chinese), pp. 75–104. Taipei: Guiguan Press.

———. 1991. "Kuan-hsi and Network Building: A Sociological Interpretation." *Daedalus* 120, no. 2: 63–84.

Kipnis, Andrew. 1997. *Producing Guanxi: Sentiment, Self, and Subculture in a North China Village*. Durham, N.C.: Duke University Press.

Kleinman, Arthur. 1980. *Patients and Healers in the Context of Culture*. Berkeley: University of California Press.

———. 1992. "Local Worlds of Suffering: An Interpersonal Focus for Ethnographies of Illness Experience." *Qualitative Health Research* 2, no. 2: 127–34.

———. 1999. "Experience and Its Moral Modes." In Grethe Peterson, ed., *The Tanner Lectures on Human Values*, no. 20, pp. 357–420. Salt Lake City: University of Utah Press.

Kleinman, Arthur, and Joan Kleinman. 1991. "Suffering and Its Professional Transformation: Toward an Ethnography of Interpersonal Experience." *Culture, Medicine and Psychiatry* 15, no. 3: 275–301.

——. 1997. "Moral Transformations of Health and Suffering in Chinese Society." In Allan Brandt and Paul Rozin, eds., *Morality and Health: Interdisciplinary Perspectives*, pp. 101–18. New York: Routledge.

Knapp, Ronald. 1986. *China's Traditional Rural Architecture: A Cultural Geography of the Chinese House*. Honolulu: University of Hawaii Press.

Kraus, Richard. 1977. "Class and the Vocabulary of Social Analysis in China." *China Quarterly*, no. 69: 54–74.

Kung, James. 1994. "Peasants in a 'Hot Pot': Pushing the Limits of Biased Strategy against Agriculture?" In Maurice Brosseau and Lo Chi Kin, eds., *China Review 1994*, pp. 11.1–21. Hong Kong: Chinese University Press.

Lang, Olga. 1946. *Chinese Family and Society*. New Haven, Conn.: Yale University Press.

Laslett, Barbara. 1973. "The Family as Public and Private Institution: An Historical Perspective." *Journal of Marriage and the Family* 35, no. 3: 480–94.

Laslett, Peter. 1971. *The World We Have Lost*. London: Methuen.

Laslett, Peter, and Richard Wall, eds. 1972. *Household and Family in Past Time*. Cambridge, England: Cambridge University Press.

Lavely, William, and Xinhua Ren. 1992. "Patrilocality and Early Marital Co-residence in Rural China, 1955–85." *China Quarterly*, no. 130: 378–91.

Leibenstein, H. 1975. "The Economic Theory of Fertility Decline." *Quarterly Journal of Economics* 89, no. 1: 1–31.

Levy, Marion, Jr. 1949. *The Family Revolution in Modern China*. Cambridge, Mass.: Harvard University Press.

Li Bingsheng. 2001. "*Cunmin zizhi xia Zhongguo nongcun gonggong chanpin de gongji wenti*" (The issue of public goods provision under villager autonomous rule in rural China), *Kaifang Shidai* (Open age), no. 3: pp. 72–81.

Li Jiangyuan. 1998. "*Nongcun ganqun guanxi jinzhang gengyuan zai tizhi*" (The tension between rural cadres and villagers is rooted in the political system), *Gaige neican* (Internal reference to reforms), no. 13, pp. 30–33.

Li Jun. 1999. "*Yinsi duoshaoqian yi jin*" (How much for a pound of privacy?), *Beijing Qingnianbao* (Beijing Youth Daily), January 24, p. 8.

Li Yinhe. 1993. *Shengyu yu Zhongguo cunluo wenhua* (Fertility and village culture in China). Hong Kong: Oxford University Press.

——. 1998. *Zhongguo nuxing de ganqing yu xing* (Love and sexuality of Chinese women). Beijing: Jinri Zhongguo chubanshe.

Li, Zhisui. 1994. *The Private Life of Chairman Mao: The Memoirs of Mao's Personal Physician*. Trans. Tai Hung-chao. New York: Random House.

Lindholm, Charles. 1988. "Love and Leaders: A Comparison of Social and Psychological Models of Romance and Charisma." *Social Science Information* 1, no. 27: 3–45.

Liu Dalin, ed. 1995. *Zhongguo dangdai xing wenhua* (Sexual behavior in modern China). Shanghai: Shanghai Sanlian Shudian.

Liu, Xin. 2000. *In One's Own Shadow: An Ethnographic Account of the Condition of Post-Reform Rural China*. Berkeley: University of California Press.

Liu, Ying. 1990. "Zhongguo nongcun hexin jiating de tedian" (The features of nuclear families in rural China), *Shehuixue yanjiu* (Sociological studies), no. 4: 35–39.

Liu Zuoxiang. 1996. "*Si quanli: yige zhide zhongshi de fazhi lingyu*" (Private rights: a noteworthy area of rule by law), *Dongfang* (The Orient), no. 4: 19–23.

Lull, James. 1991. *China Turned On: Television, Reform, and Resistance*. London: Routledge.

Lynch, Owen, ed. 1990. *Divine Passions: The Social Construction of Emotion in India*. Berkeley: University of California Press.

Ma Hong and Sun Shangqing, eds. 1993. *Jingji Baipishu, 1992–93* (The White Book of Economics, 1992–93). Beijing: Zhongguo fazheng chubanshe.

Madsen, Richard. 1984. *Morality and Power in a Chinese Village*. Berkeley: University of California Press.

McCreery, John. 1976. "Women's Property Rights and Dowry in China and South Asia." *Ethnology* 15, no. 2: 163–74.

Meillassoux, Claude. 1981. *Maidens, Meal and Money: Capitalism and the Domestic Community*. Cambridge, England: Cambridge University Press.

Millar, J., and C. Glendinning. 1987. "Invisible Women, Invisible Poverty." In C. Glendinning and J. Millar, eds., *Women and Poverty in Britain*. Hemel Hempstead, England: Harvester Wheatsheaf.

Mitterauer, Michael, and Reinhard Sieder. 1982. *The European Family: Patriarchy to Partnership from the Middle Ages to the Present*. Trans. Karla Oosterveen and Manfred Horzinger. Oxford, England: Basil Blackwell.

Moore, Barrington. 1984. *Privacy: Studies in Social and Cultural History*. Armonk, N.Y.: M. E. Sharpe.

Motsch, Monika. 1996. "The Mirror and the Chinese Aesthetics: A Study of the *Hongloumeng*." *Ming Qing Yanjiu* (Italy): 117–38.

Ocko, Jonathan K. 1991. "Women, Property, and the Law in the People's Republic of China." In Rubie Watson and Patricia Ebrey, eds., *Marriage and Inequality in Chinese Society*, pp. 313–46. Berkeley: University of California Press.

Oi, Jean. 1989. *State and Peasant in Contemporary China, The Political Economy of Village Government*. Berkeley: University of California Press.

———. 1991. "Partial Market Reform and Corruption in Rural China." In Richard Baum, ed., *Reform and Reaction in Post-Mao China: The Road to Tiananmen*, pp. 141–61. New York: Routledge.

———. 1998. "The Evolution of Local State Corporatism." In Andrew Walder, ed., *Zouping in Transition: The Process of Reform in Rural North China*, pp. 35–62. Cambridge, Mass.: Harvard University Press.

Pader, Ellen. 1993. "Spatiality and Social Change: Domestic Space Use in Mexico and the United States." *American Ethnologist* 20, no. 1: 114–37.

Palmer, Michael. 1995. "The Re-emergence of Family Law in Post-Mao China: Marriage, Divorce and Reproduction." *China Quarterly* 141: 110–34.

Parish, William, and Martin Whyte. 1978. *Village and Family in Contemporary China.* Chicago: University of Chicago Press.

Pasternak, Burton. 1972. *Kinship and Community in Two Chinese Villages.* Stanford, Calif.: Stanford University Press.

Peng Xizhe and Dai Xingyi. 1996. *Zhongguo nongcun shequ shengyu wenhua* (Community fertility culture in rural China). Shanghai: Huadong shefan daxue chubanshe.

Pieke, Frank. 1998. "Networks, Groups, and the State in the Rural Economy of Raoyang County, Hebei Province." In Edward Vermeer, Frank Pieke, and Woei Lien Chong, eds., *Cooperative and Collective in China's Rural Development.* Armonk, N.Y.: M. E. Sharpe.

Potter, Jack. 1970. "Land and Lineage in Traditional China." In Maurice Freedman, ed., *Family and Kinship in Chinese Society*, pp. 121–38. Stanford, Calif.: Stanford University Press.

Potter, Sulamith Heins, and Jack M. Potter. 1990. *China's Peasants: The Anthropology of a Revolution.* Cambridge, England: Cambridge University Press.

Prost, Antoine. 1991. "Public and Private Spheres in France." In Antonie Prost and Gerard Vincent, eds., *A History of Private Life*, vol. 5. Trans. Arthur Goldhammer. Cambridge, Mass.: Harvard University Press.

Qiu Xiaohua and Wan Donghua. 1990. "*Dui jinshinianlai woguo xiaofei xinshi de jiben huigu yu zhanwang*" (Retrospect and prospect of China's consumption situation in the past decade), *Xiaofei jingji* (Consumer economy), no. 2: 2–12.

Rebhun, L. A. 1999. *The Heart Is Unknown Country: Love in the Changing Economy of Northeast Brazil.* Stanford, Calif.: Stanford University Press.

Rosenblatt, Paul. 1967. "Marital Residence and the Function of Romantic Love." *Ethnology* 6, no. 4: 471–80.

Ruf, Gregory. 1998. *Cadres and Kin: Making a Socialist Village in West China, 1921–1991.* Stanford, Calif.: Stanford University Press.

Rybczynski, Witold. 1986. *Home: A Short History of an Idea.* New York: Penguin Books.

Sayer, Andrew. 1985. "The Difference That Space Makes." In Derrek Gregory and John Urry, eds., *Social Relations and Spatial Structures.* London: Macmillan.

Schak, David. 1974. *Dating and Mate-Selection in Modern Taiwan.* Taipei: Oriental Cultural Service.

Schlegel, Alice, and Rohn Eloul. 1988. "Marriage Transactions: Labor, Property, and Status." *American Anthropologist* 90: 291–309.

Selden, Mark. 1993. "Family Strategies and Structures in Rural North China." In Deborah Davis and Stevan Harrell, eds., *Chinese Families in the Post-Mao Era*, pp. 139–64. Berkeley: University of California Press.

Sennett, R. 1970. *Families against the City*. Cambridge, Mass.: Harvard University Press.

Shen Chonglin, Yang Shanhua, and Li Dongshan, eds. 1999. *Shiji zhi jiao de chengxiang jiating* (Urban and rural families at the turn of the century). Beijing: Zhongguo shehui kexue chubanshe.

Shue, Vivienne. 1988. *The Reach of the State*. Stanford, Calif.: Stanford University Press.

Simmons, Carolyn, Alexander von Kholke, and Hideko Shimizu. 1986. "Attitudes toward Romantic Love among American, German and Japanese Students." *Journal of Social Psychology* 3: 327–36.

Siu, Helen. 1989. *Agents and Victims in South China: Accomplices in Rural Revolution*. New Haven, Conn.: Yale University Press.

———. 1993. "Reconstituting Dowry and Brideprice in South China." In Deborah Davis and Stevan Harrell, eds., *Chinese Families in the Post-Mao Era*, pp. 165–88. Berkeley: University of California Press.

Skolnik, A. 1991. *Embattled Paradise: American Family in an Age of Uncertainty*. New York: Basic Books.

Stacey, Judith. 1983. *Patriarchy and Socialist Revolution in China*. Berkeley: University of California Press.

Stafford, Charles. 2000. "Chinese Patriliny and the Cycles of *yang* and *laiwang*." In Janet Castern, ed., *Cultures of Relatedness: New Approaches to the Study of Kinship*, pp. 37–54. Cambridge, England: Cambridge University Press.

Statistics Bureau. 1988. *Zhongguo nongcun tongji nianjian* (Statistical yearbook of rural China). Beijing: Zhongguo tongji chubanshe.

Stone, Lawrence. 1975. "The Rise of the Nuclear Family in Early Modern England." In Charles Rosenberg, ed., *The Family in History*. Philadelphia: University of Pennsylvania Press.

Sun Yuandong. 1999. "*Lun xiancun dipi dui jiceng xingzheng de yingxiang*" (The influence of local bullies on basic level administration). *Kaifang shidai* (Open age), no. 3: 38–41.

Sung, Lung-sheng. 1981. "Property and Family Division." In Emily Ahern and Hill Gates, eds., *The Anthropology of Taiwanese Society*, pp. 361–78. Stanford, Calif.: Stanford University Press.

Tambiah, Stanley. 1973. "Dowry and Bridewealth and the Property Rights of Women in South Asia." In Jack Goody and Stanley Tambiah, eds., *Bridewealth and Dowry*, pp. 59–169. Cambridge, England: Cambridge University Press.

Thornton, Arland, and Thomas Fricke. 1987. "Social Change and the Family: Comparative Perspectives from the West, China, and South Asia." *Sociological Forum*, 2, no. 4: 746–79.

Thornton, Arland, and Hui-Sheng Lin, eds. 1994. *Social Change and the Family in Taiwan*. Chicago: University of Chicago Press.

Tian Xueyuan. 1997. *Daguo zhi nan: dangdai Zhongguo de renkou wenti* (Difficulties of a big country: the population problem in contemporary China). Beijing: Dangdai Zhongguo chubanshe.

Trawick, Margaret. 1990. "The Ideology of Love in a Tamil Family." In Owen M. Lynch, ed., *Divine Passions*, pp. 137–63. Berkeley: University of California Press.

Unger, Jonathan. 1984. "The Class System in Rural China: A Case Study." In James Watson, ed., *Class and Stratification in Post-Revolution China*, pp. 121–41. Cambridge, England: Cambridge University Press.

———. 1989. "State and Peasant in Post-Revolution China." *Journal of Peasant Studies* 17, no. 1: 114–36.

United Nations. 1993. *World Population Project: The 1992 Revision*. New York: United Nations.

Walder, Andrew. 1986. *Communist Neo-traditionalism: Work and Authority in Chinese Industry*. Berkeley: University of California Press.

Walder, Andrew, ed. 1995. *The Waning of the Communist State: Economic Origins of Political Decline in China and Hungary*. Berkeley: University of California Press.

Wang Yalin and Zhang Ruli. 1995. "*Nongcun jiating gondneng yu jiating xingshi*" (The function and form of rural family). *Shehuixue yanjiu* (Sociological studies), no. 1: 76–85.

Wank, David. 1995. "Bureaucratic Patronage and Private Business: Changing Networks of Power in Urban China." In Andrew Walder, ed., *The Waning of the Communist State: Economic Origins of Political Decline in China and Hungary*, pp. 153–83. Berkeley: University of California Press.

Warren, Carol, and Barbara Laslett. 1977. "Privacy and Secrecy: A Conceptual Comparison." *Journal of Social Issues* 33, no. 3: 43–51.

Wasserstrom, Jeffrey. 1984. "Resistance to the One-Child Family. *Modern China* 10: 345–74.

Watson, James L. 1975. *Emigration and the Chinese Lineage: The Mans in Hong Kong and London*. Berkeley: University of California Press.

———. 1986. "Anthropological Overview: The Development of Chinese Descent Groups." In Patricia B. Ebrey and James L. Watson, eds., *Kinship Organization in Late Imperial China, 1000–1940*, pp. 274–92. Berkeley: University of California Press.

———. 1997. "Preface." In James Watson, ed., *Golden Arches East: McDonald's in East Asia*. Stanford, Calif.: Stanford University Press.

Watson, James, and Evelyn Rawski, eds. 1988. *Death Ritual in Late Imperial and Modern China*. Berkeley: University of California Press.

Watson, Rubie. 1984. "Women's Property in Republican China: Rights and Practice." *Republican China* 10, no. 1: 1–12.

———. 1985a. *Inequality among Brothers, Class and Kinship in South China*. Cambridge, England: Cambridge University Press.

———. 1985b. "Women, Family, and Revolutionary Chang in China." *Peasant Studies* 13, no. 1: 61–64.

———. 1991. "Wives, Concubines, and Maids: Servitude and Kinship in the Hong Kong Region, 1900–1940." In Rubie S. Watson and Patricia B. Ebrey, eds. *Marriage and Inequality in Chinese Society*, pp. 231–55. Berkeley: University of California Press.

White, Terene. 2000. "The Shape of the Society: The Changing Demography of Development." In Terene White, ed., *China Briefing 2000: The Continuing Transformation*, pp. 95–121. Armonk, N.Y.: M. E. Sharpe.

Whyte, Martin. 1992. "Introduction: Rural Economic Reforms and Chinese Family Patterns." *China Quarterly*, no. 130: 317–22.

———. 1993. "Wedding Behavior and Family Strategies in Chengdu." In Deborah Davis and Stevan Harrell, eds., *Chinese Families in the Post-Mao Era*, pp. 189–216. Berkeley: University of California Press.

———. 1995. "The Social Roots of China's Economic Development." *China Quarterly*, no. 144: 999–1019.

———. 1996. "The Chinese Family and Economic Development: Obstacle or Engine?" *Economic Development and Cultural Change* 45, no. 1: 1–30.

———. 1997. "The Fate of Filial Obligations in Urban China." *China Journal*, no. 38: 1–31.

Wolf, Arthur. 1985. "Chinese Family Size: A Myth Revitalized." In Hsieh Jih-Chang and Chuang Ying-Chang, eds., *The Chinese Family and Its Ritual Behavior*, pp. 30–49. Taipai: Academia Sinica.

Wolf, Arthur P., and Huang Chieh-shan. 1980. *Marriage and Adoption in China, 1845–1945*. Stanford, Calif.: Stanford University Press.

Wolf, Margery. 1972. *Women and the Family in Rural Taiwan*. Stanford, Calif.: Stanford University Press.

———. 1985. *Revolution Postponed: Women in Contemporary China*. Stanford, Calif.: Stanford University Press.

Wong, Siu-lun. 1985. "The Chinese Family Firm: A Model." *British Journal of Sociology* 36, no. 1: 58–72.

Wu Cangping, Gui Shixun, and Zhang Zhiliang. 1996. *Gaige kaifang zhong chuxian de zuixin renkou wenti* (The latest demographic issues during the reform of openness). Beijing: Gaodeng jiaoyu chubanshe.

Xiao Tangbiao. 1997. "*Nongcun zongzu chongjian de pubianxing fenzi*" (An analysis of the widespread reconstruction of rural lineages), *Zhongguo nongcun guancha* (Observations of rural China), no. 5: 15–18.

Xin zhoukan (The new weekly). 1998. A special report on the issue of privacy in Chinese society, no. 21: 13–25.

Xu Anqi, ed. 1997. *Shiji zhe jiao Zhongguoren de aiqing he hunyin* (Love and marriage among Chinese at the turn of the century). Beijing: Zhongguo shehui kexue chubanshe.

Yan, Yunxiang. 1992. "The Impact of Rural Reform on Economic and Social Stratification in a Chinese Village." *Australian Journal of Chinese Affairs*, no. 27: 1–23.

———. 1995. "Everyday Power Relations: Changes in a North China Village." In Andrew Walder, ed., *The Waning of the Communist State: Economic Origins of Political Decline in China and Hungary*, pp. 215–41. Berkeley: University of California Press.

———. 1996. *The Flow of Gifts: Reciprocity and Social Networks in a Chinese Village*. Stanford, Calif.: Stanford University Press.

———. 1997. "The Triumph of Conjugality: Structural Transformation of Family Relations in a Chinese Village." *Ethnology* 36, no. 3: 191–212.

———. 1998. "Girl's Power: Young Women and Family Change in Rural North China." Paper presented at the workshop "Women and Modernity in Twentieth-Century China," University of California, Santa Barbara, March 6.

———. 1999. "Rural Youth and Youth Culture in North China." *Culture, Medicine, and Psychiatry*, no. 23: 75–97.

———. 2000. "The Politics of Consumerism in Chinese Society." In Tyrene White, ed., *China Briefing, 1998–2000*, pp. 159–93. Armonk, N.Y.: M. E. Sharpe.

———. 2001. "Practicing Kinship in Rural North China." In Susan McKinnon and Sarah Franklin, eds., *Relative Values: Reconfiguring Kinship Studies*, pp. 224–43. Durham, N.C.: Duke University Press.

Yanagisako, Sylvia Junko. 1979. "Family and Household: The Analysis of Domestic Groups." *Annual Review of Anthropology* 8: 161–205.

Yang, C. K. 1965. *Chinese Communist Society: The Family and the Village*. Cambridge, Mass.: MIT Press.

Yang Ping. 1994. "*Zhangjiang nongcun jiazu zongfa zhidu diaocha*" (An investigation of the lineage and the *zongfa* system in rural Zhanjiang), *Zhanlue ye guanli* (Strategies and management), no. 1: 81–90.

Ye Wenzhen. 1998. *Haize xueqiulun: Zhongguo haizi de chengben he xiaoyong* (On demands for children: the cost and utility of Chinese children). Shanghai: Fudan daxue chubanshe.

Zeng, Yi, Tu Ping, Gu Baochang, Xu Yi, Li Bohua, and Li Yongping. 1993. "Causes and Implications of the Recent Increase in the Reported Sex Ratio at Birth in China." *Population and Development Review* 19, no. 2: 283–302.

ZGNCJTDCZ (Zhongguo nongcun jiating diaochazu (Survey group of Chinese rural families)). 1993. *Dangdai Zhongguo nongcun jiating* (Rural families in contemporary China). Beijing: Shehui kexue wenxian chubanshe.

Zha Bo and Geng Wenxiu. 1992 "Sexuality in Urban China." *Australian Journal of Chinese Affairs*, no. 28: 1–22.

Zha, Jianying. 1995. *China Pop: How Soap Operas, Tabloids, and Bestsellers Are Transforming a Culture*. New York: New Press.

Zhao, Bin, and Graham Murdock. 1996. "Young Pioneers: Children and the Making of Chinese Consumerism." *Cultural Studies* 10, no. 2: 201–17.

Zhou, Xiao. 1989. "Virginity and Premarital Sex in Contemporary China." *Feminist Studies* 15, no. 2: 279–88.

Zhu Chuzhu and Zhang Yougan. 1996. "Zhongguo xianyang bufen nongcun haizi chengben ye xiaoyi yanjiu" (A study of the costs and benefits of child-rearing in rural Xianyan). *Renkou yanjiu* (Population studies), no. 6: 13–22.

Index